MUDIE'S

CIRCULATING

LIBRARY

AND THE

VICTORIAN

NOVEL

MUDIE'S CIRCULATING LIBRARY

and the

Victorian Novel

GUINEVERE L. GRIEST

Indiana University Press

BLOOMINGTON / LONDON

Library of Congress catalog card number: 76-126210

ISBN: 253-15480-4

Manufactured in the United States of America

To my parents & my sister Jeanne

CONTENTS

ILLUSTRATIONS

PREFACE

DURING THE FIVE-YEAR PERIOD FROM 1961 TO 1966 THE circulating libraries of W. H. Smith, *The Times* Book Club, and Boots went out of business. Writers commenting at the time of these closings often nostalgically recalled Mudie's, the great circulating library that had closed its doors almost three decades earlier. Many reminiscences came from men trained in the tradition of prestige and influence that was Mudie's heritage from the nineteenth century. During the half century from 1842 to 1894, Mudie's achieved its greatest power, and it is that span of years which this account will cover.

The contents of much of the first two chapters appeared in slightly different form in *Nineteenth-Century Fiction*, Vol. XX, No. 2, pp. 103-26, and appears with the permission of the Regents of the University of California. I wish to thank the curators and librarians at the British Museum, the Henry W. and Albert A. Berg Collection of the New York Public Library (Astor, Lenox, and Tilden Foundations), the Guildhall Library of the Corporation of London, the Huntington Library, the Library of Congress, the Pierpont Morgan Library, and the Libraries of Cambridge University, the University of California at Los Angeles, and the University of Illinois at Urbana for much individual courtesy and helpfulness. I am grateful to the University of Illinois for a sabbatical leave to put this manuscript in final form.

Mr. Walter Mudie generously shared with me his recollections of the Library. Professor Walter Houghton graciously identified authors of several articles. I wish to record my gratitude to the late Professor E. K. Brown, who introduced me to the Victorian writers, and to the late Professor Morton D. Zabel, who encouraged my interest. I am equally grateful to Professor Robert E. Stange, who offered much valuable advice.

November 1969.

MUDIE'S

CIRCULATING

LIBRARY

AND THE

VICTORIAN

NOVEL

As children must have Punch and Judy,

So I can't do without my Mudie.

—NINETEENTH-CENTURY RHYME

THE AGE OF MUDIE:

BACKGROUND

· *Three-Deckers, Circulating Libraries,*
and Booming Fiction ·

SINCE MAN FIRST RECORDED HIS THOUGHTS, HE HAS gathered what he has written in collections that have formed libraries. Libraries large and small have influenced human affairs in ways almost impossible to overestimate. Unique in English literary history is the leviathan institution known as Mudie's Select Library. With its rivals it maintained in the nineteenth century a reading public that borrowed, but did not buy, original editions of novels. Publishers' advertisements of newly-issued fiction in that era tacitly confirm this fact, frequently proclaiming to interested readers, "Popular New Novels, at all the libraries, each in three volumes. . . ." These advertisements reveal the importance of these great lending organizations in book distribution and, by implication, the dominance in the fiction lists at the libraries of the novel in three volumes. Novels were announced not for sale, but as available to the public through lending organizations; their form was commonly not one volume, but three. Their cost, usually discreetly ignored in the advertisements, was a guinea and a half for the three volumes, a cost which effectively priced them out of the market for individual buyers. At the end of the century a writer for the *Spectator* claimed he personally knew of only two instances in which three-deckers had been bought on their first appearance: a man in Calcutta, eager to know whether Disraeli had anything to reveal, purchased *Endymion*; and a young man had sent a three-decker to his fiancée, who had been "inconsolable because Mudie had not sent her the new novel."[1]

Such satire effectively shows that readers who wanted recent novels were driven to the powerful circulating libraries, which exerted a significant but hitherto largely neglected influence in the Victorian literary milieu.[2] In any period, of course, the creative artist will be influenced by the social conditions—economic as well as political, religious, and cultural—in which he lives and works. In particular, the web of complex interactions uniting the writer, his reader, and his publisher will have inevitable effects on the finished product, repercussions which must be considered in any complete evaluation of the work. The ways in which literature is produced and distributed also leave impressions on the writing, and it would be valuable to ascertain the depth and quality of those impressions on nineteenth-century fiction, to see how creative work has been influenced by social conditions and has in its turn helped to shape those conditions.

The nineteenth century especially provides a rich field for a study of this type because of the spectacular growth of the reading public in that period. This growth did much to transform the economic basis of authorship and publishing, which, again, left impressions on the public. Richard D. Altick's excellent analysis of *The English Common Reader* considers the mass reading public in the nineteenth century in terms of English social and cultural history. Consideration here will be limited to the reader of novels, especially the one who, in person or by his footman, received his volumes across the counter of the circulating library; to the libraries themselves; and to their combined effects on publishing, writers, and of course novels. The dominance of fiction in the literature of the second half of the nineteenth century, the three-volume form in which it was usually first issued, the powerful circulating libraries which distributed the handsomely bound volumes, not only in London but to all Great Britain, and the relative unity of the fiction-reading public combine, in this Age of Mudie, to provide an especially rewarding subject. A brief survey of the growth of circulating libraries will indicate the base from which Mudie's developed into a Library Establishment. That development, important in itself, is inextricably united with three-decker novels, which must then be considered in some detail in order to understand the controversy which raged at their abolition.

From 1842, when Charles Edward Mudie started lending books at his shop in Bloomsbury, until 1894, when the Library Establishment—Mudie's, Limited, combined with its rival W. H. Smith's—destroyed the three-decker, for which it was largely responsible, fiction maintained a recognized supremacy in the world of letters. Contemporary writers in mid-century were noticing that the comparative lull following the great period of Scott had been broken. This awareness of the novel as the literary form typical of the age never flagged, but deepened into firm conviction with the passing years. "We have become a novel-reading people," Anthony Trollope declared in 1870, "from the Prime minister down to the last-appointed scullery-maid. . . . Poetry also we read and history, biography and the social and political news of the day. But all our other reading put together hardly amounts to what we read in novels."[3] The tyranny of the novel has never been "more irresistible," wrote Edmund Gosse in 1892; "the Victorian has been peculiarly the age of the triumph of fiction."[4] In 1894, the *Publishers' Circular*, trade journal of English publishers, described the novel as dwarfing all other kinds of literature, and a few years later Henry James observed that the place of "the prolonged prose fable" had become "in our time, among the incidents of literature, the most

surprising example . . . of swift and extravagant growth. . . .
The flood at present swells and swells, threatening the whole
field of letters, as would often seem, with submersion."[5]

Not only was the novel the chosen form of giants like
Dickens or Thackeray, but, as Saintsbury pointed out, it had
become the method by which "the professional man or woman
of letters" made "his plentiful or her scanty income,"[6] which
indicates the novel's domination of the literary marketplace.
Dickens was commanding dazzling prices for his work, but so
had Scott and Byron in earlier years. In the second half of the
nineteenth century, writers like Bulwer-Lytton, Thackeray,
Trollope, and George Eliot were receiving four-figure sums for
their novels, and the ordinary, "respectable man of letters"
could "command an income and a position quite equal to those
of the average lawyer or doctor."[7] Actually, he might achieve
somewhat greater social prestige and the incalculable rewards
of fame, or even notoriety.

The novel in three volumes was the staple of the market;
it was in this way that these writers, with the exception of
Dickens and Thackeray, issued the bulk of their work in book
form. It was in this way, too, that lesser novelists, like Mrs.
Catherine G. F. Gore, Harrison Ainsworth, and Geraldine
Jewsbury, found their public. As fiction was indisputably the
leading genre of the period, so were three volumes the virtually
inevitable form into which the words were fitted. A work written
in more than three volumes drew protests from the publishers,
primarily because of expense; a work published in fewer than
three risked loss of prestige at the counters of the circulating
library, and it was at those counters that the contemporary fate
of novels was ultimately decided.

Three-deckers and circulating libraries were inextricably
united in what the late Victorians delighted in terming the
palmy days of booming fiction; today a knowledge of the libraries
is essential to complete understanding of this form. "Leviathans,"

they were called, even then, and in their power and dominance they were unlike any similar institutions before or since. As late as 1931 the publisher Stanley Unwin felt it necessary to spell out to the International Congress of Publishers at Paris exactly how the English circulating library system operated. Although then well past its prime, the system retained a strong influence. To Europeans who smiled politely and announced that they, too, had public libraries, Unwin insisted "that the Circulating Library System, as it is in Great Britain, is a unique and elaborate organization; that its influence on booktrade conditions in England is considerable and that no one can begin to understand the British publishers' problems who ignores or is unaware of its existence."[8] In the Victorian era, publishers, authors, and public all recognized the might of the libraries, and the structure and contents of novels conformed to their wishes. That this was possible indicates the extent to which they were satisfying the demands made by their customers, so that their policies in effect mirror the attitudes and desires of the novel-reading public. All considerations of their practices, all praise of their usefulness, all protests against their monopoly must be placed against this background of steadily increasing numbers of pleased Victorians.

Mudie's circulated the works of Mary Elizabeth Braddon, Rhoda Broughton, and Mrs. Henry Wood, as well as novels by a host of anonymous writers, works castigated by George Moore as devoid of discussion of morality or politics, embodying a humanity that was "headless, trunkless, limbless, and is converted into the pulseless, non-vertebrate, jelly-fish sort of thing which, securely packed in tin-cornered boxes, is sent from the London depot and scattered through the drawing-rooms of the United Kingdom."[9] Nevertheless, at the height of its power, and even in its declining years, Mudie's was practically guaranteeing an audience for writers of a far different standard, writers like George Eliot, for whose works Mudie had an almost "insatiable" appetite.[10] Before the subscriber who obtained his books in the pillared hall in New Oxford Street is dismissed as insignificant, it should be remembered that among the three-deckers he exchanged were works by George Meredith, Thomas Hardy, and Henry James. As solid as the class which patronized it, Mudie's reflected and epitomized its age, mirroring the Victorian view of fiction in its shining counters on New Oxford Street.

Because the libraries were able to embody a part of the Victorian temperament, all efforts to overthrow their supremacy or to change the form and price of the novel were ineffectual until the nineties when the librarians themselves finally realized that the artificial fashion they had encouraged would indeed ruin them if unchecked. By that time changing trade conditions had transformed the three traditional volumes from an unassailable support to a staggering burden. With this recognition came the end of the three-decker and the end of Mudie's as a national institution. The end of the Victorian circulating library does not in fact coincide with the closing of Mudie's, but rather with the extinction of the three-decker, a method of publication so closely entwined with its prosperity that the end of the one spelled the doom of the other. The company itself survived until the 1930s, but its autocratic position was lost, and other libraries, like Boots or Harrod's as well as Smith's, which was perhaps more responsive to the changing times, were meeting the new demands of a different reading public.

The storm generated by the abolition of the three-volume novel is all but forgotten today. At the time, however, the furor filled the press, ranging from discreet discussions of "The Three-Volume Novel Question" in the more dignified quarterlies to screams of "cheap and nasty forever!" about one-volume novels in the weeklies. Sure proof of the power of the libraries was the thoroughness and speed with which they accomplished their task, while they remained publicly aloof to the controversy raging around them. In 1894, 184 three-volume novels were issued; that year the libraries banned the form. By 1897, only four appeared.[11] So complete and thorough was the disappearance, that within seven years the *Spectator* was citing the abolition of the three-volume novel as one of the reasons for the enormous expansion of the reading public.[12]

If their end was fast, it was also flashy. In their gaudy embossed covers or, to use Michael Sadleir's phraseology, "in an orgy of magniloquence, the three-decker plummeted to extinction."[13] It made room for the gradual rise of another type of novel that had been seeking a public, a dramatic novel, usually shorter, the novel, at its best, of James and Conrad. The passing was not unsung; an epitaph in verse appeared anonymously in the *Saturday Review*. Although its author, Kipling, wrote few novels and no three-deckers, he thoroughly understood the reasons for the popularity of this "ship of the line."

"And the three-volume novel is doomed."—*Daily Paper*

Full thirty foot she towered from waterline to rail.
It cost a watch to steer her, and a week to shorten sail;
But, spite all modern notions, I found her first and best—
The only certain packet for the islands of the Blest.
. . .

We asked no social questions—we pumped no hidden shame—
We never talked obstetrics when the Little Stranger came:
We left the Lord in Heaven, we left the fiends in Hell.
We weren't exactly Yussufs, but—Zuleika didn't tell.
. . .

Her crew are babes or madmen? Her port is all to make?
You're manned by Truth and Science, and you steam for steaming's sake?
Well, tinker up your engines—you know your business best—
She's taking tired people to the Islands of the Blest![14]

With her, to the Islands of the Blest, she was also carrying the "great national institution," Mudie's Select Library.

· *The Flourishing of the Evergreen Tree* ·

MUDIE'S SELECT LIBRARY WAS ALMOST A PREDICTABLE development from the circulating libraries and publishing practices before its day. Circulating libraries had been thriving in England since the second half of the eighteenth century, apparently outgrowths of two methods of dealing with the increasing reading public. One of these was the booksellers' custom of charging a small fee to customers who read books in the shop. For convenience chairs or stools were provided.[15] Lending volumes to be read outside the store was a natural outgrowth of this practice; a bookseller's advertisement in 1674 announced that the "Widow Page at the Anchor and Mariner . . . near London-Bridge" has "all sorts of Histories to buy, or let out to read by the week."[16]

A second impetus to the growth of circulating libraries was apparently the example given by the flourishing social and literary clubs. The Rev. Samuel Fancourt opened one of the earliest circulating subscription libraries in London between 1740 and 1742. (The first use of the term "circulating library" Joseph Gilburt found for the *Oxford English Dictionary* is from a Fancourt advertisement of 1742.) Although difficulties caused Fancourt to dissolve his library in 1745, the books were kept, and the library continued under a different plan. Club principles were followed in setting up a non-commercial organization to be run by a committee elected by the subscribers. Anyone who could pay the entrance fee of a guinea, plus a shilling a quarter, was eligible for membership in the library. Out of the entrance fees came rent for the rooms in Crane Court, Fleet Street, the salary of the librarian (Fancourt), new books, and the cost of printing a catalogue, which was issued in parts between 1746 and 1748. By the time Fancourt had finished listing his books, however, his library had been sorely pressed. At least one competitor was undercutting him; a book printed for T. Wright, "at the Bible in Exeter Exchange," notified its readers

that "at the said T. Wright's is opened a Library for Lending
all Manner of Books at 16*s*. a Year."[17] Fancourt's difficulties
had so multiplied that sometime after 1755 he had to remove
his library from Crane Court, and although it was subsequently
reopened in the Strand, it eventually failed, and its three thousand
volumes were sold. While Fancourt's library was one of the
earliest in London, its stock was not typical of those which
followed, since its works were primarily learned—theological
and technical.[18]

Once started, the circulating-library movement spread
rapidly, in outlying districts, as well as in London. Actually,
true circulating libraries developed first outside London. Edinburgh had one of the earliest, said to have been started by Allan
Ramsay about 1725 in connection with his bookshop.[19] Benjamin
Franklin, however, knew of no such organizations in London at
that time; it was some fifteen years later that Fancourt opened
his library.[20] By mid-century libraries had sprung up in such
places as Bristol, Bath, Norwich, Birmingham, Newcastle, Hull,
and Liverpool. At Cambridge the first subscription library was
begun about 1745 by Robert Watts, who was succeeded by his
more famous son-in-law, John Nicholson, known as "Maps,"
from his habit of calling his wares as he carried them from
college to college. His oversize portrait by Reinagle shows him
going on his rounds with his bag of books and maps; it domi-
nates the entrance hall of the present University library, attesting
the success of his work and his place in University life.

Circulating libraries were thriving. No longer was their
mere existence noteworthy; instead critics began to inveigh
against these institutions and their stock. Their strictures emphasized the corruption of taste and idleness the libraries fostered. As early as 1728 Robert Wodrow's *Analecta* had voiced
a horrified protest against the "wickedness of all kinds" obtainable for twopence a night,[21] and complaints had multiplied as
the century advanced and the libraries flourished. By 1760
George Colman's *Polly Honeycombe* closed with the earnest

warning of Polly's father that "a man might as well turn his Daughter loose in Covent-garden, as trust the cultivation of her mind to A CIRCULATING LIBRARY." In the next year the *Annual Register's* report on the life of a woman in the country included mention of a circulating library from which she borrowed her books. Fifteen years later, in 1775, Sir Anthony Absolute made his famous and much quoted remark to Mrs. Malaprop: "Madam, a circulating library in a town is as an evergreen tree of diabolical knowledge! It blossoms through the year! And depend on it . . . they who are so fond of handling the leaves, will long for the fruit at last."[22]

The rapid growth of the libraries found publishers hard put to it to fill the demand, and many old novels, refurbished and fitted with different names, were printed as new works. The last decades of the eighteenth century were not only the time of the sentimental romance, but of the Gothic novel as well, and the popular taste for these tales of terror was being stimulated by William Lane's Minerva Press and by his circulating library in Leadenhall Street. (Leigh Hunt subscribed there as a school-boy.) Lane energetically established branches of his library in the more fashionable country towns, and his firm prospered through the first quarter of the nineteenth century. His sub-scription rate, however, rose steeply, from a guinea a year in 1798 to five guineas in 1814, allowing twenty-four volumes in town, or thirty-six in the country. Although Lane gave great impetus to the increase of circulating libraries, his press became so closely associated with the romance of horror or of "stale and uninteresting incident," in Scott's phrase, that "Minerva Press" was commonly used as a scornful epithet.[23]

The charges frequently made against these "iniquitous and barbarous hosts of circulating libraries" are summarized in a diatribe by Mrs. Catherine Gore published in *Blackwood's* in 1844, just two years after Mudie had started his own counter-attack. In highly rhetorical language, she bemoans the fate of Scott, whom "the hateful factory system of twice three volumes per annum"[24] had killed. Her sympathies were undoubtedly more readily aroused because she herself chafed under the three-decker requirement, although she prudently conformed to it. Couched in colorful metaphors are charges that libraries were virtually the only buyers of new books, and that they would buy only three-volume novels for their three-sovereign-a-year subscribers. Although these accusations were echoed later in the century, reverberating then from charges against Mudie, in the 1840s his "select" library seemed to be the antithesis of the "monster-misery" of earlier years.

The expansion of the library movement is a sure indication that its wares were rapidly increasing in quantity, at least. With greater numbers came, logically enough, greater standardization; for this and other reasons the one- to seven-volume length that had come out of the eighteenth century was gradually resolved into three. Prices, too, were rising steadily; they kept pace with the cost of living, certainly, but they also reflected the higher cost of composition, itself due to wage increases and the high price of metal.[25] Furthermore, the French wars had interfered with supplies. But apart from these material factors, the increase in average novel prices from 2s.6d. a volume in 1780 to a high of 7s. in 1810 reflects the growing importance of the influence of the circulating libraries over publishers. In the eighteenth century, when the library was a department in a bookshop, it was obviously best to keep prices on a mutually advantageous level. As a separate business, on the other hand, the library actually preferred nominally high prices as a kind of insurance that readers would be compelled to borrow, and as an additional handicap to the retail bookseller, already at a disadvantage because of the extra discounts often allowed to libraries.

The phenomenally successful sales of the most popular novelist of his day also bolstered rising novel prices. Scott's *Kenilworth*, published in three volumes at a guinea and a half in 1821, set a fashion which lasted for almost the rest of the century. Although not the first novel to be so issued (Thomas Hope's *Anastasius* had come out in that form and at that price three years earlier), it was the most influential because of Scott's enormous prestige. By 1833, the form was so firmly established that Smith, Elder attempted to break "the mischievous prejudice which prevails in the trade against works in less than three volumes"[26] by issuing original novels in a "Library of Romance" at 6s. a volume. Each volume was to contain the equivalent of two in the conventional style, and monthly issue was scheduled. The series, according to the hopeful prospectus of its editor, Leitch Ritchie, would benefit almost everyone connected with novels. It would actually increase the profits of circulating libraries, benefit the booksellers, encourage authors to write more carefully and deliberately, and provide better books for readers—all these benefits to be derived from the reduced number of novels in circulation.

Fewer but better novels would ensue, Ritchie contended, because publishers would select with more discrimination when manuscripts were destined for extensive circulation instead of for the limited markets provided by the circulating library. Still, as a consequence of the improvement in novels, libraries themselves would circulate more copies, and booksellers would no longer have large stocks of unwanted fiction. Ritchie's arguments foreshadow others heard with increasing frequency as the age progressed. Unfortunately, by the fourth volume, Ritchie's series had already received a death blow; the editor's formal announcement read

> It has been suggested to the proprietors by the Circulating Libraries, that the volumes of the Library of Romance are inconveniently long, and should be rendered capable of being divided into two, so as to enable them to supply their subscribers with the usual quantum of reading at a time. This appears to be nothing more than reasonable. . . .[27]

Thus, after only four months, the libraries forced the books into the very mold against which their existence was a protest.

Two months later came the final concession. Ritchie carefully laid the blame where it was due, explaining that henceforth the books would come out at bi-monthly intervals, since "the libraries should not be cut short of their fair proportions by a new volume pushing the old one from its stool before its *run* is half over."[28] Even these appeasements were not enough, and the series ended in 1835 with a total of only fifteen volumes.

Smith, Elder's experiment is worth noting as the first of the attempts to break the high price and artificial format of the novel. Although increasing in frequency as the century advanced, other ventures were no more successful. It must be remembered, too, that the "Library of Romance" was bucking scattered opponents, lacking both the prestige and domination achieved in later years by Mudie's. Even so, their power was sufficient. It was evident even in the quality of the novels, which also contributed to the downfall of the "Library." *The Ghost-Hunter and his Family* by The O'Hara Family, which opened the series, is perhaps typical of the titles, which also included a few translations, such as Victor Hugo's *The Slave King* (*Bug-Jargal*). The difficulty, which was to dog subsequent attempts as well, lay in persuading either novices or front-rank authors to write for price-breaking series when the pervasive influence of the libraries kept profits in the three-decker. Not until George Moore, and the final capitulation of the circulating libraries, was this handicap overcome.

Another cause of the failure of the "Library of Romance" undoubtedly lay in the political and economic unrest of those years close to the Reform Act of 1832. After the publishing panic following the crash of 1825, which reflected the price fall of 1820–1821 and the ensuing financial distress, many of the circulating libraries toppled, carrying with them the rank and file of novelists. Observers at the end of the century noted the "sudden crash of the novel,"[29] and that "for a long time [afterwards] there were few aspirants for the art of fiction."[30] It appeared to Saintsbury, chronicling the literary history of the period, to be a kind of ebb or "half-ebb"[31] in the novel, and Emily Symonds declared that of all books published then, not one in fifty paid expenses.[32] Furthermore, tastes and attitudes were shifting as the Romantic movement was drawing to a close. Finally, Scott, the novelist who was considered supreme in his form, had died in 1832, leaving a vacancy that seemed impossible to fill.

Charles Edward Mudie,
founder of Mudie's Select Library

MUDIE'S: THE LEVIATHAN

· *Growth of Mudie's* ·

BY THE FORTIES, POLITICAL AS WELL AS ECONOMIC CON-
ditions were changing; that decade of turbulence and misery
often termed the "hungry Forties" saw passage of the income
tax bill, acts on working and sanitary conditions (including the
first Public Health Act), some relief from the pressure of social
problems through an increase in the real wages of the working
class later in the decade, the growth of the telegraph, and the
"Railway mania," which added three thousand miles of tracks
to the English countryside between 1843 and 1848. Along
with these developments came a wave of novels, including such
varied works as *Barnaby Rudge*, *Martin Chuzzlewit*, *Coningsby*,
Sybil, *Jane Eyre*, *Vanity Fair*, *Wuthering Heights*, *Yeast*, *Mary
Barton*, *Pendennis*, *David Copperfield*, and *The Caxtons*, many
of which directly reflected the times. The "age of fiction," as
contemporary critics were already viewing the Victorian era,
was rapidly growing. Poetry still held its audience (the poems
later collected in *Bells and Pomegranates* were being issued in

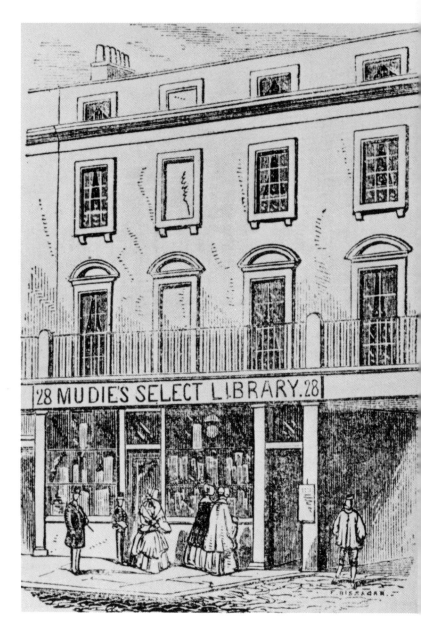

First site of Mudie's in Bloomsbury.
Courtesy of the Guildhall Library, London.

pamphlet form between 1841 and 1846, and Tennyson's *Poems* appeared in 1842), but drama was stagnant, and for the mass of the middle and upper classes, imaginative "literature" was concentrated more and more in fiction.

The forties indeed proved to be auspicious times for young Charles Edward Mudie, who began to lend books from his stationer's shop in Southampton Row (then Upper King Street), Bloomsbury, in 1842. The man who was credited with revolutionizing English reading for several generations was born in 1818 in Cheyne Walk, Chelsea, the youngest of several sons of Scottish parents. His father kept a small newspaper and stationer's shop, where books were loaned at a penny a volume. By the time he was twenty-two, Mudie had opened his own business, at first, like his father's, supplying newspapers and stationery. Within two years, however, young Mudie was lending a collection of books of a progressive kind, including American transcendental works, at the astonishingly low rate of a guinea a year. That rate, to the despair of his rivals, became as famous as the library itself and apparently as unchanging as its policies.

Just how surprising Mudie's rates were is apparent even in the discreet advertisements, with their identical small type, covering the first page of the *Athenaeum*. On March 4, 1843 four circulating libraries advertised their services. Of these, Bull's was charging six guineas a year in town; Saunders and Otley five, six, or eight guineas; Churton's four, five, or ten guineas. The prestige of their Cavendish and Hanover Square addresses hardly compensated for the three- to nine-guinea saving Mudie offered. With Scottish canniness he emphasized this differential by noting his quarterly rate of only 6*s.* That sum was less than half the 15*s.* lowest family rate charged by Horne and Company in Cheapside. The rates of the rival companies are difficult to compare exactly, because of different numbers of books allowed at a time, restrictions on borrowing new publications, and the allowance of part of the rate for the purchase of new books. Bull's, for example, allowed its six-guinea-a-year patrons to keep two guineas' worth of books. It was clear, however, even to the casual reader of the *Athenaeum*, that Mudie's rate was startlingly low.

Not so obviously different was the name of the library. Instead of "New System," "British and Foreign," or "Public Subscription," the significant word in Mudie's name was "Select." In more than one sense that term was the key to Mudie's success. Select he did, energetically ensuring that new works, on publication, were immediately available to his subscribers in quantities as large as necessary. Poetry, history, biography, travel and adventure, scientific and religious works, the English and even the American reviews, as well as fiction, were included in the new library, a marked change from the earlier ones whose shelves were loaded with volumes from, or similar to those from, the Minerva Press. Mudie's Library came to be considered the "modern" or "higher kind of circulating library,"[1] its type being virtually unknown on the continent or in the United States.

Nor were the more obvious implications of the word "select" overlooked; Mudie carefully excluded certain books for "moral reasons."[2] No longer would the head of a Victorian family need to waste his time scanning circulating library works to see whether they were suitable for his daughters; no longer would the daughter, like Lydia Languish, have to throw her book behind the sofa at the entrance of her parent; the Mudie novel, resplendent in its bright yellow cover imprinted with the Pegasus symbol, lay on the parlor table, ready for any member of the family circle to read aloud. The concept expressed by his term "select" formed the keystone of the arch which supported Mudie's great business; and the constant chipping at it through the years by authors, publishers, and even subscribers eventually contributed to the collapse of the whole structure.

Because of his careful selection, the quality of the stock sharply differentiated his books from those of the ordinary libraries of the 1840s; indeed, their failure to supply anything but trash stimulated Mudie in his venture:

Seldom could I get a book that I wished for, and I was fain to
buy what I wanted. The idea suddenly struck me that many other
young men were in similar case with myself. I had by this time
accumulated a number of books, so I determined to launch out a
library on my own lines.[3]

He was interested in the American transcendentalists; in the first
collection in Southampton Row he arranged the *Dial* and the
writings of Theodore Parker in his shop window. Within two
years from the time he started lending books, Mudie published
the first English editions of James Russell Lowell's *Poems* and
of Emerson's "Man Thinking. An Oration" ("The American
Scholar"). The small shop in Bloomsbury was soon frequented
by students from the recently founded University of London
who were drawn by the books offered by this young "radical in
politics and . . . liberal in religion."[4] Frederick Denison Maurice,
Thomas Hughes, and David Masson were soon on his subscription list, while such men as Richard Holt Hutton and
Frederick Tennyson were attending a "coffee symposium" in his
parlor. It was from Mudie, too, that Sir John Franklin obtained
the books he took on his successful but fatal voyage to discover
a northwest passage to the Pacific in 1845.

Even the times favored the energetic young librarian; the
depression in 1847 probably stimulated subscriptions. In that
year the publisher John Murray warned Lord Campbell (who
was to be one of the arbiters in the free trade "Bookselling
Question" of 1852) that sales would be slow because "books
are the first luxury abandoned; for if a man puts down his
carriage, or leaves off champagne at his dinners, all the world
discovers his poverty; but unobserved he can borrow a publication he wishes to look at from a circulating library. . . ."[5] At
any rate, Mudie's business prospered rapidly, and Mudie himself
quickly became the impressive figure Mrs. De Morgan pointed
out to her young son, William, who never forgot his delighted
awe at seeing this "king of the Librarians."[6]

In 1852 Mudie moved to larger quarters at the corner of

New Oxford Street and Museum Street, from which his cart clattered over the London streets with its load of books. By this time Mudie was employing two tactical devices that were to make his library almost synonymous with the novel in Victorian England. First, he advertised extensively "the principal New and Choice Books in circulation," itemizing the "Constant Succession of the Best New Books, Exchangeable at Pleasure." Some indication of the importance these advertisements assumed in the literary world may be seen in Daniel Macmillan's assurance to Charles Kingsley that Mudie would advertise *Westward Ho!* in both "the London and Manchester papers; that will make the other libraries buy it."[7] If Kingsley was relieved, George Henry Lewes, on the other hand, worried about Mudie's failure to include *Scenes of Clerical Life*. Writing to John Blackwood in 1858, he acknowledged that he and George Eliot "have puzzled ourselves greatly" over it, adding that she "takes it as a sign that Mudie doesn't think much of the book." The following January, George Eliot herself asked Blackwood, "Can you imagine why Mudie has almost always left the C[lerical] S[cenes] out of his advertised list, although he puts in very trashy and obscure books? I hope it is nothing more than chance."[8] A listing in Mudie's selection had become one of the best advertisements for any novel.

The second tactic by which Mudie strengthened his library was the acquisition of new works rapidly and in large quantities. In December 1855, for instance, Mudie ordered 2,500 copies of volumes three and four of Macaulay's *History of England*. When Longman's traveler sprang up the stairs at Paternoster Row with this news, the firm's glee was tempered with consternation, since the two volumes weighed about seven pounds, making a total dead weight of almost eight tons. Longman's, unable to deliver in their handcart, stipulated that Mudie would have to fetch his eight tons himself, as he did, later setting aside a separate room in his library to store and exchange the volumes.

Mudie took even more of Livingstone's *Travels* in 1857, 3,250 copies, and two years later 1,000 copies of Tennyson's *Idylls of the King*. During the ten years between 1853 and 1862, he added almost 960,000 volumes to his library, nearly half of which were fiction;[9] and by the end of the century he had acquired more than seven and a half million books, according to a *Times* estimate.[10] The annual rate of increase, as Mudie advertised it, jumped by more than 80 percent in three years—from more than 100,000 volumes in 1858 to more than 180,000 in 1861.

So, despite sour predictions from the older, established companies that few stylish carriages would find their way from Bond Street to such an unfashionable place as New Oxford Street, Mudie's stream of customers steadily increased. Outgrowing his second premises, he built a new hall, opening it in December 1860, with festivities attended by "nearly all the best names in literature and the trade," in the *Athenaeum's* succinct phrase. Among "the vast number of literary and artistic friends,"[11] who attended what Anthony Trollope termed "Mudie's great flare up,"[12] were (besides Trollope himself) George Henry Lewes, Monckton Milnes, Theodore Martin (the future biographer of the Prince Consort), Thomas Chandler Haliburton (whose Sam Slick had found his way into the pages of the Mudie catalogue), George Cruikshank, Charles Knight (who had contributed much to the movement for cheap literature), Augustus Sala, Henry George Bohn, John L. Motley (who had already published his *Rise of the Dutch Republic*), and Sir Leopold McClintock (of whose account of the search for Franklin and his lost expedition seeking the Northwest Passage Mudie had taken 3,000 copies). Soon to be one of the landmarks of the street, the stuccoed Regency building was, in the *Athenaeum's* judgment, one of the most successfully designed classic structures in London. At semi-circular counters customers exchanged their books in the great round hall, which was reminiscent "of the British Museum Reading Room on a small scale."[13] There, under a wide lantern, attendants procured orders from shelves lining the two-story walls. The roof was supported by Ionic columns, whose forms were repeated by pilasters on the walls, and the pure white walls and columns contrasted vividly with the varied colors in the rows of books.

Extensive advertising and large orders of popular "select" works were proving profitable. Branches were opened in the City, Birmingham, and Manchester, and arrangements were made to supply book clubs and societies, as well as provincial libraries, where the yellow label with the Pegasus symbol put in the shop window informed patrons that boxes from New Oxford Street would periodically bring fresh supplies of the latest books. John Loder, the bookseller whom Edward Fitz-Gerald patronized at Woodbridge, followed this common practice. Some twenty years later, George Gissing wondered whether the Church Institution in Wakefield had *Demos*. "It is a branch of Mudie's, and nothing but persistence is wanted," he assured his sister Ellen.[14]

In 1858 Mudie did, however, refuse to start libraries at W. H. Smith's railway bookstalls. Whatever his reasons—whether he felt that the idea was unsound, or that Smith's offer (rumored to be £1,000 a year) was too low, or that he himself would be over-expanding—his rejection forced Smith's into the competing business that survived until 1961, outlasting Mudie's by almost a quarter of a century. Meanwhile Mudie steadily enlarged his own business. Instead of one cart, a fleet of Mudie vans was dispatched daily to exchange books at London houses. Boxes carried books with the Pegasus imprint to the most remote parts of England, enabling the country parson or doctor to keep up with the literary world. Although other libraries remained in business (for example, the Grosvenor Gallery Library, Mitchell's, Day's in Mount Street, and Cawthorn and Hutt's "British Library" in Cockspur Street), Mudie's had become the leviathan that had sharply revised the system of distributing fiction in England in less than two decades.

Its most spectacular opposition came in the early 1860s from the Library Company Limited of Pall Mall, which attempted to undermine Mudie's with a half-guinea subscription. Floated with a capital of £100,000, in shares of £1 each, the company proposed to allow holders of a certain number of shares "to rank as subscribers as well as to divide whatever profits may accrue."[15] Thus offering hopes of dividends in addition to a library subscription, the company easily lured stockholders, but it was in trouble almost from the beginning. In the first place, Mudie's rate was already surprisingly low. (Thomas Hookham, whose firm eventually succumbed to Mudie's, expressed the general feeling in the trade about Mudie's charge when he noted that the young librarian had "invented a scale of terms of subscription, cutting . . . much lower than he need have."[16]) To slash that rate by half was in itself almost suicidal, but added to it was the burden of the "free" subscriptions for shareholders.[17] It is small wonder that in August 1864, little more than two years after its prospectus had been issued, "A Deluded Shareholder" was complaining in *The Times* about the shortage of books in the company, its failure to pay dividends, and the worthlessness of the shares.[18]

The apprehensions of the "Deluded Shareholder" proved justified, for the firm went under within the year. Its significance lies in the boom it created in the market for fiction, a boom which itself reveals the extent to which the libraries had become a primary market for fiction. From the publisher's point of view, the situation was too good to last. Tinsleys', which was just starting in business, attained almost immediate success with such works as *Lady Audley's Secret*. Indeed, William Tinsley remembered the sales of that novel as almost a race between Mudie's and the Library Company Limited to see which firm would purchase the larger number of copies. Other publishers as well profited from the greatly increased demand for novels resulting from the competition.

· *The Limited Company* ·

WHETHER AS A RESULT OF THIS COMPETITION, OR OF THE boom in joint-stock companies which was reaching its climax in 1864–1865, or of other factors, Mudie formed his own library into a limited liability company in 1864. Of the £100,000 capital, £50,000, and the management, were reserved by Mudie; the remaining £50,000 was immediately subscribed by John Murray, Richard Bentley, and other publishers. As manager Mudie also drew a salary of £1,000 a year. For the next thirty years of three-volume supremacy, the single most powerful library was half owned by publishers; one of them, Bentley, could be called (in language of a later date) the "king of the three-decker." Not only was Mudie already an indispensable buyer of Bentley novels, but after 1864 his firm was paying dividends to the publisher. On February 7, 1881, for example, George Bentley received notice from the library of a 7½ percent dividend for a six-month period.[19]

Meanwhile, the Select Library's competitors were either outdistanced or bought; Thomas Hookham's account of the fall of his library testifies eloquently to the fate of many small firms. Mudie, with his low rate, his persistent advertising, and his apparent genius for organization, not only made his own name, but also brought "the ruin of many lending libraries in London and the country, and the surrender to the public at large of almost all that made the library business worth doing." After Mudie moved to New Oxford Street, Hookham, like "all the principal librarians to the west of him declined to give up what they thought was their legitimate or fair mode of trade." Assisted by profits from their opera and theater departments (ticket sales formed a definite part of most circulating libraries[20]), the libraries contrived to stay in business for a time. As subscribers altered their carriage drives to include New Oxford Street, however, it became apparent something would have to be done. "We were the first to alter our terms to a competing scale," Hookham goes on, "but it was too late."[21]

In its attempt to meet Mudie's competition, Hookham's was then converted into a limited company, under the name of the English and Foreign Library Company, Limited. It started with a capital of £25,000, and although it was in difficulties in eighteen months, it struggled on for six years, until September 1871. What was left after the collapse was finally taken over by Mudie's, which had also swallowed Booth's of Regent Street a few years earlier. The size of Mudie's in comparison to its rivals is indicated in an 1875 letter of B. A. Van Homrigh in the Bentley Collection. Writing to his employer, George Bentley, he listed the number of copies of one of the firm's recently-published novels, *Leah* (by Mrs. Annie Edwards), which he had sent to London libraries:

Smith's	25
Day	13
Cawthorn	13
Mitchell	6
Mudie	125

Although this is an instance selected at random, it is noteworthy that Mudie's took five times as many copies as its nearest competitor. Mudie's Select Library became more and more the Victorian leviathan whose patronage seemed to Mrs. Oliphant "a sort of recognition from heaven."[22]

Expansion continued after 1860; new construction was required to handle the quantities of books demanded in the London branches, in the provinces, and overseas. Volumes were shipped in specially built tin-lined boxes to such places as Germany, Russia, China, India, Egypt, Baghdad, and South Africa (a subscription came from the Kimberley Public Library). Such was the solidity of the firm and even of its containers that it was confidently asserted that its boxes had been dug out of the sea after shipwrecks with no damage to the contents. Mudie himself maintained tight control over the company, actively determining policies as well as supervising operations. His elder son Charles Henry entered the firm when he came of age in 1871 and was groomed to assume control. When the younger Mudie died in 1879, his grief-stricken father was unable to resume his usual routine at New Oxford Street, precipitating some minor crises and delays in the business. In January 1880, James Payn, a reader for Smith, Elder who was concerned about the effect of all this on his own three-decker, *Under One Roof*, remarked in a letter to Andrew Chatto, "Our people complain bitterly of Mudie's absence affecting his orders."[23] Mudie apparently never recovered from his loss, and took progressively less interest in the business. About 1884 he relinquished all active duties to his younger son Arthur and to others.

As the years went by, however, the novels on the shelves tended to become merely reworkings of the same material, and volumes piled up in Mudie's catacombs, his storage cellars. The popularly-priced reprint added to the difficulties in ways that will be examined in detail later. Finally, in 1894, Mudie's united with Smith's in an action which effectually banned the hallowed three-decker from their shelves. The firm's problems, however, were not solved. Perhaps it clung too tenaciously to Victorian principles and practices. William H. Matthews, a member of the firm for almost the last fifty years of its existence, recalled resistance to the telephone (except for private lines connected with London branches) and insistence on hand-written correspondence.[24] At any rate, orders from Mudie's were small even before the First World War, according to English publishers, and not long after it, the firm was forced to leave the New Oxford Street landmark for smaller premises in Kingsway. Basically sustained by the three-decker, Mudie's apparently was unable to cope with changed conditions or meet the competition of Smith's and Boots in the provinces, or of Harrod's and *The*

Times Book Club in the West End. The pendulum was swinging away from centralization and back to the decentralization Mudie's had originally replaced. Both Smith's and Boots had many branches; Smith's had its railway bookstalls and its newspaper agency, and Boots had the chemist's shops, from which the library had grown, to bolster their lending departments.

In the London of the 1920s, Mudie's seemed to Wyndham Lewis a survival from another era, a "superbly Forsyte institution, solid as roast beef. . . . It was about the only place in London where you could still find muttonchop whiskers, lorgnettes, tall hats from late-Victorian blocks, feathered and flowered toques, . . . and that atmosphere of unhurried, fastidious leisure which has quite gone."[25] Even the retrenchment of moving to Kingsway was insufficient, however; the firm struggled along there for a few years, and finally, on Saturday, July 12, 1937, a court order shut the doors of Mudie's Select Library. Its stock was eventually bought by one of its competitors, Harrod's, but the New Oxford Street building, "a historical literary landmark,"[26] stood empty for many years as a melancholy reminder of its former prominence, and was finally destroyed by the German air raids of the Second World War. What the bombs destroyed was only the shell of the institution many had thought of as a permanent feature of English life, closed after ninety-five years of providing the British middle-class reader with suitable literature. During its years of eminence, however, years of great development in the English novel, Mudie's had been the single most important distributor of fiction, and had exerted such a profound influence that its creator had become a symbolic "Dictator of the London Literary World."[27]

· *Inside Mudie's* ·

FROM CONTEMPORARY ARTICLES IT IS POSSIBLE TO RECONstruct the operation and organization of the firm at the height of its power in the second half of the nineteenth century. Basically it was separated into four divisions: London, country, bookselling, and bookbinding. The London section, with its branches in the City and the West End, was probably the most important; it itself consisted of two parts.

In the main hall of the New Oxford Street building a steady procession of customers approached the semi-circular counters, separating themselves by the initials of their last names, which were emblazoned on signposts set on ornamental stands topped with the familiar bronze Pegasus symbols. Here was housed the main accumulation of approximately one million volumes; it was so large that, to an awed writer in the *Spectator* of 1863, the collection "of the famous Bodleian sinks into the shade, and that of the Vatican becomes dwarfish, as far as quantity is concerned."[28] The books were arranged on the shelves, first by size, then alphabetically by author, with fiction the only separate classification. The bright bindings of the most popular works decorated iron shelves lining the great hall, where a gallery behind the counters gave access to the upper levels. Less frequently demanded books were relegated to the "catacombs," or cellar, which spread out beneath the great hall under adjacent New Oxford Street. The muffled roar of traffic overhead rumbled through these bookstacks, which were connected with the main floor by iron staircases, some kind of speaking tubes, and lifts. Writers describing Mudie's always pictured the bustle of this great hall. There customers lined the counters, assistants in their frock coats and striped trousers hurried to and fro on the main floor and the gallery, lifts constantly disgorged their contents, and calls from the tubes rose over the hum of voices. Mudie himself often procured orders, then ceremoniously handed his preferred patrons to their waiting carriages.

If it was inconvenient for a customer to exchange his books personally or by sending a servant, the London Book Society, the other part of the London branch, delivered his choices to his door. This Mudie patron, who had to subscribe for at least three volumes weekly at two guineas a year, sent in his list to

New Oxford Street, and a few hours later his choices were delivered by van any place within a twenty-mile radius of London. Nine vans covered the 170 districts into which London was divided for this service.

> New boxes come across the sea
> From Mr. Mudie's libraree

wrote W. S. Gilbert in *Bab Ballads*. Those beyond the limits of the London Book Society were served by the second division of the organization, the country department, which shipped boxes to all parts of England and overseas. One thousand boxes, carrying 10 to 100 books each, were dispatched weekly to country and colonial subscribers, many of whom were provincial or colonial libraries, holding the larger subscriptions of 100 to 500 volumes, or occasionally even more.

Although definitely subsidiary to the lending department, bookselling, the third division of the business, was a profitable adjunct. First, of course, it provided a market for some of the many volumes of three-decker novels that had run their course in the library. Since the average Victorian reader seldom bought a three-decker until he had sampled its worth at the circulating library, and since Mudie could easily afford to slash prices well below the 31s.6d. asked for new three-volume novels, the bookselling department was an important section. It was said to have been frequented by Gladstone, with his eye out for a likely bargain. In 1860, he could have picked up these three-deckers, all originally priced at 31s.6d.: *The Mill on the Floss* for 7s., Mrs. Oliphant's *Laird of Norlaw* for 3s.6d., *Richard Feverel* for 5s., or *Castle Richmond* at the rather high 9s. Publishers kept a sharp eye on these prices as one of the best gauges to popularity and possible profits from a cheap reprint. Thus Daniel Macmillan wrote Mrs. Charles Kingsley in 1856: "We see that Mr. Mudie charges 15s. for second-hand copies of *Westward Ho!* while he sold Thackeray's *Esmond* at 9s. This shows that though Thackeray's book was much more successful at first . . .

yet Mr. Kingsley's book has proved more permanently interesting to the English public."[29] Besides selling individual titles, Mudie offered books in large lots, for example, 100 volumes, for small provincial libraries.

Binding Department

In another phase of its activities the bookselling department stocked the handsomely decorated books used for prizes and awards, books advertised as "adapted for gentlemen's libraries and drawing-room tables and for wedding and birthday presents." They were bound in the bookbinding division, the fourth branch of the company, found on the upper floors of the New Oxford Street building, where the repairing of worn library volumes and the stitching of the numerous catalogues were also done. The style of calf binding developed here became famous as "Mudie calf."

More than 250 workers were required to run the library, and employment by Mudie was regarded by many as the equivalent of a government position. There was even a "select" club for employees of this "select" library, the Pegasus Club, with a limited membership.

With a large stock of novels, most of which were in three volumes, the problem of disposing of copies of works no longer in demand was great. If there were any chance of renewed interest (because of a new work by the author, for example), the volumes were stored in the catacombs. Others were offered for sale, individually, or in large parcels. Still others were sold for waste paper, doubtless to the ubiquitous Victorian trunk maker. Finally, the copies in the worst condition were disposed of to make fertilizer. This problem of surplus volumes was one of the gathering number of difficulties which eventually brought about the downfall of the three-decker in the 1890s.

· *Competitor: W. H. Smith's* ·

MUDIE'S ONLY COMPETITOR WORTH THE NAME WAS THE company that owed its library department to him—W. H. Smith's. In a sense, it might be said to antedate Mudie's, for Smith's, "Newspaper Agents, Booksellers, and Binders," in Duke Street, Grosvenor Square, opened a reading room in the Strand in 1820,[30] where for a fee of a guinea and a half, a subscriber could read 150 papers, as well as magazines and reviews. In the early years of the nineteenth century Smith's had been the leading newspaper agents of Britain, a position which was not relinquished when the firm started to expand with the railway bookstall business in 1848. Young William Henry Smith, who had recently been admitted into partnership with his father, initiated the new enterprise, which seemed to *Punch* so similar to circulating libraries that it quipped "a Railway is decidedly the best vehicle going for circulating a Library."[31] Smith quickly earned the title of "The Northwest Missionary" for his success in eliminating the "unmitigated rubbish"[32] previously found on the platforms of the London and Northwestern Railway.

By 1862, with a monopoly of the bookstalls on almost all the railways, Smith's had expanded in two more directions. Having secured the copyrights for Lever's novels in 1854, the company began to issue 2s. reprints of popular fiction under Chapman and Hall's imprint. Although highly successful (the firm reaped dual profits by both publishing and selling), these early "yellow-backs" were abandoned by the firm after about thirty years, probably because of a decision to restrict activities to distribution. The second expansion, into circulating libraries, grew out of Mudie's refusal to conduct such operations for the firm. These libraries were modeled on the Mudie pattern, as the *Athenaeum* noted:

> Messrs. W. H. Smith and Son, taking advantage of the convenience afforded by their railway bookstalls, are about to open a Subscription Library on a large scale, something like that of Mr. Mudie. The bookstalls will, in fact, become local libraries, small but select, with the immense advantage of hourly communication by train, with a vast central library in London.[33]

Thus providing the same kind of "select" book Mudie offered, Smith's libraries prospered, developing by 1862 into a network of 185 branches in railway bookstalls. Soon the most powerful rival of the original Select Library, Smith's also included all the services that had attracted subscribers to Mudie's: London delivery, country and overseas shipments, and bookselling.

The similarity in the characters and careers of these "twin tyrants of literature," as Mudie and Smith were dubbed by Wilkie Collins, is striking. They were born within seven years of each other, developed their businesses about the same time, withdrew from the active management of their firms in the same decade, and died within months of each other. Both men had a strongly religious bent: Smith's intention to take orders had been forestalled by his father's insistence that he enter the business; Mudie's non-conformist sympathies led him to preach occasionally and to write hymns.[34] It is not surprising, therefore, that the two library systems adopted similar standards, so that, while there are individual exceptions, a book banned by one was not likely to be found on the other's shelves. Both men had remarkable abilities in organizing and directing a business combined with a keen sense of their moral responsibilities to their great reading public. As with many of their contemporaries, these responsibilities were reflected by their attitude as paternal protectors. Both were convinced that, with a few dangerous exceptions, the public did not want books which questioned the generally accepted Victorian standards, a judgment verified by the increasing numbers of satisfied subscribers. They served together on the first London school board, both from Westminster. Although Mudie's public career stopped there,[35] Smith went on to Parliament. He rose to be First Lord of the Admiralty with so little experience that the general astonishment was reflected by W. S. Gilbert, who drew on Smith's career for the character of the Right Honorable Sir Joseph Porter, who sang in *H. M. S. Pinafore*:

> I grew so rich that I was sent
> By a pocket borough into Parliament
> I always voted at my party's call
> And I never thought of thinking for myself at all
> . . .
> Stick close to your desks, and never go to sea
> And you all may be Rulers of the Queen's Navee!

Both men had died before the two firms united in 1894 to issue the circulars which suppressed the three-decker, but the stamp of their powerful personalities was still molding policies and practices. In the two businesses there had apparently never been any cutthroat competition, perhaps because Mudie's rested primarily on the flourishing three-decker, whereas Smith's leaned more towards the cheap reprint in one volume. It was much more suitable for railway lending than the three-decker, since one complete volume could conveniently be withdrawn at one station and returned at the destination. Smith's library, too, formed only a department, and the least profitable department at that, of the large firm. Although their markets overlapped, differences existed, and it was Mudie's that provided the mainstay for the three-decker.

MUDIE'S AND THE

THREE-DECKER

· *The Library Establishment* ·

THOMAS CARLYLE, MEETING CHARLES EDWARD MUDIE AT A reception given by Lady Ashburnham in 1850, looked sharply at the rising young librarian and said, "So, *you're* the man that divides the sheep from the goats! Ah! it's an *awfu'* thing to judge a man. It's a *more* awfu' thing to judge a book." Mudie's answer to this brusque greeting typifies the replies he was to make, publicly and privately, to the growing number of attacks on his selective policies. With characteristic firmness he said, "In my business I profess to judge books only from a commercial standpoint, though it is ever my object to circulate good books and not bad ones."[1]

What Mudie thought good became more and more important as his library flourished and expanded. Within two years of Carlyle's observation, he had moved from his original premises in Southampton Row to New Oxford Street. Eight years later that "vast number of literary and artistic friends" gathered to open his large new hall. Mudie's had become a force to be reckoned with in the distribution of reading matter, especially fiction, and to be depended on by publishers for large purchases of three-volume novels. Consequently his orders for material profoundly affected the literary world, and yards of stuff, printed

Party celebrating the opening of Mudie's Great Hall, December 1860.

in the prescribed pattern and in approved colors, were carefully produced. The length he preferred, the plots he enjoyed, the subjects he approved, the attitudes he endorsed, were perpetuated in the pages of the elaborately bound volumes lining his shelves. What is not found in these volumes indicates indirectly the kind of reticence thought necessary and desirable not only by the librarian but by his Victorian subscriber; for the middle- or upper-middle-class reader who exchanged his volume regularly under Mudie's dome received, besides entertainment, confirmation or definition of many of his beliefs.

Like other institutions created by an age, the circulating library extended and emphasized the ideas with which it began, solidifying them until, at the height of its influence, it appeared to be the originator of these ideas, and was so attacked. It is as a disseminator of established attitudes towards literature that the circulating library, especially Mudie's, becomes almost identical with the reader. It is a good base on which to build a study of some of the characteristic assumptions and theories which influenced the literature of the Victorian age, and the ways in which these assumptions and theories were affected by the established customs of publishing and distributing books. To evaluate the effects of this Library Establishment on authors, publishers, and the reading public, it will be helpful to have some knowledge both of the subscription practices of the library at the height of its influence and of the three-decker form itself.

If the term "circulating library" was virtually synonymous with "Mudie" in the mid-nineteenth century, "Mudie" meant fiction, or more specifically, novels. Although Charles Edward Mudie had started his library to oppose the eighteenth-century libraries which had stocked novels almost exclusively, and although Mudie himself was proud of the "inclusive character of the collection,"[2] novels bulked large in his business, both in numbers and in turnover. More subscribers were likely to ask the Mudie attendant for *The Bertrams* or *Adam Bede* than for *The Origin of Species*, for *East Lynne* than for *The Science of Languages*, for *Lady Audley's Secret* than for Kinglake's *Crimea*.

It is to Mudie's credit that he did much to establish and maintain the character of his library through large orders for non-fiction: 3,250 copies of Livingstone's *Missionary Travels in South Africa*, 3,000 copies of McClintock's *Voyage of the "Fox,"* and an initial order of 1,000 copies of Lady Brassey's *Voyage in the "Sunbeam,"* an order so large it amounted to the entire first printing, and indeed necessitated a delay in publication until Longman's could strike off more copies.

Describing his books, Mudie advertised in 1855, "The preference is given to Works of History, Biography, Religion, Philosophy, and Travel. The *best* works of Fiction are also freely added."[3] In 1860 Mudie wrote to the *Athenaeum* that he had added over 391,000 books to his collection between January 1858 and October 1859. On the basis of numbers of volumes, about 42 percent were fiction, 22 percent history and biography, 13 percent travel and adventure, and 23 percent miscellaneous. According to his own analysis, the figures were

	NUMBER OF VOLUMES
History and Biography	87,210
Travel and Adventure	50,572
Fiction	165,445
Miscellaneous, including works of Science and Religion, and the Principal Reviews	87,856[4]

Spectator figures for his additions in the decade 1853–1862 show substantially the same percentage of fiction.[5] At this point it must be remembered that Mudie listed volumes, and that the fiction category included many multi-volumed works. By title, then, a fair estimate would give fiction about one-third of Mudie's total stock (the same percentage as that cited by John Francis in 1888[6]). Nevertheless, fiction was the largest single category Mudie listed, and it was as a distributor of stately three-volume novels that he came to be best known, so that the pervasive influence of the circulating library is most clearly perceived in fiction.

The virtual standardization of the novel into three volumes is the most obvious influence on fiction. Novels in three volumes were naturally good business for the circulating library. By Mudie's terms in 1858 (substantially the same as those in force from his opening until the doors finally closed almost a century later), a subscriber could have one exchangeable volume for a guinea a year, or four volumes at two guineas. Larger sub-scriptions, intended for country houses, clubs, or other organizations, were also available: eight volumes for three guineas, fifteen for five guineas, thirty for ten guineas, and sixty for twenty guineas. In 1863, Mudie advertised his rates as from "One Guinea to One Hundred Guineas Per Annum." In 1869, the London Book Society charges for three or six volumes (with delivery service) were

	3 MONTHS	6 MONTHS	12 MONTHS
Three volumes	15s.	£1. 5s.	£2.2s.
Six volumes	£1.1s.	£1.18s.	£3.3s.

In 1882, advertisements, noting discreetly that "Two or Three Families in any Neighbourhood may unite in One Subscription," described two types of large subscriptions: Class A, which provided fifteen volumes of the "newest books" at one time for five guineas a year; and Class B, which for the same price furnished twenty-five volumes of "older books."[7] According to the *Pall Mall Gazette*, one public office in London took over twenty thousand volumes for two hundred guineas a year.[8] Special "Liberal" terms were available for "Book Societies and Literary Institutions." Leading periodicals were available on the day of publication to "Town Subscribers," each issue counting as one volume. The importance of the periodical division, which tends to be hidden behind the volumes of three-deckers, may be inferred from such comments as one in the *Quarterly Review* by Henry Longueville Mansel, who attributed the low quality of the frequently serialized sensation novels in part to the widespread practice of borrowing periodicals.[9] From the country the patron had to pay two guineas for his volume, and was also responsible for the cost of carriage to and from the central library. The most famous rate, of course, was the guinea a year with which Mudie had first attracted widespread attention.[10]

With such terms, then, Mudie could circulate one three-decker to three separate subscribers, paying a total of three guineas a year, or an entire novel for two guineas to families or to those readers who were too impatient for news of the outcome of the proposal to wait until the volume could be exchanged. Works in three volumes enabled the librarian to double or triple the profit he would have from a single-decker. Furthermore, while tripling his intake, he also tripled the number of subscribers he could serve with one title. In addition, Mudie's discount on the three-decker, frequently amounting to fifty percent of the nominal price and sometimes more, was proportionately greater than for one-volume or even two-volume books. It is not surprising, then, that Mudie's was first of all reluctant to stock a one-volume first edition, and moreover, if obliged to stock, even less inclined to list, advertise, and circulate the work. Finally, of course, the market for borrowing three-deckers was captive because the 31s.6d. bookstore price was obviously prohibitive for the middle-class buyer, who might have been able to stretch his budget to include some novels at 6s., 7s.6d., or even 10s.6d.

· *Three-Deckers* ·

THE NUMBER THREE WAS NOT CHOSEN ARBITRARILY BY Mudie to fit into his business of course, but through circulation from his counters "three-decker" soon became synonymous with the type of novel on his shelves. The term itself was derived, according to the *OED*, from the eighteenth-century three-decked ship, specifically "a line-of-battle ship carrying guns on three decks" (the usage Kipling drew on for his poem). In the eighteenth century novels were usually issued in two to seven volumes: Richardson's *Clarissa* (1748) in seven, Fielding's *Amelia* (1752) in four, Goldsmith's *Vicar of Wakefield* (1766) in two, and Fanny Burney's *Cecilia* (1782) in five. The three-, four-, and five-volume forms were most common, and by the opening years of the nineteenth century, novels in more than three volumes had become noticeably unusual.[11]

Scott did much to further the three-volume fashion with *Waverley* in 1814, and by publishing fourteen three-deckers in the next fifteen years. Even without Mudie, Scott's enormous popularity would have insured a temporary vogue for this form of issue, because Scott's influence on publishing, as well as on the novel itself, was powerful. With Mudie the fashion soon solidified into something that looked to many writers like an instrument of torture, a Procrustean bed on which novels were placed to be dragged out or broken into the statutory length.[12]

Scott's prestige is apparent not only in the emergence of three volumes as standard, however; it was also felt in size and price. By 1832, the year of his death, these had become fairly uniform; each volume was post octavo, priced at 10s.6d. The novel had grown from the duodecimo, frequently used in the eighteenth century, to a post octavo book measuring about 5 by 7½ inches, roughly the dimensions of the modern "Everyman" series. This size played a part in the length of the novel, and figured prominently in the controversy that rose over the end of the three-decker, when almost the only logical argument for the established system was the convenience of the volume. Scott's example also gave considerable impetus to the steadily rising price of fiction. In the middle years of the eighteenth century, novels had averaged 2s.6d. a volume in plain paper wrappers or 3s. bound. Richard D. Altick points out that in the 1770s it would have cost a woman in one of the London trades the proceeds of a week's work to buy a three-volume novel, say *Evelina*.[13] From this time, the cost of fiction rose slowly and regularly, adding from sixpence to a shilling a volume with each decade.

The cost of living was rising too, forced up by the Napoleonic wars, and circulating libraries, now usually separated from booksellers, also contributed to the spiral. The five volumes of *The Scottish Chiefs* sold for 35s. in 1810,[14] and 7s. a volume had become the average price for substantial fiction by 1814. Five thousand copies of *Waverley*, which appeared in three volumes for a guinea, were sold that year. Scott's three-deckers quickly rose in popularity; four years after *Waverley* the 10,000 copies of the first edition of *Rob Roy* were sold out in three weeks. Their prices, too, were going up; *The Antiquary*, 1816, cost 24s.; the next year *Ivanhoe* brought 30s.; and in 1821 *Kenilworth* at a guinea and a half set the 10s.6d. a volume level Scott was to keep for the rest of his novels. By 1830, eighteen out of twenty-eight three-deckers sold for 31s.6d.; in 1840 fifty-one out of fifty-eight brought that price.[15] Two years after that Mudie opened his library, and the three-decker at the price Scott had made popular and profitable was well on the way to the position of unquestioned supremacy it maintained until the last decade of the century.

Changing conditions were reflecting the rapid growth of the reading public and the expansion of publishing. Charles Knight estimated that between 1800 and 1827, 588 new books a year were issued, an increase of 216 percent over the average for the last eleven years of the eighteenth century.[16] The very increase in numbers undoubtedly suggested benefits to be derived from greater standardization in publishing practices. While Scott, as an individual author, was doing much to stabilize the form and price of novels, publishers also were systematizing as well as expanding their activities, to include bookbinding, for example. Mudie is one of those credited with helping to establish the new custom. During the early days of the three-decker, novels were usually priced in quires, and sold to distributors who first bound the sheets and then rushed them to the circulating libraries. On notice by a publisher that the sheets would be ready at noon, the distributors would line up, buy, and begin their race to see which one could get copies to the libraries first.[17] Mudie soon started to buy the sheets himself, binding them to suit his own requirements. Because of the growth of publishing and of Mudie's, and the highly speculative nature of the middleman's market, this early practice was generally abandoned, and publishers soon started to issue their novels bound, usually in cloth. During the second half of the century, however, W. H. Smith occasionally negotiated with a publisher for sheets. Michael Sadleir traced a copy of *Felix Holt*, in bright blue instead of Blackwood's brown binding, to such a sheet purchase.[18] In this case the library was probably trying to cut costs, because the publisher, resolutely resisting library demands for large discounts, was charging a high 22s.6d.

Although Scott's publishing practice provided a good recommendation, it alone would not have sufficed to maintain the guinea-and-a-half price for some sixty years, during which part-issue and other forms of cheap literature threatened it, without the backing of the circulating library. Scott's poetry had been sold at high prices, too; *The Lady of the Lake*, for example, brought two guineas. This amount, however, was not standardized, and poetry generally was reasonably priced during the Victorian era. When a guinea and a half was still prevalent in novel publishing, Browning's volumes sold for 5s. to 7s.6d. (*Dramatic Idyls*, 1879, cost 5s., for instance, and the four volumes of *The Ring and the Book*, 1868–1869, cost 7s.6d. each); Arnold's *Poems*, 1853, cost 5s.6d., and *Enoch Arden*, 1864, 6s. Poetry was, of course, bought more often than borrowed, although Mudie stocked large numbers of some editions. Its comparative inexpensiveness undoubtedly stimulated sales, and indirectly indicates the power of the libraries to maintain an arbitrary form and price. Poetry, in other words, issued for a small group of buyers, was priced to meet its market; first editions of novels, on the other hand, had virtually no market except the circulating library, to whose advantage it was to maintain a nominal 10s.6d. on each volume.

Authors and publishers acknowledged the three-decker as necessary and planned accordingly, recognizing it as the easiest and most effective way to bring a novelist's name to public attention. Writing to George Eliot of her *Scenes of Clerical Life* which he was about to issue in two volumes, John Blackwood wished that "the Series had been long enough to make the statutory three volumes as that would have afforded time to fix your reputation more firmly and familiarly in the public mind."[19] In the same letter Blackwood admits that "a permanent or extended sale" would depend on the one-volume reprint, but the rigidity of the system in 1857 was such that it did not then occur to him to break it by publishing only a one-volume edition. The way to establishing a reputation lay through the circulating library, and almost the only way to its shelves, for the novel, was through the three-, or more rarely, the two-volume issue, at a half guinea per volume.

The cracks in this solid wall of respectable three-deckers were serialization and publication in monthly parts, the latter form largely popularized by Dickens and consistently used during the years in which he was writing. By this method, the reader spent a pound for a novel on a kind of installment plan, at a shilling a month. Part-issue was usually most successful with established authors, since profit depended on large sales. Later in the century, serial publication in the successful new monthly magazines like *Macmillan's* and the *Cornhill* largely superseded part-issues. In effect serialization contributed to the strength of the three-volume form. Novels issued in monthly parts usually came out later in only one or two volumes, but serials often preceded appearance as a standard three-decker. By 1863 Trollope could term the original publication of *Rachel Ray* in volume form as "old-fashioned."[20] At any rate, the cracks remained surface flaws which never split the solid three-decker wall. Even if authors had to stretch and expand their work to meet a quota of pages, even if printers had to widen margins and lead pages to piece out suitable volumes, still the all-powerful libraries demanded and got their quota of three volumes. The reason was simple and economically sound as far as it went. The libraries could count on being able to circulate enough copies of an ordinary novel to warrant placing an order with the publisher sufficiently large to guarantee a profit on the edition. Even with the large library discounts which often brought the price of a novel down from 31s.6d. to 15s. or even less, publishers had a handsome profit margin.

· *The "Procrustean Bed"* ·

PROFIT MARGIN ALONE WAS ENOUGH TO SUSTAIN THE THREE-decker in any storm of criticism. One of the most frequent of the contemporary complaints protested the "Procrustean length" imposed on both authors and readers. Actually, however, neither the upper nor the lower limit of words was rigidly defined, and there was a trend, even while three-deckers were most popular, towards shorter novels. Writing some years after the libraries' ultimatum that quashed the form, Sir Arthur Quiller-Couch agreed with a *Morning Post* explanation of this gradual shrinkage in the novel. From a length of about 250,000 words in the times from Scott to Dickens and Thackeray, the novel had dwindled to 150,000 words when serialization in magazines became popular. After the disappearance of the three-decker there came a further reduction to 70,000 or 80,000 words.[21]

While there was certainly a general tendency to shorter novels as the century advanced, and while the serial, which ran anywhere from twelve up to an occasional twenty months with about 10,000 to 12,000 words in each installment, definitely influenced length, a three-decker's cargo of words varied widely throughout the nineteenth century. One of the shortest, Mary Wollstonecraft Shelley's *Frankenstein*, 67,150 words, appeared in 1818; Henry James's *Portrait of a Lady*, with 223,165 words, was published in 1882. On the other hand, Thomas Hope's *Anastasius*, 1819, ran to 273,996 words, although Robert Buchanan's *Foxglove Manor*, 1884, carried only 97,845.[22] Usually a three-volume novel ranged from 120,000 to 200,000 words, and less frequently from 200,000 to 250,000. In rough figures, *Guy Mannering* and *Oliver Twist* contain about 161,000 words each; *Henry Esmond*, 186,000; *Romola*, 227,000; *A Pair of Blue Eyes*, 131,000; and *Tess of the d'Urbervilles*, 151,000. Trollope, with a practiced eye on the market, estimated the "proper length of a novel volume" as 66,000 words,[23] or 198,000 for the usual three. Charles Reade approached the upper limits with *Hard Cash* at 260,498 words. If it seemed difficult to squeeze the text between the covers of a three-decker, or for other reasons, the novel might be expanded to four volumes (as were Bulwer-Lytton's *My Novel* and George Eliot's *Middlemarch*), although this practice remained exceptional.

Many factors besides publishing practices determined length of course, but the three-decker form did set boundaries (even if somewhat elastic ones), especially for minimum requirements. To reach that lower limit was becoming increasingly difficult for writers like George Gissing, attempting what he termed the "dramatic" novel. With a leeway of 150,000 words, however, the three-decker had room for varied lengths—for Mrs. Henry Wood's highly successful *East Lynne*, whose 251,866 words appeared in 1861, as well as for J. M. Barrie's *Little Minister*, some 137,000 words shorter, but also widely popular thirty years later. What was important about the length of a manuscript for a novel from the typographical standpoint was that it fit into three volumes, so that the published work could reap the advantages inherent in that form.

The prestige of the three-volume novel, in part attributable to Scott, was nurtured and strengthened by Mudie's, catering as it did to the middle and upper-middle classes. It is difficult for twentieth-century readers to evaluate the status which the Select Library's complex organization helped to confer on the three-volume form. It was customary, certainly, for successful three-deckers to be re-issued in single volumes, but there hovered over a first edition in three stately tomes an aura of dignity and worth which tended to obscure those works unfortunate enough to be issued originally in a meagre one volume. Even Dickens, who in effect bypassed the libraries by selling his works in monthly parts directly to his readers, recognized and accepted this prestige throughout his career. When it had been decided to stop *Master Humphrey's Clock*, Dickens thought it might be better for him to publish nothing for a year, "and then come out with a complete novel in three volumes and 'put the town in a blaze again.' "[24] Dickens was obviously interested in obtaining some respite from his rapid pace, and afraid that he might be pushing his success too far. Still, it is apparent that he regarded the three-decker with respect as a means of maintaining his reputation. A quarter of a century later, he was warning an aspirant to the pages of *All the Year Round* that he had insufficient "knowledge of life or character" to attempt the eminent three volumes. Dickens advised him to try first for success in short fiction, "and in the meantime put your three volumes away."[25]

So accepted, in fact, was the triple-issue convention in fiction that critics and writers casually referred to the third volume in much the same way as a last chapter or conclusion might be mentioned today. A novel "may hurry the reader onward through its three volumes,"[26] George Henry Lewes wrote in 1847; "my third volume ended when I was sixteen, and was married to my poor husband," Thackeray's Mrs. Mackenzie tells Pendennis (*The Newcomes*, Chap. XXIII). Critics did not attempt to discourage individuals from buying three-volume novels they deemed worthless; rather they hoped, as did James Fitzjames Stephen, to induce "one circulating library not to order this work."[27] To some, the task of wading through three volumes became so burdensome that they claimed they felt "almost exhilarated" to find a novel in only two. The term even crept into common metaphorical use. "The impatient public has been allowed to peep into the third volume of the great Chinese romance, and all the absorbing interest is gone," *The Times* commented about the end of the Chinese war in 1860.[28]

Three volumes were expensive, and considered substantial by public and authors alike. Typical is the lament of Minna Fetherstonaugh, a minor novelist of the period, in a letter to her publisher, that her new manuscript was the wrong length:

too much for a magazine story, "and too little to make more than a 1 vol. book."[29] For an unknown author to try to publish in one volume even at 2*s*.6*d*. would be sheer folly, a publisher wrote to the *Daily News* in 1871: "The trade would fight shy of him, the public would not buy him, and the press would inevitably snub him."[30] Reputations and money were made in the three-volume market.

The relative absence of single-volume fiction from the lists of the Select Library must have done much to lower readers' opinions of it as a form. Geraldine Jewsbury, a reader for the publishing firm of Bentley, epitomizes the distinction in her reports, advising that one manuscript "is more fitted for a railway book than the three volume dignity." Another, she finds, "would make a very good addition to those works which you publish . . . for railway reading and for *that* purpose and in *that* shape I would recommend you to take it."[31] In thus relegating some novels to first issue in single volumes, Geraldine Jewsbury separated "literature" from "light amusing reading." Such a distinction, buttressed by the comforting bulk of the three-decker, would have been accepted and approved by Mudie's subscribers.

The custom of issuing a cheap, one-volume edition of a popular novel about a year after it had "run the gauntlet of the three volumes and received the approval of the press"[32] actually reinforced the distinction of the original, adding to the lustre held by any first edition, the apparent merit of the three-volume form. Any one-volume novel tended to be thought of as a railway novel or a re-issue, so that first editions in that form risked being mistaken for the "Cheap Reprints," with smaller type and narrower margins, which were "almost invariably excluded" from Mudie's, as the catalogue declared. In a letter to his friend Fitzjames Stephen, the younger Lytton clearly indicated the position of the one-volume novel. Writing first about his father's *Zanoni* and *A Strange Story* (issued in three and two volumes respectively), he goes on to mention that he had "picked up . . . a little anonymous one volume novel."[33] To him, as to Geraldine

Jewsbury, the former were literature, and worthy of serious discussion. Even making allowances for filial partiality, the tone of the second reference is sharply different, implying a story fit only for whiling away an hour or two, comparable to "something to read on the plane" today. At best, the single-decker might be a light, perhaps whimsical work, of the sort described by Alexander Macmillan to Henry Kingsley. Outlining a story related by Jane Welsh Carlyle, Macmillan concluded it might not expand to fit a three-decker, "But it would make the charmingest little one-volume affair in the world."[34]

The three-volume first edition was substantial, accepted, conventional; its one-volume sister seemed light, charming perhaps, but often questionable. Exceptions were novels of religion and of adventure; like juvenile works, they frequently appeared in single volumes. The difference between the two forms of issue involved not merely length, but more importantly, content. The one-volume novel, free from Mudie's scrutiny, might contain material considered immoral, either intrinsically or through the author's treatment of it. On the other hand, some critics saw in the one-volume form a mid-century tendency to the psychological novel. Such was the view expressed by the *Saturday Review* in 1859, when the three-decker was at the height of its power, and the *Saturday* itself was on the way to establishing its reputation as one of the most influential of the English literary periodicals. Analyzing the differences between the two kinds of publication, the writer expressed an almost universal judgment of literary critics on the library edition: "Three-volume novels are the children of the circulating libraries. They are articles of commerce. . . ." and were therefore so constructed.[35]

Altogether different was the one-volume novel, which the *Saturday* believed was almost always the work, usually the first, of a clever young author. Against such merits as original plots framed by well educated writers with lively talent, the *Saturday* set two main objections. First, it criticized one-volume novels as masks for indulging the "dangerous habit" of self-description, the characters being simply the author in varying moods, in high spirits or low, or in love, and revealing their creator's intense interest in life. Furthermore, these novels perpetuated a transitory, even sometimes diseased, state of mind, and presented their readers with a mass of contradictory opinions. As such, the *Saturday* considered them mere pretences by which authors were relieved of the trouble of making up their minds. The *Saturday's* critic thus saw three-volume novels as works manufactured for a certain market, with hackneyed plots by plodding authors. The one-volume novel, on the other hand, illustrated what happened to fresh talent channeled in directions which seemed wrong to him, but appear surprisingly modern to us. To him, as to others, the form reflected the type of fiction between its covers.

Complementing the general attitude of disparagement of the one-volume novel was an elevation of any work worthy of notice to three volumes. Julian Hawthorne writes of visiting Wilkie Collins, who praised *The Scarlet Letter* as a great novel. "Even the second volume, where most novelists weaken, is fine, and the third fulfills the splendid promise of the first," said Collins, nor would he believe Julian's protests that it was only one until he found it on his bookshelf. "You are right. One volume and not over 70,000 words in all! It is incomprehensible!"[36] While this is an extreme example, Collins's assumption would nevertheless not have seemed strange to readers conditioned by the libraries to equating fictional worth with the three volumes in which it was contained.

Nor was this equation confined to fiction. Biographies, memoirs, works of travel and adventure—all reflected the effects of the three-decker. The triple issue was not such an ironclad regulation for them, of course, and frequently the length justified the form. Still, biographies like Fanny Kemble's *Records of a Girlhood* and *Records of Later Life* were issued in three volumes, and Mary Russell Mitford, in the midst of moving her

estimated four tons of books to Swallowfield, was called upon
to supply material for another volume of her *Recollections*. She
had intended two volumes, but her publisher desired a third.
Bentley issued these works, and his success with fiction probably
strengthened his disposition toward a three-decker. With all
allowances for Victorian delight in detail, for justifiable, even
inevitable length, and for numerous exceptions both over and
under the regulation number for novels, it seems clear that the
method of publishing fiction was strong enough to exert an influence on non-fiction. Especially if a book were planned for library
circulation, the publisher or the author might be tempted to
expand until the result would be, as Edmund Gosse described
a two-volume biography, "a publication . . . like a vast sarcopha-
gus in the manner of Bernini, with weeping angels blowing
trumpets over tons of marble . . . a shapeless monster of a
book."[37]

Whatever the general prestige of the three-decker, critical
opinion, like that advanced by the *Saturday Review* writer, came
to regard the average example of the form at its best as light,
and at its worst, worthless and sentimental. George Henry Lewes
expressed his shock at Dickens's lack of intellectual interests by
noting that there were "nothing but three-volume novels and
books of travel" on his bookshelves early in his career, although
two years later three-deckers "no longer vulgarised the place."[38]
By the nineties this attitude had become so general it afforded
material for satire in a play. In *The Importance of Being Earnest*,
which Oscar Wilde wrote in the summer of 1894 when the
controversy over the banning of the three-decker was at its
height, the identity of Jack Worthing turns on the manuscript
for a three-volume novel. "In a moment of mental abstraction,"
his nurse, Miss Prism, had dropped the infant Jack into the
handbag intended for her text ("of more than usually revolting
sentimentality," according to Lady Bracknell). The nurse then
checked the bag at Victoria Station; the manuscript itself, which

she had written during her "few unoccupied hours," was in turn put in the perambulator and abandoned when she discovered her mistake, too late of course to recover the child.

The guinea-and-a-half price of the three-decker did more than contribute to its prestige and strengthen its monopoly; it was a part of that monopoly. Attacks were often made on the "exorbitant price" of fiction; others were directed against the triple-issue; actually they were virtually inseparable: it was the three-decker at 31s.6d. that ruled. To publish one volume at 31s.6d. or even half that amount would obviously have been disastrous to any publisher. The price was already high enough to discourage individual buyers, and the profits of the circulating libraries would have been cut by two-thirds, since only one subscriber could read the book at a time. For publishers to reduce the guinea-and-a-half price, on the other hand, while continuing to float the three-decker, was never successful because even at a reduced price the work was still too expensive for individuals, and as long as libraries wanted three volumes, they also required, whatever they actually paid, a nominal price high enough to rule out purchasers.

· *Anatomy of Publication* ·

AFTER MID-CENTURY, A SUCCESSFUL NOVEL MIGHT RUN through several modes of publication. Starting as a serial in a magazine, it would soon appear in a standard "library" edition of three volumes. Mudie's subscriber had the advantage of learning the final outcome of the proposal three to six weeks before the serial reader. If magazine buyers also patronized Mudie's, there may even have been runs on last volumes of popular works. Charles Reade's agreement with Dickens and William Henry Wills for *Hard Cash* spells out a typical arrangement. Reade retained the copyright and was "at liberty to publish the story as a complete work three weeks before the final portion . . . be printed in 'All the Year Round.' "[39]

Actually more was involved than capitalizing on the impatience of readers: the three-decker found its most urgent demand before bound copies of the magazine were available. Bentley's experience with *Poor Miss Finch* shows what could happen when a library waited for the magazine volume. In this case, the villain was not Mudie's, but Smith's. According to Wilkie Collins's own account,

> Mr. Bentley purchased of me the right of issuing an edition of the book [*Poor Miss Finch*] . . . —relying of course on the Libraries to take *his* issue of the story, in place of Cassell's issue in the shape of the volume of their magazine. . . . Mudie stood by us. But the Railway Circulating Library kept their subscribers waiting until Cassell's Miscellaneous volume came out—and then bought four hundred copies of it, and served my story out to their customers in *that* form. The subscribers submitted—and the result is that Mr. Bentley has not made a halfpenny by his bargain.[40]

The threat of buying magazine volumes also gave Mudie and other librarians the chance to squeeze an extra discount from the three-decker. Later in the century, when novels began to appear in newspapers this threat diminished, as authors and publishers were quick to perceive. Writing to Andrew Chatto in 1882, Charles Gibbon recalled a previous "injury to the sale of the 3 vol. edition by the libraries using the bound volumes of the magazine," but pointed out that as his new novel was "appearing in newspapers the libraries will not be able to get hold of it except in your edition."[41]

After the library edition had been circulating at Mudie's for about a year, a one-volume reprint (perhaps revised or cut) was sold, usually at 6s., though this varied. One of Dickens's rare three-deckers, *Great Expectations* (1861), appeared first in *All the Year Round*, for example. Within five months after its appearance as a book, it had gone through five editions in three-volume form; a reprint in one volume at 7s.6d. was issued in 1862, and one at 5s. in 1863. Dickens's enormous popularity, however, caused variation in the standard pattern. More typical instances were such three-deckers as *Romola* (1863), originally in the *Cornhill*, with a one-volume, 6s. reprint in 1865; *Put Yourself in His Place* (1870), also originally in the *Cornhill*, with an 1871 reprint; *The Eustace Diamonds* (dated 1873, but actually issued in December 1872), originally in the *Fortnightly*, with an 1873 reprint (in two volumes); *The Return of the Native* (1878), originally in *Belgravia*, with an 1879 reprint (dated 1880); and *Diana of the Crossways* (1885), originally in the *Fortnightly*, with an 1890 reprint. Finally, when the first reprint market was exhausted, a 3s.6d. form or a 2s. "yellowback" for railway bookstalls was issued. For these methods, the three-decker provided the pivot, not only because of its guaranteed market, but because success at Mudie's, or lack of it, provided a gauge by which publishers could estimate the market for cheap editions. When Charles Reade was negotiating about *The Cloister and the Hearth*, he summed up the situation neatly: "I shall be happy to sell Mr. Bentley the new work for such a period of time as may enable him to go at his leisure . . . from the dear edition to a 10s. edition then 5s. then 2s.6 and to reap the full benefit of all. I see no other way of doing business so long as Mudie is Emperor of England."[42]

Authors who had difficulties with Mudie for one reason or another had to wait until the cheap edition was issued to appeal to the buying public. One such author was Wilkie Collins, who in 1881 wrote of *Fallen Leaves* (already serialized in the *World* and published as a three-decker), that he was waiting until it "has been circulated in the third, and cheapest, form of publication, among a far wider circle of readers than any to which the book has yet appealed."[43] Single-volume reprints were preferred by some writers not merely because of the greater numbers of buyers, but for artistic reasons. Although towards the end of his life Harrison Ainsworth was no longer in the top rank of popular novelists, Routledge's issued a uniform illustrated edition of his works at 6s. a volume. Commenting on it to James

Crossley, Ainsworth admitted, "I quite agree with you that the books read better in this form than as originally published in three volumes."[44]

Four- and two-volume novels maintained a somewhat higher reputation than single volumes, but the three-decker was "a closed burrow" as George Moore put it. "Even the two-volume novel enters with difficulty."[45] Sometimes it was not even attempted; when *Wuthering Heights* was issued, for example, it was combined with *Agnes Grey* to form the conventional three volumes. Nor did the unscrupulous publisher Newby reveal that *Wuthering Heights* itself did not fill the regulation quota until the unsuspecting reader reached the final page of the second volume. The title page of the last volume reads: "Agnes Grey / A Novel / by / Acton Bell / Volume III." Publishers were more ready to take a chance with a three-volume novel; John Morley, reading manuscripts for Macmillan's, considered George Bernard Shaw "a man to keep one's eye upon," because he knew how to write, but for his *Unsocial Socialist* he "would not prophesy a financial success (it is not more than two small volumes)."[46] Macmillan then requested, as Victorian publishers frequently did with promising authors, to see anything else on a larger scale, a euphemism for three volumes.

Two volumes instead of three might mean the difference between rejection and acceptance of a manuscript by an unknown author; for a writer with an established reputation it amounted to pounds, shillings, and pence. When Bentley was negotiating with Rhoda Broughton, who at that time had several circulating library successes to her credit, he offered her £1,200 for *Second Thoughts* if it ran to three volumes, only £750 for two. Miss Broughton, who had difficulty stretching most of her manuscripts to three-decker proportions, could not manage it, and so reluctantly accepted the lower sum.[47]

Even novels by American authors, one volume in the United States, bowed to the three-decker, 31*s*.6*d*. edict of English publishing. Most of James Fenimore Cooper's tales were thus issued by Bentley, who also put out Melville's *The Whale* in that form. Others in the circulating library style included Hawthorne's *Transformation* (*The Marble Faun*), Mark Twain's *The Gilded Age*, and the novels of Henry James. The artificiality of the English price is strikingly shown by a comparison of costs on either side of the Atlantic. *Moby Dick*, to cite one instance, in one volume, sold for $1.50, while the tag on its English counterpart read 31*s*.6*d*., or the equivalent of more than $7.80.[48] Anthony Trollope records in his *Autobiography* that one of his three-deckers was published in the United States at 7½*d*. Although lack of international copyright, a sore point for nineteenth-century English authors, affected the American price, it could not account for a difference of more than six dollars.

For unknown authors, or for authors with doubtful talent, the three-decker and the circulating library offered a comparatively open avenue to publication. The *Daily News* thus explained the situation in 1871:

A, the novelist, brings to B, the publisher, a MS. work, which is printed and offered to C, the librarian. A may be an ass. Should the press and the public make this discovery, the book will not be successful; but A and B will lose very little, because C has . . . taken a certain number of copies at 15s. or 18s. each.[49]

In other words, any loss was distributed; "the publisher, the librarian, the public, and the unlucky reviewers are all sufferers to a small extent, the loss not falling heavily on any one." Although the *News* wondered what happened to such writers in other countries, it was positive that "at all events England may be regarded as the Paradise of inefficient or unknown novelists." The comparative ease with which fiction could be issued and the subsequent attraction to the form felt by writers seeking an audience, then, were contributing to the growth and development of the novel in the Victorian era.

In spite of protests against the circulating library, like

Matthew Arnold's declaration that "the system of lending libraries from which books are hired," which kept up "the present exorbitant price of new books in England," was actually "eccentric, artificial, and unsatisfactory in the highest degree . . . machinery for the multiplication and protection of bad literature, and for keeping good books dear,"[50] Mudie's flourished and sustained the three-decker. References to the New Oxford Street library abound in contemporary novels, testifying not only to the powerful impression it made on authors, but also to its importance in establishing verisimilitude for the faithful depiction of contemporary life. Thus in *Orley Farm* Mrs. Furnival, whose creator Anthony Trollope was himself a patron, explains her reasons for coming unexpectedly to the office of her husband, who is about to comfort Lady Mason, "Mr. Furnival, as I happened to be in Holborn—at Mudie's for some books—I thought I would come down and ask whether you intend to dine at home today." In Gissing's *Workers in the Dawn*, Maude Gresham, recently divorced after a loveless marriage à la mode, writes to her friend Helen Norman: "I cannot tell how much or how little you know of my story, which really I may some day be tempted to present to you in the familiar three volumes. I think it might go down excellently with the patrons of Mudie's, especially if the character of the heroine were a trifle idealised. . . ."

These characters from the pages of novels reflected reality; the Englishman borrowed his novels, even when they were written by personal friends. Robert Browning wrote his "Dearest Isa" that he had been unable to finish her book "because Mudie's stupidly sent the second volume twice."[51] George Gissing, struggling to make ends meet in London, was another Mudie patron; in a letter to his sister Ellen he commented, "I am just going to Mudie's, though goodness knows how I shall get there through this heat."[52]

4

PUBLISHERS, PROFITS,

AND THE PUBLIC

· *The Guaranteed Market* ·

WITH SUCH PRESTIGE AND PATRONAGE, IT IS NOT SURPRISING to find publishers catering to Mudie's. What was good business for the circulating library formed a sound economic basis for established and reputable general publishing firms as well as for fiction houses of dubious standing. Mudie's was not only buying books from publishers like Blackwood's, Chapman and Hall, Longman's, Macmillan's, Bentley's, Tinsleys', and Newby's, but paying dividends to some of them as well. Although to aspiring authors, the "Grand Old Men of the publishing world of that day" (as George Bernard Shaw called Alexander Macmillan, Longman, and Bentley), may have seemed "so powerful that they held the booksellers in abject subjection,"[1] they were actually highly sensitive to library requirements, as far as novels were concerned. Some production figures for the three-decker will show why it was so financially inviting to these companies.

Anthony Trollope, who had a long and close association with Chapman and Hall (he purchased a one-third interest in the firm for his elder son Harry), outlined the expenses for a three-volume novel in 1876. Paper, printing, and advertisements for an average edition of 600 copies (with an allowance for spoilage) amounted to about £200. With a sale of 550 copies (and 500 copies were "a good success for a novel" according to George Eliot[2]) at the libraries' discount price of 15s., the receipts would total £412.10s., leaving £212.10s. for the author and publisher.[3] Bentley's actual expenses in 1865 for Florence Marryat's *Too Good for Him* correspond with Trollope's estimate: 500 copies cost the publisher £235 (again including advertising). At the end of the century, S. Squire Sprigge, using Society of Authors figures, set production costs and advertising for 500 copies at under £130.[4] As late as 1894, the *Author*— probably specifically its editor, Walter Besant—felt that with non-union labor a novel could be produced for only £80, and that it would, with a sale of just 250 copies at 14s., yield a return of £175.[5] William Heinemann, on the other hand, expostulated that both union and non-union prices were uniformly 25 to 33 percent more than those shown by the Society of Authors,[6] whose figures undoubtedly reflected more zeal than accuracy. Even George Gissing, who had had some unfortunate experiences with publishers, noted that Besant had failed to take into account the risk incurred by the publisher and had furthermore "neglected to consider the ordinary business expenses of a publisher—his offices, clerks, warehouses etc."[7] Since Trollope paid careful attention to business, and was in a position to see both sides, his figures probably represent a fair estimate for good work from a reputable firm.

With a larger edition, profits were of course proportionately greater. Writing to Lady Strangford, one of his authors, in 1875 or 1876, George Bentley cited advertising and production costs for 2,000 copies as £568: ". . . for many years past the large libraries pay us only 15/- a copy for novels and . . . 4 copies are given in every 100 copies still further reducing the price to about 14/6. The practical result of this is, that 1500 copies yield about £1100."8 This would have netted £532 for the publisher and his author or, if 1,800 were sold, £737. Even if Mudie did not take "1500 of any Bentley novel, sight unseen," as John Carter believes he did,9 1,500 copies would seem to be a reasonable estimate of his order for a work from an established writer.

Taking these figures into consideration, it is difficult to understand how Tinsley could have legitimately charged Hardy £15 for the publication of his first novel, *Desperate Remedies*.10 In January 1871, Hardy paid Tinsley £75 in Bank of England notes. If the gross receipts covered the costs of publishing, this sum was to be repaid, and anything over those expenses was to be divided equally between Hardy and Tinsley. While not a striking success (scarcely three months after its issue Hardy was shocked to see it listed in Smith's surplus catalogue at the Exeter Station at 2s.6d. for the three volumes), it had a respectable sale. According to the accounting sent by Tinsley a year after its publication, 500 copies had been printed, and 370 sold; a check for £60 was enclosed.

If Trollope's estimate of £200 is used for production and advertising costs (and Tinsleys', lower in reputation than Chapman and Hall, may well have spent less), and if 370 copies were sold at 14s.6d., gross receipts would have exceeded expenses by about £68.5s. Thus Hardy would have received his £75 back, plus £34.2s.6d., or a total of £109.2s.6d., instead of the £60 he actually got. It is possible, of course, that Tinsley could not sell the novel for as much as 14s.6d.; but even at 10s.6d. a copy, the book would have come within £6 of covering a cost of £200. Just how the sum of £60 was determined is not clear. Hardy's letter to Tinsley states explicitly that if expenses were met, the full £75 was to be repaid, but there is no mention of any smaller sum or partial repayment. Mrs. Hardy comments simply that Tinsleys' indicated the £60 amounted to "all that was returnable to him . . . after the costs and the receipts were balanced, no part of the receipts being due to him."[11] Hardy himself was apparently so gratified at the small loss of £15 that he did not examine the figures closely. Perhaps sales came within £15 of covering expenses, so Tinsley charged Hardy only for the deficiency, or perhaps Tinsley paid the novelist from receipts that were in excess of expenses. At any rate it seems likely that Tinsley, who had a reputation for driving good bargains, at least cleared expenses, since he offered Hardy £30 for *Under the Greenwood Tree* about a year later.

An ironical sidelight, which also reveals the pervasiveness of library influence, is that W. H. Smith's bore some responsibility for the publication of Hardy's first novel as well as for his decision to abandon fiction. Edmund Downey, Tinsley's assistant, records that William Faux, manager of Smith's library department, read the manuscript of *Desperate Remedies* for Tinsley almost as a joke, but returned a glowing report of it. Some twenty-four years later, after the Bishop of Wakefield announced he had burned his copy of *Jude*, Smith's withdrew it from circulation, and the resulting furor caused Hardy to give up novel-writing.

These financial details concerning *Desperate Remedies* illustrate how profitable a three-decker could be for a publisher when he could persuade an author to pay at least a part of the expenses of production. This practice was sufficiently widespread to be satirized in the 1888 *Confessions of a Publisher*. What made it especially applicable to the "library edition" was the guaranteed market, which enabled the publisher to issue the work at a lower price for the author than would otherwise have been possible. Unscrupulous publishers, of course, took advantage of this to print worthless books, like the one written by the heroine of this satire. Her novel is, in the first place, only in one volume which, the publisher tells her, "is especially difficult to place successfully." When it becomes apparent that she has funds sufficient to cover the cost, he suggests revision by one of his writers to improve it and to bring it up to regulation size. She writes a check, and her career as an author is launched.[12]

Closely related to the cost of production in the overall expense of a novel was advertising. Here also Mudie influenced the practices of publishers, because his "Select, Varied, and Comprehensive" lists in the *Athenaeum*, *Spectator*, and other journals took much of the burden of announcement from the publisher. As far as three-deckers were concerned, publishers might simply state that new novels were "ready at every library," or to use Tinsleys' favorite phrase, "in Reading at all libraries." No appeal for actual purchase was made; on the contrary the reader was urged to borrow, to "Ask at the libraries."

Whether a simple listing, with the austere admonition that "These Lists, be it remembered, represent the main sources of the general information now in vogue,"[13] or an account of the number of individual works in circulation (1,000 copies of *It Is Never Too Late to Mend*, 1,200 copies of *Two Years Ago*, 2,500 copies of *Adam Bede*), Mudie notices provided the finest advertising available. A certain worth was implied by the simple inclusion of a book in the "select" library. In addition to this, the number of copies of a work taken not only showed how well Mudie was taking care of his patrons, but also stimulated demand through a bandwagon appeal. Well aware of the advantages gained by publishers from his advertising, Mudie often used it as a weapon in driving his bargains. "I wish to do what I can for 'Burgoyne,'" he wrote Bentley in 1873, "and if you will let me have 520 as 480 in the terms proposed I will place it near the top of my list . . . and give it a leading position in a few special advertisements." Again, in 1878, he was offering to "go on *advertising* the book if I can have say *50 or 100 at 18/*."[14]

Mudie advertised his favorite three-decker more readily than its one-volume counterpart, of course, and thus added to the difficulties of that struggling form an increased cost. If production expenses amounted to £300, and £100 was spent for advertising, the latter would amount to 25 percent of the whole, John Chapman explained in 1852. If, on the other hand, a pamphlet cost £10, and £10 was spent on advertising, 50

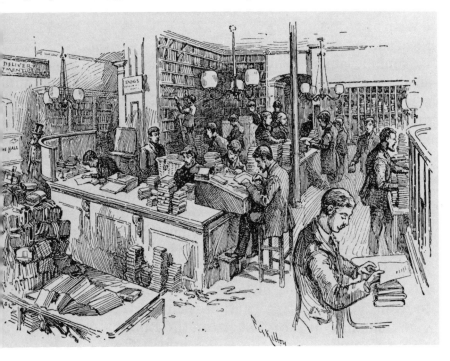

The London Book Society supplied delivery service in London.

percent of the entire outlay had been expended, continued Chapman. The relatively high cost of making an inexpensive book known was, Chapman maintained, one of the main reasons that "novels, narratives of voyages and travels, and indeed nearly all the most entertaining books" were "either spread out into the most ludicrous state of attenuation, or remorselessly cut down . . . for the publisher's Procrustean bed of three volumes post octavo." Thus the proportionately high cost of advertising one volume as opposed to three, added to the benefits accrued from Mudie's lists, contributed to making it "easier and more profitable" for publishers "to sell 500 copies of a work at a guinea and a half per copy, than 5,000 at half a crown, or 50,000 at a shilling."[15]

The publisher, then, was really issuing novels for the circulating library only; the owner of a chain of seven bookshops told the *Pall Mall Gazette* "for a three-volume novel I don't suppose I get one order in three months."[16] Since the sale of a small edition—400 copies or even fewer—sufficed to provide an adequate profit to such a publisher, the prices he charged Mudie throughout the second half of the century indicate his wide margin of profit. Before any discussion of these prices, however, it should be pointed out that after 1852 free trade prevailed in bookselling as in the rest of British economic life. Unlike the publishers, whose profits were more certain with limited sales at an established price, authors preferred the largest possible sales, and hence low prices. John Chapman, aided by authors like Dickens (who had presided at a meeting in Chapman's shop protesting the booksellers' practice of maintaining advertised prices), by Gladstone, and by such powerful journals as *The Times* and *Athenaeum*, finally brought the Booksellers' Association to submit to arbitration. That association had been formed four years earlier with the object of maintaining advertised prices. A commission headed by Lord Campbell agreed with general contemporary public feeling and found for free trade.[17] Because of that decision, from 1852 until after the disappearance of the three-decker, books could usually be bought for 2d. to 3d. on the shilling off the list price.

Not all publishers fell docilely into the libraries' pattern. Some resisted the discounts Mudie demanded; some launched original novels in series, attacking both the stipulated price and the format; some experimented with different forms and prices for individual works. Exactly what Mudie had to pay depended not only on such factors as the number of copies taken, the author, and the popularity of the novel, but especially on the ability of the publisher to drive a bargain. In 1850 Bentley offered three-volume fiction to Mudie's at a pound, as a "private arrangement." This was a general proposal; specific works might vary from that level. In addition there was a progressive reduction for large orders. Bentley offered *The Channings* to Mudie at 15s. if 1,000 copies were taken, at 20s. for any smaller number on the day of subscription, and at 22s.6d. thereafter. By 1862, when Bentley made this offer, the libraries had managed to increase their usual discount. These prices were higher than usual; Bentley explained them by the sum he had to pay Mrs. Henry Wood for the manuscript.[18]

Bentley, who headed a great fiction house and later invested in Mudie's limited liability company, was more responsive to library pressure than some other publishers. Even he, however, resisted the librarian's price-cutting; his pencilled note on Mudie's offer of 12s. for 25 copies of a three-decker read: "We can sell out probably all at 18/- elsewhere."[19] John Blackwood held out against Mudie's demands for discounts as much as possible, although eventually he capitulated. At the end of 1855 he was instructing his London manager Joseph Langford to "manage the Leviathan Mudie as best you can. . . . I dislike giving him the commission, but we must sometimes yield to expediency."[20] Apparently that "yielding" involved only an additional 10 percent discount, but Blackwood cautioned George Eliot against mentioning it in the case of *Scenes of Clerical Life*, because "as a general principle it is a doubtful policy."[21]

Blackwood's letters to George Eliot contain a running commentary on his battle with the Leviathan, the discounts he thought "wise" to offer, the times the librarian succumbed to him. Encouragement from George Eliot reveals her own interest. "There had need be some authors and publishers strong enough to resist his tyranny, which threatens to thrust poor books down the throats of the public, and to strangle good ones," she wrote in 1860, when Blackwood may have been charging

29s. for *The Mill on the Floss*. He told her at that time, "I chuckle considerably over Mudie having to take the 3,000. You may recollect that he offered to take that number if we would make the book sell at 21/. Confound his impudence it would have been simply diverting something like 3,000 times 8/- from the pockets of author and publisher into his voracious maw."[22] George Eliot agreed, and in 1861 acknowledged, ". . . indeed, to me personally, the satisfaction is unspeakable of having publishers whose transactions are known to be genuine. There was an article in the Athenaeum some time ago which assumed that Mudie got *all* novels at his own price: I suppose he takes care not to boast of the exceptions."[23]

As a result of Blackwood's firm policy, as late as 1866 W. H. Smith was paying 22s.6d. for *Felix Holt* (and incidentally buying few copies); but by the 1870s Blackwood had been forced to drop his price to 18s.[24] Even this was 3s. over the probable average of 15s., which Bentley and Chapman were then getting, and which was the level maintained, with a few exceptions, until the end of the three-volume novel. In the twenty years between 1850 and 1870, then, the actual price paid for the three-decker dropped by at least 25 percent, from 20s. or higher, to 15s. Although it is true that actual publishing expenses were also falling, this price reduction provides striking evidence of the generous profits carried by the three-decker in mid-century.

With these profits, it is easy to see why the three-decker prevailed. Still, publishers chafed under library stipulations. Nor was resistance limited to taking a stand against discounts. Some tried to appeal directly to the public with general price reductions or with price-breaking series of original novels. Smith, Elder made an attempt in the thirties, before the rise of Mudie's, and Chapman and Hall initiated a monthly series in 1845. Four 3s. parts, issued at monthly intervals, were to provide the equivalent of a three-decker in two volumes for 14s. (the extra shilling a volume for binding part-issues was a customary charge). Chapman and Hall thus cut the standard price of a guinea and a half by 17s.6d. The conservative *Athenaeum* praised the idea of providing "works of imagination in a cheaper form," and by "destroying the old three-volume system of mechanical symmetry, to deliver the author from an incubus, which has borne heavily on his fancy, and constructive power."[25]

Although three volumes seemed peculiarly adapted to circulating libraries, it must be remembered that Mudie did not originate that method of publication but developed a library suitable to distribute the form, in turn strengthening the form until what had been merely frequent became almost inevitable. Chapman and Hall's series entered into direct competition with the established form when Mrs. Marsh's *Emilia Wyndham* was brought out by Colburn in three volumes at 31s.6d. at the same time (1846) that her *Father Darcy* was being published in the monthly series. Unfortunately for Chapman and Hall, the three-decker, which proved to be the most successful of all the author's productions, completely swamped its lower priced rival. Whatever the literary merits of the two, however, the success of the three volumes of *Emilia Wyndham*, and the utter failure of *Father Darcy*, from which the series never fully recovered, seemed to indicate the futility of attempting to defy the established system. The last title advertised as part of the series was Geraldine Jewsbury's *Half-Sisters* (1848), at the increased price of 18s. for the two volumes. The same format, however, was used for *Mary Barton* (1848) and *Alton Locke* (1850).[26]

Nevertheless another price reduction, and a dramatic one at that, was initiated about ten years later by Bentley himself, who lowered prices while still adhering to three volumes, thus attempting to tap two markets—the libraries and the individual buyers.[27] His plan was enthusiastically approved by two novelists who were just beginning to publish. In August 1853, Wilkie Collins wrote to George Bentley that he was "delighted to hear that your house is about to lead the way in lowering the present extravagantly absurd prices charged for works of fiction. I should be inclined to doubt the propriety of this adhering to the three volume form, if I did not believe that you know the 'manner and customs' of Librarians much better than I do. . . . I heartily wish the new experiment, what I believe (if properly supported by really good works) it will certainly obtain—encouraging and genuine success."[28] Charles Reade reiterated this sentiment a month later, "You are about (*entre nous*) to lower the price of Novels in other words to invite the Public to buy instead of borrow, or to buy as well as borrow. Good!"[29] Bentley himself, in financial difficulties and trying to stimulate sales,[30] announced in the *Athenaeum* of October 15 that all new novel prices would be reduced by two-thirds, so that three volumes would sell for 10s.6d. rather than 31s.6d., with corresponding reductions for works in two volumes or one. The "First Original Novel published" on the "New Plan" was *Margaret, or Prejudice at Home and Its Victims*. A two-decker, it sold for 7s. Also advertised in the "New Arrangement" was Collins's *Basil*, a recently issued three-decker reduced to 10s.6d.[31] The experiment was short-lived, however; within two months Bentley's prices were back at the standard guinea and a half.

Probably the most significant result of this brief trial by Bentley was a competitive price reduction by Routledge's, also short-lived. Routledge's tried again in a year or two with a series, "Routledge's Original Novels," and about fifteen years later, in 1871, Samuel Tinsley (who had no connection with the firm of Tinsley Brothers whose mainstay was the three-decker), was complaining to *The Times* that authors and publishers were suffering under the system imposed by the libraries.[32] Within two months he had announced a "Series of New and Original Novels (usually published in three volumes at a guinea and a half) . . . , Price Four Shillings."[33] This series, with its spectacular 87 percent price reduction, received favorable attention in the press; the *Spectator* expressed its satisfaction with "the portable and readable size" of this example of a "very wholesome one-volume-edition system."[34] Still, it lasted only a few months and included only two titles. Furthermore, while Tinsley was maintaining that cheap, single-volume novels would increase profits to publishers, he prudently continued to issue the standard library editions.

Sporadic attempts by other publishers were made until the actual extinction of the three-decker. One of the last was in 1891, when William Heinemann launched his 5s. "Crown Copyright Series."[35] Advertising it as containing "New and Original Works," by the "First and Most Popular English, American, and Colonial Authors," Heinemann explicitly disclaimed the three-decker: "These novels will not pass through an Expensive Two or Three Volume Edition, but they will be obtainable at the Circulating Libraries."[36] What arrangements he had made to assure purchase by the libraries is unknown; he may have negotiated with Sidney Pawling, a nephew of Charles Edward Mudie, who ended his fifteen-year connection with the library the following year to join Heinemann's firm. At any rate, the publisher's specific reassurance that the volumes would be in the libraries confirms Mudie's reluctance to buy such works. By 1892, however, the need for a 5s. series had diminished because the libraries themselves were feeling the pressures which were to force them to ban the three-decker less than two years later. Six-shilling novels, for one thing, were being issued in increasing numbers; Heinemann himself brought out Kipling and Balestier's *Naulahka* that way in 1892. The Crown Copyright volumes (by such writers as Maarten Maartens, Robert Buchanan, and Mrs. Hungerford) were not spectacular bargains among the numbers of 6s. novels released after the library edict.

All the series were unsuccessful primarily because of the great influence of the circulating library. With a stake in high prices, the library had usually refused to stock the one-volume original series, and one publisher, acting independently, could make little headway against a powerful, centralized library like Mudie's. Finally, one-volume original editions failed because the quality of the fiction was not high enough to command a wide market. Without any guaranteed profit from the libraries, and with difficulty in selling to a "borrowing public," even at a fraction of the inflated price, publishers were unable to pay enough to lure competent writers.

It was only natural that the relations between authors and publishers should reflect the circulating library policy. Although the *Saturday Review* ironically exaggerated when it said that publishers believed "there is only one thing worse than a two-volume novel—namely, a one-volume novel,"[37] contracts and agreements frequently specified "a three-volume story" or its equivalent. Richard Bentley, urging Susan Ferrier to write another novel, assured her that if three volumes appear "too arduous, . . . the public would be glad to receive two, or even one volume," but he warned her that "they might not be so advantageous to your publisher."[38] Authors, too, offering manuscripts, carefully noted their length. Typical are Mortimer Collins's hearty query to Bentley, "Can't you make me an offer for a III Vol. novel? I've a capital one finished";[39] Augusta Marryat's more diffident, "I have written a novel in three volumes—Will you like to see it. . . ?"[40] and Wilkie Collins's inflated, "Having nearly completed an Historical Romance in three volumes, . . . I have thought it probable that such a work might not inappropriately be offered for your inspection."[41]

If an accepted manuscript were short, and the author could not or would not revise it, he could be asked to contribute a preface. But an author did not necessarily need to be consulted; a publisher had his own ways of stretching. Standard devices included widening margins, adding more lead between the lines, and increasing the size of the type. Since each chapter started well down on a page, multiplying the number of those divisions could lengthen a book without changing the text.[42] Such practices were in fact so common that a writer in *All the Year Round* in 1863 could thus describe a three-decker: "The Legitimate Novel, in three fat octavos, with three hundred and twenty pages in each of the two first volumes, and three hundred and fifty at least in the last, and not many lines in any of the pages, and not many pages in any of the chapters!"⁴³

Sometimes, indeed, publishers spaced out manuscripts surreptitiously, without consulting their authors. Rhoda Broughton "cried out against the publisher of *Not Wisely but Too Well* for stretching the tale over three volumes,"⁴⁴ and Trollope's well-known fiery temper flared up several times against typographical subterfuge. To Alexander Strahan he delivered this stinging rebuke: "I have always endeavored to give good measure to the public—The pages, as you propose to publish them, are so thin and desolated, and contain such a poor rate of type meandering thro' a desert of margin, as to make me ashamed of the idea of putting my name to the book. The stories were sold to you as one volume and you cannot by any argument be presumed to have the right of making it into two without my sanction to the change—."⁴⁵ On that occasion, Trollope won his point, and *Lotta Schmidt* appeared in one volume.

Trollope's integrity stood firm on this point of giving his readers fair measure. Answering the contention that it was none of his affair if publishers chose to lead out his pages, he pointed out that "the public would have to suffer, seeing that they would have to pay Mudie for the use of two volumes in reading that which ought to have been given to them in one."⁴⁶ Trollope consistently refused to compromise; to Alexander Macmillan, who was concerned in arranging a two-volume edition of *Sir Harry Hotspur of Humblethwaite*, he maintained, "But the fact is that as one pound of tea wont make two by any variance in packing the article—so neither will a one-volumed tale make two volumes."⁴⁷ Although Macmillan doubted that profits would be realized on a one-volume issue, he yielded, and the novel was finally brought out in that form by Hurst and Blackett.

Trollope's vigilance may have been sharpened because some four years earlier, ". . . on one occasion, and on one occasion only, a publisher got the better of me in a matter of volumes.

He had a two-volume novel of mine running through a certain magazine, and had it printed complete in three volumes before I knew where I was,—before I had seen a sheet of the letterpress. I stormed for a while, but I had not the heart to make him break up the type."[48] In his work-table for *The Belton Estate*, to which Trollope was apparently referring, which indicates plans for a two-volume book, Trollope further reproaches Chapman and Hall with the endorsement, "Surreptitiously printed in three volumes."[49] The opposite viewpoint was taken by Charles Reade, who washed his hands of the whole affair, and told Bentley he could print his novel as "one honest or two dishonest vols."[50]

While some publishers bowed to the seemingly inevitable and stretched manuscripts into three volumes with all their ingenuity, others were restless under the steady pressure from the libraries. One of the latter was John Blackwood, who also resisted Mudie's discount demands. As early as 1849, Bulwer-Lytton had written to him "that I am more and more inclined to think that for great sales the usual three-volume form is wearing out, and think something great might be done by a popular book in a new shape."[51] What the "new shape" was to be, Bulwer did not specify, although his opposition to part-issue eliminates that method. Some years later it turned out to be four volumes, the form Blackwood also used in the seventies for George Eliot's last two novels. Blackwood had kept the price of *Felix Holt* up, but at the expense of sales; Lewes was even advised by Frederic Chapman that he would have offered it at 15s.—instead of 22s.6d.—"and they [the libraries] would take no end." When, therefore, Blackwood suggested an "experiment in a new form," George Eliot quickly agreed. Nothing came of it, however, until it was apparent that *Middlemarch* would require at least four volumes, when Lewes proposed to Blackwood, ". . . as you have more than once spoken of the desirability of inventing some mode of circumventing the Libraries and making the public *buy* instead of borrowing I have devised the following scheme . . . to publish it in *half-volume parts* either at intervals of one, or as I think better, two months,"[52] at 5s. each.

This arrangement was finally agreed on after some discussion of details. Lewes, for example, wondered whether an advertisement sheet should be bound in every part, not only for the income, but for the appearance it would give of a larger volume, an important consideration with the British reader who, he believed, was accustomed by Mudie to the size of a three-decker. Although Langford, in London, had from the first objected that the form and price did "not even appear to give any advantage to purchasers," he went along with the experiment because he deemed it "so important . . . to get out of the clutches of Mudie." Langford's fears were apparently justified; Blackwood summed up the sales to Lytton about a year later: "In confidence I may tell you that the sale of Middlemarch has not reached an average of 5,000, and with the author's full possession of the public ear and the voice of the Press I think this may be looked upon as testing the greatest sale that can be reached by an expensive Novel."[53] It was successful enough so that Blackwood repeated the form with *Daniel Deronda*, but sales to individuals were disappointing, and the four-volume novel was never generally adopted.

Blackwood's experiment was an individual attempt with a single novel (not a price-breaking series) to free himself from the librarian's control. About ten years later, Longman tried Mrs. Oliphant's *In Trust* at 12s.6d. for three volumes. This was two shillings higher than the Bentley price of almost thirty years earlier, but Bentley's was to apply to all his new novels, not just to one. The widespread interest in Longman's venture expressed in literary periodicals indicated the growing dissatisfaction with the form. Still, little chance of success was foreseen. The novel itself was well chosen for such an experiment, the *Athenaeum* observed, because "it is not a work of genius, such as the public would buy at any price; it is an excellent representative of the better class of current fiction, such as most intelligent people ask for at the circulating library, but have not hitherto been in the habit of buying and placing on their shelves." Furthermore, the good type, paper, and binding made it "a far more serious and noteworthy attempt to abolish the English system of hiring books than any number of sixpenny reprints of books already popular."[54]

The *Spectator* echoed these points, adding that 12s.6d. was as low as any publisher could reasonably be expected to go. If the experiment were successful, continued the *Spectator*, the guinea-and-a-half price would receive its death blow. Nevertheless, the reviewer went on, reiterating a common belief that was in fact fostered by the three-decker, "we hardly expect success, believing . . . that the English are not a book-buying people."[55] It was the *Saturday Review*, however, which most accurately indicated the inherent weakness in Longman's attempt. Wishing well to the "spirited experiment," the *Saturday* nevertheless cautioned that success would not result in "the desired revolution in the relations between the writers and readers of novels."

> We are afraid it is almost as much out of the question that book buyers should purchase a three-volume novel for twelve shillings as for thirty-one shillings and sixpence. No private house can find room for the fictions of voluminous authors. This is not the only reason for their sinking out of sight, but it is a sufficient one.[56]

Another Mudie influence on publishing practices was his requirement of an interval (about a year) between the first edition and the reprint (usually at 6s.), sufficient to allow full circulation for the earlier issue as well as for its sale in the bookselling department. Mudie frequently asked for such pledges before confirming his orders, pledges which publishers justifiably resented. William Blackwood refused to bind his firm thus, writing to Langford with the decisiveness that characterized his dealings: "With regard to Mudie, we cannot bind ourselves not to publish a 12/ edition until a twelvemonth is past, or till any other time." He conceded that it was inadvisable from the standpoint of both author and publisher to issue a cheaper edition "until the three volume one has had it's [*sic*] full swing." Still he reiterated "when this will be we could not fix just now," and concluded, "Looking therefore both to the inconvenience to the author and ourselves . . . and to past effects in a similar case, upon Mr. Mudie's interest of such an edition, we do not think he has any reason to ask us for such a guarantee as he requires."[57]

Publishers had to strike a fine balance between what was to be gained from the virtually guaranteed library circulation and possible profits to be realized from sales to individuals of 12*s.*, 6*s.*, and later 3*s.*6*d.*, or cheaper editions. Mudie's sales of three-deckers withdrawn from circulation also helped publishers establish probabilities for the success of a cheap reprint and of possible future works by the author. If Mudie's volumes did not sell readily, reprint plans were delayed or abandoned. If, on the other hand, the used three-decker brought the 15*s.* that *Westward Ho!* did (see above, p. 29), the publisher might confidently encourage his promising author. Daniel Macmillan deduced from the Mudie price how much he could offer Kingsley for his next novel. If Kingsley made "a book equal to himself with the plot he sketched out," Macmillan felt justified in offering "to print a first edition large enough to yield him 1,000 *l.*"[58]

Publishers also considered Mudie in other, more minor ways, in choosing the title of a novel, for instance. Byron Webber thought Moore's *A Modern Lover* "A good title, but I am afraid it will get Bill [Tinsley] into trouble with the libraries."[59] Another time Mudie asked Bentley to alter the title of Wilkie Collins's *The New Magdalen*. Indignantly the author wrote his publisher that

> Nothing will induce me to modify the title. His proposal would be an impertinence if he was not an old fool. . . .
>
> But the serious side of this affair is that this ignorant fanatic holds my circulation in his pious hands. Suppose he determines to check my circulation—what remedy have *we*? what remedy have his subscribers?[60]

Geraldine Jewsbury, with her usual forthright vehemence, expressed her indignation about such interference to Bentley: ". . . about *Mudie*. I am *disgusted*—the hypocritical pretence of being frightened at a title—when the book & its tendency is not only moral but above morality—. . . ."[61]

Mudie's presence was also felt when publishers determined dates of issue. If these did not suit the librarian, he grumbled. B. Van Homrigh, Bentley's assistant, wrote to the publisher, "Mr. Mudie's Son called today to complain of the Numbers of Novels we publish the 3^d of this month. . . ."[62] Such expressions of dissatisfaction were common along Paternoster Row (or, in Bentley's case, New Burlington Street), as were also proposals that a publisher curtail all issues for a period of months, like Arthur Mudie's request, again to Bentley, "I wish to ask you to hold what books you can *back* for the next half year."[63] From the publisher, Mudie's preferences were relayed to authors, who planned their schedules accordingly. Thus Henry Kingsley, the younger brother of Charles, reassured Macmillan about a forthcoming work: "I have entirely absorbed myself in this, and it will be done in two months, the time which Mudie especially recommended, which is what I have been driving at."[64] Furthermore, if Mudie bought, he might ask to return his surplus volumes; the librarian was in a position to make applications like this one to Bentley: "I am sorry to trouble you in a matter of overstocking. . . . Can you allow me to *return nearly all!!*"[65] The close and complicated relationship with the library, all but forgotten today, was keenly felt by the publisher; if he should happen to forget it, the powerful Mudie did not hesitate to remind him of it.

One last influence, at least on one firm, can be traced to the libraries: the brilliantly colored and lavishly ornamented bindings that made three volumes from the house of Bentley recognizable anywhere—even in the gloomy Mudie catacombs. Many covers which bore their titles or distinguishing illustrations in deeply embossed designs enabled the Mudie attendant, filling a particular order or the frequent request for "a good novel," to locate the Bentley works almost by touch. In 1884, for example, he could have easily picked out *The Knave of Hearts* in this way, for it had a full-size playing card inset obliquely in the cover. Library influence is further discernible in that some of the generous profits Bentley received from three-deckers were converted into bindings that reveal his Victorian delight in embellishment. As John Carter described those issued just before the end of the form, "Peacock patterns, fancy stripes, lincrusta fabric; cloth fashioned to look like wood, like stone, like grass; visiting cards let into the sides, silk bows on the back, edges gauffered, zebraed, sprinkled with butterflies—no bizarre extravagance was too fantastic for Bentley," who himself compared the performance to "Mata Hari painting her mouth before the firing squad."[66] *A Girton Girl* (another work by Mrs. Annie Edwards) had inset in its pale mauve cover a wood-engraved medallion depicting the girl herself, resplendent in a flowing black and white cap and gown, leaning nonchalantly on a bit of Greek carving, and looking thoughtfully towards the outside of the book.

The shadow of Mudie's Great Ionic Hall fell from New Oxford Street across the conference tables of many Victorian publishers. Blackwood's testimony before the Royal Commission on copyright understated the case. "You may rely upon it," he assured Her Majesty's Commissioners, "that the publishers and authors have considered the subject [of the circulating library system] thoroughly, and act according to the best of their light."[67] Actually Mudie was more than "considered," he was attended to respectfully, and his wishes became the reality of publishing. The number of volumes for a book, its price, the date of its issue, the size of the edition, the number of individual titles to come out at a specified time, the title, even the binding—all these Mudie actively, if silently, helped to determine. Besides external matters, Mudie's power touched internal considerations, such as typical attitudes and plots in the triple-volumed editions lining his shelves. The Victorian novelist, with a few exceptions, responded to his public not directly, but through its representative in the person of Charles Edward Mudie.

· A Guinea a Year: Mudie and His Subscribers ·

WHETHER FOR GOOD OR EVIL, THEN, MUDIE'S LOOMED importantly in Victorian publishing, especially fiction. Even more obvious than the influence on publishers were effects on the reading public, the borrowing public, as it was developed by the libraries. On their way to finding readers, three-deckers always detoured through New Oxford Street. Authors and publishers accepted this intervention, and eventually grew to rely on it. Because he met his public through the circulating library, the novelist achieved one of the early steps towards success when his work rested on library shelves. Hardy and his wife first realized the amount of interest excited by *Far from the Madding Crowd* from the numbers of copies "with Mudie's label on the covers" which they saw carried about the streets in London.[68] Mrs. Humphry Ward, too, received proof of the astonishing success of *Robert Elsmere* at Waterloo Station. An excited woman who shared the author's compartment clutched "the familiar green volume," and leaned out the window to explain to a friend, "They told me no chance for weeks—not the slightest! Then—just as I was standing at the counter, who should come up but somebody bringing back the first volume. Of course it was promised . . . but as I was *there*, I laid hands on it, and here it is!"[69]

Publishers, too, reassured anxious authors by soothing references to the great library. The destination of a book was not a personal library, but Mudie's; not individual possession, but borrowing. Accurately embodying this attitude is the remark of N. T. Beard, a Bentley employee, who concluded a letter to Edith Somerville, the Irish novelist, explaining an apparent delay in publication, "You will see that a M.S. has to pass through many vicissitudes before it reaches the hands of the readers with Mudie's labels on its covers."[70]

Any attempt to show Mudie's influence on the Victorian reading public immediately touches interactions between the two. First of all, what was this reading public? Henry James defined it at the time as "the public that subscribes, borrows, lends, that picks up in one way and another, sometimes even by purchase."[71] Further qualification is necessary, however, to indicate the extent of this public accurately. A primary restriction on Mudie's direct influence was of course the guinea-a-year subscription. Compared to a guinea and a half this was a bargain, providing the patron with as many Mudie novels as he could read for a sum just two-thirds the list price of a single novel. Still, the number of families who could afford even 21s. was relatively small. In 1872 the *Spectator* estimated that "the number of really comfortable families, of families from which a guinea subscription might be expected . . . cannot . . . exceed 60,000 out of the 4,600,000 within Great Britain."[72] Of these "comfortable" families, a large percentage subscribed to a circulating library. Mudie's patrons numbered about 25,000 at the time of its founder's death in 1890; Smith's about 15,000 in 1894. By the 1890s, too, the trend towards a one-volume, 6s., first edition was growing stronger, so that these figures are probably lower than they were when the circulating library was at the height of its power in mid-century. When Mudie's finally closed its doors, *The Times* estimated, for example, that "at one time" the firm had had over 50,000 subscribers.[73]

The middle- and upper-middle-class reader, it must be remembered, was practically forced to Mudie's doors by the combination of high prices and the absence of public libraries. Adherents of the circulating library system reiterated that the English reader of fiction was a borrower and not a buyer, and even attributed the entire system to readers. One publisher, for example, held that since it was to the obvious advantage of both author and publisher to meet the wishes of the public, it was clear that "the decision at which the public has arrived is that the three-volume form is the one which it prefers to all others, and moreover it

The Country Department shipped books outside the London area.
The brass-bound boxes were famous in England and overseas.

will sturdily adhere to the old-fashioned price of a guinea and a half."[74] The last point, with its rhetorical appeal to tradition, is particularly ironic, since exactly the opposite was true. The public was not adhering to the price, but was actually deterred by it from buying. A guinea and a half for a single novel was exorbitant; by the time a book was reprinted in a cheap form, or in a series, the urgency had worn away. Time is almost as important in the sale of a popular novel as in the sale of a dress. It is the latest thing, it is what people are talking about that is bought. So, to accuse the nineteenth-century reader of being a "borrower," as if it were an inbred characteristic like red hair, was really to ignore the question. By the time he could afford a novel it was forgotten, pushed out by the latest three-decker at Mudie's. The Victorian attitude which considered fiction subordinate to history or poetry also contributed to the creation of a "borrowing public."

The second element which impelled the Victorian reader towards New Oxford Street for his novels was the lack of public libraries. The Ewart Act, the first free library legislation, received Royal Assent in 1850, but it was only a permissive measure and scarcely alleviated the situation. Boroughs of over 10,000 inhabitants could, with the consent of more than two-thirds of the ratepayers, levy a tax of not more than a halfpenny (raised to a penny in 1855) on the pound for public libraries, although they were not empowered to spend any of it on books.[75] Other laws in the next two decades broadened the original provisions, but public libraries grew slowly, especially in London. Ten years after the passing of the bill, only 28 library authorities had been set up; by 1880, just 95. Six years after that, only two parishes of the 67 in metropolitan London had taken advantage of the act. Nor were the few free libraries that were established of any great size; in the 1860's, when Mudie was advertising that he was increasing his collection at the rate of more than 170,000 volumes a year, the entire stock at the Liverpool Free Library totaled only 49,277 volumes,[76] not a third of what Mudie was adding annually and a tiny fraction of his stock.

Borrowing was not only undeniably cheaper than buying, it afforded a method by which readers could cautiously sample the wares to determine their worth before actually purchasing. This advantage was stressed by the advocates of the orthodox novel, who went so far as to point out the yards of space on the bookshelves saved in this way! After reading a selection from Mudie's, the subscriber could decide what was worth owning, and buy it when the cheap edition came out or used copies became available in the sales department of the library. The English novel-reader, it was so maintained, had the best of both worlds.

Certainly he did not seem dissatisfied with the status quo. As the Select Library continued to expand after 1850, readers became less and less disposed to buy, and more and more inclined to feel that if it was worthwhile, Mudie's would have it. Gladstone, discussing the question of free trade in books before the Commons in 1852 indicated how deeply ingrained borrowing had become:

> The purchase of new publications is scarcely ever attempted by anybody. You go into the houses of your friends, and unless they buy books of which they are in professional want, or happen to be persons of extraordinary wealth, you don't find copies of new publications on their tables purchased by themselves, but you find something from the circulating library. . . .[77]

Free trade was not really the crucial issue as far as borrowing books was concerned, however. After twenty years of free trade, the habit was only more deeply ingrained. George Henry Lewes attributed it to the libraries in a letter to John Blackwood in 1872. A wealthy friend who intensely admired George Eliot, he wrote, drove to Cawthorn's to get *Romola*. It was out, however, and so, she told Lewes, "I drove away disappointed." By that time a 2s.6d. edition was available, but it never occurred to his friend to buy, Lewes continued; "She relied on the Library. Buying books was not in her habit. What is one to do. . . ?" Blackwood could, however, offer little comfort or advice on what he acknowledged was an "infamous habit."[78]

Thus three elements—literary worth, the three-volume form, and subscriptions to Mudie's—became intermingled, and the Mudie patron became habituated to borrowing novels. It was natural enough for authors to tend to lose sight of him, behind the massive facade of the library, and to forget that while publishers watched the librarian, Mudie's own fingers were on the pulse of his subscriber. The Library had been created to satisfy a demand for "select" books, and Mudie conscientiously strove to uphold the standards both he and his readers approved. As he did this, however, he solidified tastes and attitudes in some patrons, and actually created them in others. Alexander Macmillan saw the situation more objectively and more clearly than many of his contemporaries; he wrote of Mudie: "I think his power . . . has been exaggerated, and his willingness to use that power too. He must be the servant of the public in the main, and only in a very general sense its master."[79]

George Moore, on the other hand, rankling under the combined effects of the banning of *A Modern Lover* and his dealings with Tinsley, poured out his indignation in "A New Censorship of Literature" in the *Pall Mall Gazette*. "The literary battle of our time lies not between the romantic and realistic schools of fiction, but for freedom from the illiterate censorship of a librarian," he protested. What had happened was this: "Mr. X," as Moore dubbed Mudie, had bought 50 copies of *A Modern Lover*, but had refused to circulate them unless specifically requested. He explained to the author, still according to Moore's account, that the book "was considered immoral. Two ladies from the country wrote to me objecting to that scene where the girl sat to the artist as a model for Venus. After that I naturally refused to circulate your book."[80]

Moore accused the libraries of forcing publishers into the three-volume form to secure their dictatorship, which amounted to "the intolerable jurisdiction of a tradesman" over literary matters. Moore's charge, although understandable, was hardly justified, since Mudie's had buttressed, rather than built, the form. In addition, Moore's quick temper flared primarily at the librarian, and did not consider the mutual relationship between that tradesman and his subscriber.

In the flurry of letters to the editor that appeared in the *Pall Mall Gazette* after Moore's denouncement, every viewpoint from wholehearted approval of the library system to complete endorsement of Moore's opinions is represented with, as usual, anecdotes of personal experiences to support claims on both sides. George Gissing, however, was the only one to spy the English novel-reader, dwarfed as he was by Mudie's great Ionic hall. Admitting the annoyance of having one's works supervised by a tradesman, still, Gissing points out, this indicates that "the prevailing taste of the public has made it indispensable to success in the circulating business." The course of literature, he goes on, is directed by the artist, and the artist is to blame if art decays. Finally, he observes that "If you abolish the library system tomorrow, you are no nearer persuading the 'two ladies in the country' (typical beings!) to let this or that work lie on their drawing room tables."[81] Privately, Gissing supported Moore's position, although he detected "a strain of vulgarity" in the man. The style of Moore's "New Censorship" made Gissing "shudder," and he summarily dismissed *A Modern Lover* as "unspeakable trash."[82] Gissing's analysis of the situation was indeed more perceptive than Moore's, who wanted not so much an end of the library censorship as a change of taste. When that change finally occurred, of course, Mudie's great days were over.

Until it came, however, Mudie's was indispensable to the middle- or upper-middle-class reader, to the "more intelligent families of Victorian London," as *The Times* put it at the demise of the library.[83] Although complaints like Moore's were made about the selection of books, censorship, and other policies, the general satisfaction of the patrons of the New Oxford Street firm was expressed by Fanny Kemble, who had taken out a subscription for her daughter: "Of all the devices of our complex and complete civilization, I think this huge circulating library system one of the most convenient and agreeable; to be able . . . to have . . . volumes of excellent literature for one's exclusive use, seems to me a real privilege, and capital return for one's money."[84]

How much this idea of good "return for one's money" influenced readers to become subscribers, it is difficult to estimate, but at least one social historian felt the prevailing attitude was that "to buy volumes that can be borrowed or hired is accounted wanton extravagance."[85] Certainly it may have contributed to Mudie's becoming a part of the fashionable world of its day, and then, as such, it undoubtedly attracted some patrons who simply wished to be seen at its counters. "Nothing could be more reminiscent of Victorian society than the picture of it drawing up in carriages—victorias, phaetons, or dogcarts—at Mudie's door, sweeping in upon the counters and shelves and emerging again, followed by flunkeys carrying loads of the newest books. Majestic 'three-volumers'. . . . It was almost as much of an afternoon duty as a drive in Rotten Row."[86] This is the way Mudie's is pictured by one who knew it in its strength.

A combination of economic and social pressures, as well as Mudie's own enterprising methods and services, drew readers to his firm. If much of what appeared in his catalogues was worthless, still it must be acknowledged that much of the best Victorian literature found its contemporary audience primarily through Mudie's. George Henry Lewes drew an accurate picture of both the arrival of a box from Mudie's and the probability of its worth in 1862, when the library was flourishing. On a rainy afternoon at a country house comes the sound of wheels;

> it is the carrier with a box from the library! . . . That box will certainly contain some volumes which one would not read in the wettest of weather, . . . but . . . it must contain volumes which one wants to read, if only because "everybody" is talking of them. A box of *new* books from the library is not all bon-bons. The despot of a librarian will have his way, and, Napoleon-like, is certain to fling his columns of raw conscripts upon our centre at the first onset, as mere food for powder; but he has his *vieille garde* in reserve, which can be brought up to decide the wavering fortunes of the day. . . . Out tumble feeble novels, and watery travels; but they are speedily dispersed, and we fall upon the small but effective reserve.[87]

Whether a Londoner or a provincial, a member of literary circles or a country squire, a reader of manuals of comparative anatomy

or Rhoda Broughton, the Mudie patron might well have agreed
with the sentiment in the doggerel rhyme of the time:

As children must have Punch and Judy
So I can't do without my Mudie.[88]

NOVELISTS, NOVELS, AND
THE ESTABLISHMENT

· *From George Eliot to George Gissing:*
The Novelist's Viewpoint ·

SINCE MUDIE SUBSCRIBERS PROVIDED A STABLE AND RELA-
tively uniform audience in all parts of England as well as in
London, and since they were virtually the only public for the
first editions of three-volume novels, library influence on writers
of fiction, consequently on fiction itself, was inevitable. The question became one of degree—of how much. Whether from success,
failure, or an indifferent fate at Mudie's counters, authors were
keenly aware of the distributor of their novels. How many Mudie
took was a matter of first importance to novelists. Throughout
the George Eliot correspondence with her publisher, John Blackwood, Mudie's runs like a leitmotiv. For two decades the Scottish
publisher reassured his diffident author about her success in the
firmest way he knew—by citing the Mudie subscription: Mudie's
has "finally succumbed," taking 500 copies of *Adam Bede*, then
another 100, and another, eventually making up his number
to 1,000; "the magnanimous Mudie has taken 3,100 copies of
Silas Marner"; there has been some difficulty getting Mudie "up

to the mark" of 1,500 with *Felix Holt*; it looked "as if Mudie wanted to go in for a cropper to redeem himself" for some small order; Mudie wanted the usual thousand of a *Middlemarch* volume in cloth; "Mudie has written from Rome ordering 500 copies of *Theophrastus Such*."[1]

The George Eliot–John Blackwood letters provide an unusually complete account of her transactions, and they are undoubtedly typical of much of the correspondence between the Victorian publisher and his novelist. As George Eliot was encouraged to hear of the hundreds or even thousands of copies Mudie took, so were lesser authors happy to hear of smaller numbers. Daniel Macmillan cheered Charles Kingsley with the news that Mudie had ordered 350 copies of *Westward Ho!*; Gissing was heartened to hear that Mudie's Select Library "took 60 copies of *Thyrza* to begin with, and has sent for another 25 since,"[2] even if his delight in his "steadily increasing" sales was sobered by the knowledge that Mudie had "just taken 2,000 of Rider Haggard's new book." Haggard's sale must have been especially galling because, after the success of *King Solomon's Mines*, *She* had been issued in one volume, while economic necessity compelled Gissing to labor in the confines of the hated three-decker. When Mudie made one of his frequent requests for a change in publication dates, the author's spirits rose or fell accordingly. Robert Browning wrote Isa Blagden that Chapman said her novel "was to be delayed a little at Mudie's request—is it not a good sign?"[3] Even if they were not thus singled out for special attention by the librarian, authors scanned his columns in the weekly journals for titles of their works; appearance there indicated readers. "Certainly my book [*Workers in the Dawn*] is finding some readers," Gissing could believe, "for Mudie puts it in his selected list for the new year."[4]

More established writers also kept their ears open for information from New Oxford Street. When James Payn, editor of the *Cornhill*, heard "that Mudie reports 'The Burnt Million' as being much asked for," he immediately prodded his publisher,

Andrew Chatto. "Perhaps it would be as well to ask them if they want more copies,"[5] the practical author suggested. Not all advice came from authors as familiar with the business side of publishing as Payn, who was also a reader for Smith, Elder. George Gissing had to caution his brother Algernon, who was struggling to make his living from fiction, that publishers knew "exactly how to reckon with the libraries, & so on."[6] Authors also watched more minor indicators of probable success for a novel. Trained by their enterprising employer, Mudie's clerks often suggested titles to patrons who wanted "a good novel." When Gissing heard "that Mudie's assistants are 'keen on' my novels,"[7] his hopes rose accordingly. Then, as now, authors were willing to leave their desks and pens to try to promote their works. During the eight-year period when Harrison Ainsworth was turning out one three-decker annually, he acknowledged to his publisher, "I was so hurried when I was in Town last week that I could not make up the little dinner which I want to give Mudie, but I will make a point of it next time."[8]

So conscious, in fact, were authors of the Mudie system and the three-decker, that the professional, popular writer with no literary pretensions was frequently pictured in novels as grinding out the requisite number of words at regular intervals, so that "three new volumes, in green, in crimson, in blue," could appear every few months, "on the booktable that groaned with light literature." Greville Fane, one of Henry James's characters, had plots by the hundred, and "though she had contributed volumes to the diversion of her contemporaries, she hadn't contributed a sentence to the language."[9] Another such writer was Lady Carbury of Trollope's *The Way We Live Now*. Because her publisher advised her that novels, on the whole, did better than anything else, she set to work on one. "The length of her novel had been her first question. It must be in three volumes, and each volume must have three hundred pages. But what fewest number of words might be supposed sufficient to fill a page?" Although she realistically did not pride herself much on her literary merit, "if she could bring the papers to praise it, if she could induce Mudie to circulate it . . . then she would pride herself very much upon her work" (Chap. LXXXIX).

If authors generally were conscious of the great circulating library, to those who had been excluded from its Great Hall it loomed as notorious. Wilkie Collins, Charles Reade, and George Moore were among those who, for various reasons, fulminated publicly and privately against the librarian.

> But the truth is we have a rotten trade for the upper 10,000, and a healthy trade for the nation. The rotten trade is the hiring trade; of course, it operates on books just as it does on piano-fortes—it reduces the customers to a handful, and artificial prices become a necessity of that one narrow market. The 31s.6d. is all humbug, the public does not buy a copy, the sale is confined to the libraries. . . . But it is a calamitous system. . . .[10]

Such indignant outbursts as this one by Reade reveal Mudie's power more clearly than statistics about numbers of subscribers. If a novelist's work was not found in the Mudie catalogue, he had lost his best, sometimes his only, chance for that essential part of any literary composition, a reader.

The financially pressed author, or even the author who depended on his pen for his living, simply could not afford to ignore Mudie and his requirement of the three-decker. It was by far the easiest novel to sell, especially when the writer was unknown. Charlotte Brontë, for example, could find no market for *The Professor* in one volume, but at Smith, Elder, the seventh firm to which it was sent, Smith Williams "courteously and considerately" criticized it. As she later related, "It was added, that a work in three volumes would meet with careful attention. I was just then completing 'Jane Eyre,' at which I had been working while the one-volume tale was plodding its weary round in London. . . ."[11] Thus began her close association with both the firm and its reader.

Commenting on the limitations of a novelist's income, the industrious James Payn pointed out "there are few men who can write a three-volume novel, worth reading, under nine months."[12] For Payn, the three-decker was the way to success in fiction, and its profits were limited by the amount of time necessary to produce it. In his negotiations with William Longman about *Barchester Towers*, Trollope maintained "that if a three vol. novel be worth anything" it was worth £100, and he carefully repeats both the stipulated number of volumes and the amount. Not every novel would be worth that sum, but a three-decker was. Years later, when Trollope was asking £2,800 for a three-volume novel, his price for a one-volume "tale"[13] was £200, a difference of £2,600.

Although Dickens had received dazzling prices for novels that were not in the conventional form, it was for a three-decker that Longman's gave one of the largest sums paid till then for a work of fiction. Lord Rowton, who was conducting the negotiations for *Endymion*, conveyed his success in a note to Disraeli when both were attending a debate in the House of Lords: "House of Lords, Aug. 4, '80.—There are things too big to impart in whispers! . . . Longman has today offered *Ten Thousand Pounds* for *Endymion*. I have accepted it!"[14] Whether the sum was due to Disraeli's fame as prime minister or to his reputation as a novelist, it was offered for a three-decker. With such amounts before them it is little wonder novelists looked to that form for income. Even when they did not aspire to this kind of success, authors recognized the multi-volume form as the most remunerative. "An Obscure Author," for example, told the *Daily News* in 1884 of submitting "to a celebrated publisher" a manuscript he thought suitable for a cheap volume. At the publisher's suggestion, it was enlarged into a two-volume library edition which, with a guaranteed sale and a higher price, would give author and publisher "something of a margin" for themselves. As a result, the author made more than he had expected. To this case, he contrasted another, in which he had insisted on an inexpensive, one-volume edition. Although the work was more favorably received than the preceding venture, "it barely paid expenses," he concluded, ruefully attributing its failure to its form.[15]

Hence, whether he admired or abhorred it, the Victorian novelist recognized the importance and prestige of the form. Respecting it for part of his career at least, Charles Reade saw the three-decker as "a great prose Epic."[16] At the other extreme were writers who scorned it as "a triple-headed monster, sucking the blood of English novelists,"[17] or sighed about a new book, as Gissing did, "Alas, it must be in *three* volumes."[18] The sharp contrast between the idea for a novel and the nine hundred pages of the reality often struck both beginning and experienced writers. Advising young authors, James Payn urged them to "consider, when you have got your germ . . . half a dozen lines, perhaps— . . . how small a thing it is compared with, say, the thousand pages which it has to occupy in the three-volume novel!"[19] Eliza Lynn Linton explained to an interviewer that a large pile of manuscripts were not her own, but from people seeking her judgment about whether the material was worth spinning out into a three-volume novel.[20]

With a certain form of publication in mind, novelists planned their work accordingly. Casual references to the established convention frequently recur in the novels themselves, in *Vanity Fair*, for instance, when Thackeray in his burlesque "low" plot for a novel contrives a professional burglar who "carries off Amelia in her night-dress, not to be let loose again till the third volume" (Chap. VI). Again, in his final pages, Thackeray announces, "Here it is—the summit, the end—the last page of the third volume." The difference between the romantic marriage concluding the conventional three-decker is ironically contrasted with his own final, more realistic view of the relationship between Amelia and Dobbin, presented in the pages following the so-called "end"—a contrast more apparent in the nineteeenth century than to readers today. Arthur Pendennis's novel was a three-decker, and Thackeray pictures Pen's mother, coming out of her room at one in the morning with the second volume, to discover

Laura in bed, devouring the third (Vol. II, Chap. III). Mr. Omer was delighted with the sheer physical effect of David Copperfield's novel: "When I lay that book upon the table, and look at it outside—compact in three separate and indiwidual wollumes; one, two, three—I am as proud as Punch" (Chap. XXXI). As indications of the prevalence of this form of publication, these instances are all the more striking because of the satirical tone adopted by their authors who did not usually publish "Legitimate Novels."

Again, in *Barchester Towers*, Trollope remarks on the "difficulty . . . of disposing of all our friends in the small remainder of this one volume. Oh, that Mr. Longman would allow me a fourth! It should transcend the other three as the seventh heaven transcends all the lower stages of celestial bliss" (Chap. XLIII). Although, as has been indicated, some novels were indeed published in four volumes, the exceptional nature of that form is clearly shown by this excerpt. Trollope's easygoing reference reveals he had no fear that the public, thoroughly habituated to three, would misinterpret his playfulness. In his *Autobiography*, however, Trollope seriously summarizes the position of the professional novelist with reference to the three-decker:

> In writing a novel the author soon becomes aware that a burden of many pages is before him. Circumstances require that he should cover a certain and generally not a very confined space. Short novels are not popular with readers generally. Critics often complain of the ordinary length of novels,—of the three volumes to which they are subjected; but few novels which have attained great success in England have been told in fewer pages. The novel-writer who sticks to novel-writing as his profession will certainly find that this burden of length is incumbent on him. How shall he carry his burden to the end? How shall he cover his space?

Continuing his discussion, Trollope stresses the importance of proportion to the novelist, specifically so that he can "teach himself so to tell his story that it should fall naturally into the required length."[21] He might have added that it should fall also into the required number of volumes. These served at least as convenient signposts for writers who, like Gissing, planned in a tripartite construction, noting the completion of the second, or first, volume, or struggling to the end of the third.[22] Not all could supply the official diplomatic red dispatch box into which Disraeli put each individual volume of *Endymion*, of course, or the original red tape with which they were carefully tied,[23] but they could take care to furnish manuscripts which would fill the equivalent. *John Caldigate*, Trollope promised, would be "3 full volumes"; *Marion Fay* was "*exactly* . . . the same length as my other 3 vol. novels."[24]

To the professional, conscientious Trollope, writing with a plan which would fill the required number of pages was not difficult, and a writer like Mary Elizabeth Braddon could turn out seventeen three-deckers in ten years; but others chafed under such restrictions, particularly in the last two decades of the century. It was not always convenient or artistically possible to compose a novel that would exactly fill three volumes of 275 to 325 pages. Those that were forced into the mold were likely to appear manufactured. Israel Zangwill was prompted to devise the following recipe for them:

> One idea makes one paragraph.
> Two paragraphs make one page.
> Twenty pages make one chapter.
> Twelve chapters make one volume.
> Three volumes make one tired.[25]

Frequently, an author did not have enough material. Charles Reade, who was acutely aware of the difference between triple and single issue, worried a great deal about filling pages at the beginning of his writing career. He hoped to make "a decent three-volume novel"[26] of his first, *Peg Woffington*, but finally had material sufficient for only one. His second venture, *Christie Johnstone*, proved no longer. Still, in common with most new novelists, he looked on the three-decker with respect. "For the next ten years the 1 volume novel will not be profitable," he told his publisher in 1853; "but I do not think money will be lost by those I write and it is my wish to make myself known by one or two of these before I strike a heavier blow."[27] Reade, the Oxford don, coupled prestige and profit in his evaluation of the "heavier blow."

In early September 1853, a critic in the *Spectator* expressed delight with the size of *Christie Johnstone*: "In these days of literary gold-beating, when an ingot of matter is generally hammered out into that acreage of flimsy leaf which subsequently figures in a three-volume form on the shelves of the circulating library, it is refreshing to take up a novel in one volume."[28] By the end of the month, Reade himself was swinging around to the *Spectator's* position, declaring unequivocally to Bentley,

> The 3 vol Novel is the intellectual blot of our Nation—it is the last relic of our Forefathers' prolixity & d—d digressive tediousness—
>
> It is the remnant of a past age and can no more stand before the increasing intelligence of this age than an old six horse coach can compete with a train whirled past by a single engine—
>
> The principle of the 3 vol Novel is this.—Write not what you have to say only—but what you have not got to say as well.[29]

In mid-century Reade felt the three-decker had been outmoded, left behind in the rush of progress many Victorians felt: "the forms go with the age which is intelligent & rapid & has learned the value of time and space. The Novels lag behind the age—." When he looked at journals and reviews, he was struck by their conciseness: "Is a small pot of matter ever spread out thin over a 3 gallon loaf in a leading article of The Times . . . No, all these writers write for the *English people* & shun prolixity because they know *the Nation* loathes it." His own penchant for facts as a basis for fiction, for the "Matter-of-Fact romance," led Reade to admire succinct expression. He made plain, however, that "I do not say these things because I condense—it is the other way. I condense because the time is come that *you must*

with Novels written upon my plan.. viz the
condensation of good matter, not its liquidation &
diffusion –

I will give you my reason.

At present we have the Novel principally in two
Shapes – 3 vols. 1 Guinea – or the same 3
vols. bound in one 1 shilling –

Now the Public will give 1 shilling for the 3 vol novel
as an investment – because the binding & the paper
are worth in their opinion 10 d. or so.

But to sell the Public any large number of a Novel
at 7.s. we must I think improve the Novel in the
aspect I have named –

The 3 vol Novel is the intellectual blot of our Nation
it is the last relic of our Forefathers' prolixity & d-d
dyspeptic tediousness –

It is the remnant of a past age and can no more
stand before the increasing intelligence of this age than
an old four horse coach can compete with a
Train whirled past by a single engine –

The principle of the 3 vol Novel is this.. Write not what
you have got to say only – but what you have not got
to say as well –

Look at our journals & reviews. these always represent
the true taste of the people – is a small pat of matter
ever spread out thin over a 3 gallon loaf in
a leading article of the Times – or the Edinburgh
Review. No. all these writers write for the English
people & shun prolixity because they know the Nation
loathes it.

And the moment you & I come to write novels for
large masses of Englishmen we must condense our
matter in a novel as in everything else, or they won't have

condense or go to the trunkmaker after 12 months—." Later he reiterated to Bentley his determination not to pad: "I know I can produce 450 pages of *matter*, but I am not sure about 600."[30]

Ironically, Reade's collection of facts in the form of great files of newspaper clippings led him even beyond the length he condemned. His next novel, *It Is Never Too Late to Mend*, was far from "a small pot of matter . . . spread thin over a 3 gallon loaf"; it was so crammed with material it extended to over three volumes. Such was the power of the form that Reade acknowledged there was "therefore nothing to do but to reduce it by excision,"[31] although he feared that even then it would reach 1,200 pages.[32] In his extensive revision, Reade removed "The Autobiography of a Thief," which later formed a part of *Cream*, whose banning Mudie was to defend in the press. By this time Reade had come to look on the three-decker as a "great prose Epic," worthy of time and labor, and justified delays to his publisher: "I am a writer. I *cannot scribble*."[33]

During the dominance of the three-decker, professional authors unquestionably could secure a better living from it than from shorter tales, Rhoda Broughton after all relinquished £450 when she was unable to stretch *Second Thoughts* into the conventional length. Frances Eleanor Trollope (the second wife of Anthony Trollope's brother, Thomas Adolphus Trollope, himself a novelist) also resigned herself to the inevitable; she wrote to Bentley on December 21, 1886:

> Thank you very much for your letter, which enables me clearly to understand the reasons in favour of 3 vols. *versus* 2 vols. The only thing to be done, is to endeavor to lay out one's story so as honestly to fill a bigger canvas, without too much mere talkee talkee. People who have only struck ink and not oil, must consider the profit question. . . . So it is evident that both publishers and writers must for the present stick to the 3 vols.[34]

Edwin Reardon, the struggling young novelist in George Gissing's *New Grub Street*, caught in a similar predicament, suffers from such extension. "The misfortune was that you had to make three volumes of it. If I had leave to cut it down to one, it would do you credit," is the verdict of the successful Jasper Milvain. Milvain's rise in the literary world through clever and worldly maneuvers is counterpointed by the fall of Reardon, who, still attempting to cling to his artistic integrity, is unable to "manufacture" three volumes in nine weeks to support himself and his family. The harder he is driven, the less capable he becomes, even while clearly perceiving his situation. Fiction is the form for men who must make their living by literature, and yet "can't journalise." Given these circumstances, he reasons

"For anyone in my position, . . . how is it possible to abandon the three volumes? It is a question of payment. An author of moderate repute may live on a yearly three-volume novel—I mean the man who is obliged to sell his book out and out, and who gets from one to two hundred pounds for it. But he would have to produce four one-volume novels to obtain the same income; and I doubt whether he could get so many published within the twelve months." [Vol. II, Chap. XV.]

Reardon's words provide an accurate picture of the situation facing an aspiring author. In portraying him Gissing drew on his personal struggles, and this is probably a fair statement of his own opinions. His earliest novels—*Workers in the Dawn*, the unpublished *Mrs. Grundy's Enemies*, and *The Unclassed*—conformed to the convention, as novels by beginning writers frequently did. The year after the publication of *The Unclassed*, however, his letters show that he was beginning to chafe under the system. On August 9, 1885 he wrote to his brother Algernon, "I shall stick to the plan of two volumes, it is speedier work. I believe it will come to one before long with most writers." Four days later he declared firmly, "I have made up my mind to finish the next two volumes (I don't think I shall ever again write three), before winter. It is high time to . . . face the publishers resolutely." Still later in the same month he rejoiced, "It is fine to see how the old three volume tradition is being broken through. One volume is becoming commonest of all. It is the new school."[35]

His firmness, however, faltered. The two-volume work with which he was going to "face the publishers resolutely" was *A Life's Morning*, issued in three volumes in 1888. Whether the publisher extended the manuscript by his own methods, or whether Gissing revised it, it must have been Gissing who gave in, since his words to his brother imply not only two volumes in manuscript, but two volumes on the shelves. With resignation Gissing wrote his brother that two volumes were "against the publishers' predilection," adding wearily, "but on the other hand three are terrific toil."[36] Furthermore, his next novel, *The Nether World*, also appeared in the conventional form. No one affords a better example than Gissing of the serious writer, dependent on his work for his living, forced to cast his material in a length and shape uncongenial to him.

He was certainly not the only writer to alter his work, however. Rhoda Broughton was one who paralleled Gissing's case on a more popular level. Although she was not concerned with schools of fiction or their implications, she asserted in 1871, "I am resolved never to write a 3 vol. again,"[37] but, like Gissing, she yielded to pressure for the following two decades. Of the six novels she published during those years, only one deviated from the norm—and that one was in two volumes.

Although Elizabeth Gaskell said *Mary Barton* grew imperceptibly, so that she could not tell why or how a part was written, there was one exception. Her publisher, after having had the manuscript for more than fourteen months, sent word that it was insufficient to fill two volumes. She had already given up her title. It was her first novel, and she thought of it as a "tragic poem,"[38] centering on the life of *John Barton*. Her publisher, like many of his brethren before and since, preferred a heroine's name. Then, in spite of her repeated remonstrances and her offer to reduce her price, Chapman and Hall insisted on more text. She finally added Chapter 37, which contains "Details Connected with the Murder." She interpolated a conversation between Mr. Carson, the factory owner, Job Legh, and Jem Wilson and makes clear that future improvements in factory conditions in Manchester were caused by the increased understanding the employer gained through his suffering. As the book originally stood, all this would have been left implied; the multi-volume requirements really altered this author's presentation of her material. Although Chapman did not specify the nature of the addition, anything beyond the original manuscript intruded into her concept of the "tragic poem," and the authorial comment only weakens its impact, especially for modern readers conditioned to dramatic presentation.

Gissing also had to add text to a skimpy manuscript; revising and proofreading the three-decker, *Born in Exile*, in 1892, he found the last volume too short, and "wrote in two days a supplementary chapter to be inserted before the last."[39] There Gissing elaborates the motivation of Sidwell Warricombe's refusal of Godwin Peak, "born in exile" from her comfortable class. Although the fourteen-page chapter amplifies, it does not develop what has been revealed by Sidwell's brief note in the preceding chapter:

> "I cannot. It is not that I am troubled by your accepting this legacy. . . . But I am too weak to take this step. To ask you to wait yet longer, would only be a fresh cowardice. You cannot know how it shames me to write this. In my very heart I believe I love you, but what is such love worth? You must despise me, and you will forget me. I live in a little world; in the greater world where your place is, you will win a love very different." [Part VII, Chap. I.]   S.W.

Gissing's concept of the novel and his own abilities were leading him towards a "dramatic mode of presentment," as he termed it: "Far more artistic, I think, is the later method, of merely suggesting; of dealing with episodes, instead of writing biographies. The old novelist is omniscient; I think it is better to tell a story precisely as one does in real life, hinting, surmising, telling in detail what *can* so be told and no more."[40] The dramatic method, however, the suggestions and hints in Sidwell's letter, yielded to the method of the "old novelist" and to the three-decker.

This feeling of interference in the construction of the novel, evident from the middle of the century, sharpened in its last two decades when more and more writers were reacting against the Victorian profusion of detail. As long as the three-decker was in power, however, chapters continued to be added by authors who could not fill its pages. At the opposite extreme, passages were removed by those prolix writers who had difficulty compressing their work into the accepted form. Charles Reade shortened *It Is Never Too Late to Mend*, and Mrs. Humphry Ward had to cut and revise *Robert Elsmere* at George Smith's firm request, a difficult task for one who admitted her own "tendency to interminableness!"[41] By making publishers reluctant to go above the charmed number of three and unwilling to settle for fewer (especially for the lowly single volume), the pervasive influence of the three-decker penetrated beyond Paternoster Row to writers and the construction of the novels themselves.

· *Prose Epics or Triple-Headed Monsters?* ·

THE WAY IN WHICH THE NOVELS REFLECTED THE TRADITION is most readily apparent in their structure. It is obvious also in the use of incident, the tendency to extended description, multiple plots, encouragement of character portrayal, lavish details, and the author's digressions, reflections, or chats with the reader. During the years of Mudie's ascendency, practically all great novels were also highly popular. Many authors and critics were convinced that the growing reading public both understood and appreciated a well-told story. Such a conviction was undoubtedly one reason Dickens and other writers paid such careful attention to the reception accorded their novels issued in monthly or weekly parts. Writers like Hawthorne, on the other hand, were criticized for addressing their work to an intellectual audience, when "the novelist's true audience is the common people—the people of ordinary comprehension and everyday sympathies. . . ."[42] This principle of the novel as the literature of the people, replacing the ancient epic, recurs again and again in the rapidly growing criticism of fiction during these years.

Similarity to the epic was enhanced by the apparent length of the three-decker. The multiple volumes were not conducive to the single dramatic incident or to the simple reminiscence. As budding writers took up their pens, consciousness of what they had to fill made many sensitive to the necessity for pattern. If their own artistic consciences did not so prod them, literary advisers and critics did. Eliza Lynn Linton, writing privately to a hopeful novelist, admonished, "You must know what you want to say—what you want to show—else you simply ramble round about . . . your nine hundred pages."[43] Using the volumes as convenient markers to show the progress of a novel in manuscript also encouraged a tripartite structure.

Novelists of all ranks and abilities were affected. Anthony Trollope was a successful, professional novelist, who depended on the reading public for his income, but at the same time he strove to uphold certain standards. Even before the publication of his *Autobiography*, his practical attitude could be discerned in his fiction; take, for example, his comment on a remark by the indolent and improvident Bertie Stanhope in *Barchester Towers*. " 'No real artist could descend to the ornamentation of a cathedral,' said Bertie, who had his ideas of the high ecstatic ambition of art, as indeed all artists have, who are not in receipt of a good income." (Chap. XLII.) The effects of triple volumes on the structure of fiction were often as clearly marked as the act divisions of a play.[44] The first volume of Trollope's *Framley Parsonage* ends just after the young heir of the manor, Lord Lufton, has proposed to the minister's recently orphaned sister, Lucy, a girl of wit and high spirits, if not conventional beauty.

Knowing the match is opposed by his mother, she has refused, saying that she cannot love him. Thinking over her situation after he leaves, she asks the question with which the volume closes, "But how was she to forgive herself the falsehood she had told?" Although the reader had previously been aware of her feelings, it is only in this climactic last scene that Lord Lufton's emotions are revealed.

After exploring the intricate financial affairs of Mark Robarts, the minister, and related matters appropriate to the domestic novel, Volume II is climaxed by the second proposal, conveyed through Mark. Lucy admits her love this time, but qualifies her acceptance with the apparently insuperable condition that his mother must ask her. After this emotionally charged scene, and with no indication of any means of resolving the dilemma, the volume ends with the paragraph, "On the next day Lord Lufton left Framley; and started, according to his arrangements, for the Norway salmon fishing." For the second time the reader must put down a volume unsatisfied. Not until almost the last chapter of Volume III does Lady Lufton herself ask Lucy to marry her son, thus clearing up all the difficulties.

The twin crises in the story and the basic structure of three variations on a proposal correspond to the form in which the novel was printed, and a similar pattern will be found in many three-deckers. Such repetition with differences may seem especially appropriate for a novel in which the portrayal of character is a major interest, but the impact of the form is clear. Even when the novel was serialized before its appearance as a book, the effect of the three volumes is apparent. *Framley Parsonage*, it is true, did inaugurate the *Cornhill*, but as the first of Trollope's novels to be serialized, its structure may reflect more of the book than of the magazine form. *Great Expectations*, on the other hand, provides an example of a novel focusing on the development of character by a writer conditioned to publication in parts. Although it was serialized in *All the Year Round*, Dickens's indication of the volumes is obvious even to today's reader, as he finds the plainly marked first and second "stages" of Pip's expectations, the hope of the first contrasting to the reality of the second.

Novels with more emphasis on incident, including those serialized prior to appearance as a complete book, also clearly show the influence of the triple volumes. Even though Wilkie Collins claimed that one of his three efforts in writing was "to keep the story always advancing, without paying the smallest attention to the serial division in parts, or to the book publication in volumes,"[45] his novels show little success in that effort. *The Woman in White*, which appeared first in *All the Year Round*, is plainly divided into three "epochs," corresponding to the volumes, and thus, like *Great Expectations*, retains for modern readers a little of the impact of the three-decker publication. The first volume ends with the dramatically foreboding crisis of Laura Fairlie's marriage to Sir Percival Glyde; the second with the equally dramatic reappearance of Laura, veiled and in white, beside her supposed tomb (the living embodiment of a dream motif Collins has stressed through the volume). Each ending was calculated to send the reader back to New Oxford Street for the next volume, and each contrasts with the end of the novel: Laura, in a serene domestic scene, happily married to Walter Hartright and the mother of a young heir. Other devices may also be traced to the prevailing pattern, for example, Count Fosco, who is mentioned at the beginning of the first volume, is pointedly brought up in its final pages to prepare the stage for his actual appearance early in the second volume.

Outwardly *The Moonstone* seems less dependent on the triple-volume form than *The Woman in White*; the "periods" do not correspond with the volumes, and the volume divisions actually interrupt the "narratives." Having the same narrator continue from one volume to the next allows Collins to achieve continuity and in no way lessens the effectiveness of the crises. Volume I ends with the discovery of Rosanna Spearman's death at the Shivering Sands and looks ahead to "the trouble and the terror . . . at the house." Volume II is climaxed by Franklin Blake's own discovery, again at the Shivering Sands, of apparently incontrovertible evidence that he himself has stolen the Moonstone. Volume III opens with the letter Rosanna Spearman wrote before her suicide. The pivotal role played by the faithful Gabriel Betteredge is apparent in the structure: he is the narrator of all of the first and the beginning of the second volume; he is present as Franklin Blake finds "proof" of his own guilt and when he reads Rosanna's letter; and Gabriel's conversation concludes the book. (A brief epilogue, like the prologue, stands apart from the novel.)

Thus the "three separate and indiwidual wollumes" stimulated writers at all levels to consider aspects of form. When Bentley declared Lady Margaret Majendie had produced a dull first volume, she replied, "Surely artistically a first volume should be as quiet as the first volume of life itself, uneventful and dull."[46] Even if the first volume was the embodiment of tranquility, most writers, like Trollope, Dickens, and Collins, felt the necessity of a crisis; the end of a volume provided too easy a way to stop reading a novel. Charlotte Brontë told William Smith Williams she stopped "at the close of the 1st Vol."[47] of Julia Kavanagh's *Daisy Burns*. Her own first volume of *Jane Eyre* had concluded with the mysterious "demoniac laugh," the midnight attempt to burn Mr. Rochester, Jane's rescue of him and the growing consciousness of her love—any one of which might have sent the reader hurrying back to Mudie's counters.

If some kind of crisis was often desirable at the end of the first volume, it was practically imperative at the end of the second. Charles Reade advised James T. Fields to cut a passage because the American public would never miss it. "It ends a Volume with us," he told his American publisher, "so that a coup is required but it will come in the heart of your second volume where no coup is required."[48] Reade's "coup" in this case apparently was the roaring fight which closed the second volume of *It Is Never Too Late to Mend*. In the Wild West tradition of a future date, four ruffian prospectors "with shaggy beards and wild faces and murderous eyes" are defeated by George Fielding (the romantic hero), Tom Robinson (the reformed thief), and Jacky (the native Australian), as the trio are discovering gold. Reade's inclination to drama (*Never Too Late* was partially based on his play *Gold*) may have stimulated his predilection for a "curtain" at the end of an act, but he was not alone in his concern.

Charles Gibbon, a minor novelist, strove for "a particular effect for the end of the 2nd volume,"[49] an effect the more to be sought as critics complained increasingly of the tedium of the middle volume. A tripartite pattern can be basically pleasing to the human imagination of course, but with three volumes it was difficult to avoid a structure which might not have been the most effective for the writer's material. At the end of the century, one *Spectator* critic summed it up as "That Sad Second Volume,"[50] a judgment later echoed by Saintsbury, who compared the three-decker to a sort of preposterous sandwich with meat on the outside and "a great slab of ill-baked and insipid bread between."[51]

That common critical complaint against the three-decker, padding, frequently was directed specifically against the second volume. The *Spectator* critic admitted that the "retarding element," the forces working against the resolution of the plot, might be as effective in fiction as in drama. In the "sad second volume," however, the narrative was not retarded; it had ground to a complete halt. According to his theory, a novel should first state its narrative problem and explain the nature of whatever conflict is to be cleared up. Whether the problem involves events or characters, its natural division should be statement and solution, a division which the three-decker shattered by its requirement of a third volume, "which only fulfills the mechanical purpose of filling a number of pages."

The *Spectator* critic carefully restricts his remarks to average three-volume fiction, excluding at one extreme the novel which is good all through, whether in one volume or in seven, and at the other, the one which is so bad no curtailment or enlargement could improve it. Unless the novelist can acquire the power of producing an effective retarding element, or can shorten

Mudie's on New Oxford Street.
Courtesy of the Guildhall Library, London.

his work so that it can be dispensed with, the critic concluded there would always be a pitfall in the second volume. After a "bright and promising opening," and before a "vigorously worked-out and satisfactory denouement," the reader is compelled "to plod wearily . . . through a sandy desert or a spongy morass." The best examples of the "sandy desert" are deservedly gathering dust today, but the plot of *The Gold of Ophir* (the *Spectator's* representative three-decker) illustrates the objection. In the melodramatic opening a supposed corpse returns to life, but life without memory. The victim recovers knowledge of his identity in the last volume, but the second is padded with incidents and characters attached to the central plot only mechanically and obviously incorporated. Lady Margaret Majendie padded in the same way. She acknowledged to her publisher, "I already at your request threw in a railway-accident."[52]

The *Spectator* critic attributed lack of compactness and deficiencies in structure to the three-volume requirement of the circulating libraries. His points are well made, striking a judicious balance seldom found in three-decker criticism, which tended to praise the system unequivocally on the one hand, or condemn it equally drastically on the other, without any real consideration of the principles of fiction involved or of the methods of its distribution. Today, when novels are usually reprinted in one volume with no indication of the original divisions, we have lost much of the effect of triple issue on the structure. Although the framework remains the same, it is deprived of decided emphasis by the change. It was almost inevitable that single volumes were judged on their individual merits. Charlotte Brontë readily acknowledged that a work "should not be judged piecemeal." Still she wrote to her publisher of *Henry Esmond*, "My objection to the second volume lay here: I thought it contained decidedly too much History— too little story."[53] To the nineteenth-century reader, considering each volume individually, any deficiency in the second volume, separated as it was from its opening and from its conclusion by cloth-bound covers, became much more striking.

The third volume, with its inherent qualities of climax, was more likely to be satisfactory, as the *Spectator* critic noted. When Mrs. Gaskell had sent two manuscript volumes of *Sylvia's Lovers* to William Smith Williams, she felt she should forward "a sketch of the third vol.: to make you see how everything in the first two 'works up' to the events and crisis in that."[54] Charlotte Brontë found in the last volume of *Esmond* "the most sparkle, impetus, and interest." George Eliot's comments as she was completing *The Mill on the Floss* show that the writer himself was often aware of the pressures which contributed to that "sparkle, impetus, and interest." To John Blackwood she explained, "The 3d volume is, I fancy, always more rapidly written than the rest. The 3d volume of 'Adam Bede' was written in six weeks, even with headachy interruptions, because it was written under a stress of emotion—which first volumes cannot be." In a later letter she added, "I am rather in a drive of feeling and writing with my third volume: that is in the nature of third volumes."[55]

Unity in the three-decker thus involved not only the entire work but individual volumes as well. Because it was read individually, a volume required some kind of internal cohesiveness, the exact kind determined by its place among the three. The crisis at the end of either of the first two volumes often represented a culmination as well as a continuing conflict. The volumes could not, on the other hand, be so independent that they separated from the whole, as a sad second volume did. George Eliot, reading proof for *The Mill on the Floss*, felt she had attained a satisfactory balance: "The three volumes will certainly have the advantage of being very various while they have the psychological unity that springs from their being the history of two closely related lives from beginning to end."[56]

Besides a tripartite structure, the three-decker by its spaciousness encouraged a profusion of incidents. With plenty of room, novelists tended to be lavish with them; Reade had so many in *Never Too Late* he could neatly excise even a "coup" in the American edition, and still be confident his American public would never miss it. The tendency to a multiplicity of events, often organized for the reader by summaries or motifs, and to contrasting or parallel plots, is typical of the product fostered by Mr. Mudie's library. When much was dependent on incident, writers often had to provide summaries to keep the pattern of events clear to the reader unable to turn back to a previous volume to refresh his memory. So, for example, at the beginning of the second and third volumes respectively, Marion Halcombe and Walter Hartright recapitulate events related to the mystery

surrounding the woman in white. At the opening of Volume III
of *Dr. Thorne*, Trollope summarizes the events surrounding
Frank Gresham's proposal to Mary Thorne at the end of the
previous volume, but avoids strict repetition by recalling them
from the point of view of Mary's cousin and frustrated suitor,
Louis Scatcherd.

In *Old Saint Paul's* a single unifying motif runs through all
three volumes: the course of Leonard Holt's love for "the fair
Amabel," who is in turn pursued by the Earl of Rochester.
While there is nothing unique about such a motif, it was
especially helpful to coherence in a three-decker. As there is
little attempt at characterization beyond indications of virtue
and vice (the characters almost never perform any unexpected
action), *Old Saint Paul's* provides a good example of how the
author filled out his required pages without confusing the reader
by too many unrelieved occurrences.

In the first place, Ainsworth gives much historical data
about London in the plague years, frequently in the form of
startling scenes of pictorial clarity, so that the effect of the
work as a whole is one of tableaux interspersed with action.
One such picture, for example, concerned the activity found
in Old Saint Paul's:

> Besides booksellers, there were seamstresses, tobacco merchants,
> venders of fruit and provisions, and Jews—all of whom had stalls
> within the cathedral, and who were now making preparations for
> the business of the day. Shortly afterwards, numbers who came
> for recreation and amusement made their appearance, and before
> ten o'clock Paul's Walk, as the nave was termed, was thronged
> by apprentices, rufflers, porters, water-carriers, higglers, with
> baskets on their heads or under their arms, fishwives, quack
> doctors, cut-purses, bonarobas, merchants, lawyers, and serving-
> men, who came to be hired, and who stationed themselves near
> an oaken block attached to one of the pillars, and which was
> denominated, from the use it was put to, the "serving-man's log."
> Some of the crowd were smoking, some laughing, others gathering
> round a ballad-singer, who was chanting one of Rochester's own
> licentious ditties; some were buying quack medicines and remedies

for the plague, the virtues of which the vender loudly extolled; while others were paying court to the dames, many of whom were masked. . . . Here a man, mounted on the carved marble of a monument, bellowed forth the news of the Dutch war. . . . There, at the very font, was a usurer paying over a sum of money to a gallant. . . . [Book II, Chap. VII.]

Other sketches show St. Paul's by moonlight, the sweep of the city viewed from the roof of the cathedral, deserted London streets at the height of the plague, the plague-pit, and the Great Fire of 1666.

The incidents necessary to fill a three-decker could alternatively be organized by multiple plot threads, which Ainsworth also used in *Old Saint Paul's*. To Leonard and the fair Amabel as the main action, he joins the fortunes of a blind fiddler and his daughter Nizza (whom Leonard eventually marries), the pursuit of Amabel by Rochester and Etherege, the fortunes of a plague nurse and her friend the coffin-maker, and numerous other figures, not so essential to the action. Not the least of these is the weird figure of Solomon Eagle, a religious fanatic who appears throughout the novel with a prophetical brazier on his head. By his presence he draws together many of the plot strands, until finally, at the climax of the tale, he kindles the Great Fire. The narration was probably also influenced by its serialization in the *Sunday Times*, although Ainsworth retained the copyright, and undoubtedly looked on its appearance in three volumes as the definitive form, the one by which it should be judged. Serialization was more likely to affect details of suspense and recapitulation than to change typical plots.

This interweaving of plots and sub-plots is also found in those three-deckers which emphasize the delineation of character. Such was the case with Trollope's novels. Although the Lord Lufton–Lucy Robarts romance provides the pivot around which the rest of *Framley Parsonage* revolves, it does not in itself fill three three-hundred page volumes. Two other romances proceeding through numerous hazards to ultimate marriage, a family surviving severe trials, a man falling steadily to almost complete ruin, and numerous domestic and satiric sketches of daily life round out the book. In *The Three Clerks*, which incidentally was not serialized but made its first appearance in three volumes, the incidents turn upon the fortunes of the three young civil servants who are conveniently attracted by three sisters. But even with these triple loves, there is plenty of room for satire of the Civil Service and Parliament, as well as of stockjobbing in the dubious speculation involving a bridge over the Thames at Limehouse.

Contemporary critics often noted this multiplicity of plots in a three-decker. The *Spectator* critic who deplored the "sad second volume" remarked of *The Gold of Ophir* (his representative three-decker), that at the opening of the third volume, "we have the feeling of returning to a story which we have left for a while in order to read something else." The *Saturday Review* thought *It Is Never Too Late to Mend*, which Reade had first struggled to develop into three volumes and then struggled to reduce to that number, deficient in plot. The imperfection lay in the three stories of which the novel was composed: one tale of bucolic love, one of the history of a badly managed gaol, and one of the adventures of prospecting for gold in Australia. Although admiring the skilful contrivance of each separate plot, the *Saturday* (like many a later critic) concluded that they were insufficiently integrated into a single story.[57] To a writer who had difficulty filling the large canvas required by the form, the idea of separate, multiple plots requiring only sketchy connections must have been very appealing.

Contrasting plots, like the ones involving Milvain and Reardon in Gissing's *New Grub Street*, were also frequent. Gissing portrays the rise of the clever but unscrupulous Milvain against the decline of Reardon, whose artistic integrity is shattered against the material conditions of literature. Here, too, there was ample room for the depiction of scenes and incidents outside the main stream: pictures of the life of a literary hack married to a woman of the lower class, and of a struggling realistic novelist who saves his manuscript at the expense of the life of a drunken man who had inadvertently started a fire.

In any form, multiple plots were likely to end in chapters which existed only to tie loose strings together neatly. In this kind of filing-system chapter at the end of *Never Too Late*, Reade hastily marries his young lovers, erects a model prison, sends his reformed thief back to a happy marriage in Australia, and determines the fate of the minor characters according to their deserts. In *Barchester Towers*, Trollope bewails the problems that beset an author in his last chapter:

> And who can apportion out and dovetail his incidents, dialogues, characters, and descriptive morsels, so as to fit them all exactly into 930 pages, without either compressing them unnaturally, or extending them artificially at the end of his labour? Do I not myself know that I am at this moment in want of a dozen pages, and that I am sick with cudgelling my brains to find them? And then when everything is done, the kindest-hearted critic . . . invariably twits us with the incompetency and lameness of our conclusion. We have either become idle and neglected it, or tedious and overlaboured it. [Chap. LI.]

This is not mere padding, in spite of Trollope's humorous implication, but a conscious justification of his method. Trollope's endings, like those of many three-deckers, necessarily seem a final tying of those loose strings. Once the proposal is made and accepted, the book is really over, but he must carry the two principal lovers, as well as the assorted minor ones, through the ceremonies and tidily dispose of the other characters.

In addition to affecting the way in which the events of a novel were to be arranged, the three-decker probably encouraged novelists in the portrayal of character. The spaciousness of the nine-hundred-page minimum allowed characters to be revealed gradually or developed to great advantage. Thus Trollope presents the progressive deterioration of Alaric Tudor, one of the *Three Clerks*, from the brandy-punch when he first takes a bribe, through his precarious rise to the height of a Civil Service Commissioner, his dealings in the stock market, and his embezzlement of his ward's money, to the ultimate degradation of the Old Bailey and Millbank as a convicted felon. Within the covers of the three-decker, there was abundant allowance for the contrapuntal depiction of the other two clerks, Harry Norman and Charley Tudor. If Harry Norman's character does not indeed develop, it solidifies, so that his youthful tendencies have hardened by the end of the action into an unchangeable disposition. Charley Tudor follows neither of these examples, but is led from his provincial ingenuousness to the dissipations of London by his associates. Although almost pulled under by the weight of his debts and low companions, he is ultimately rescued by Katie Woodward, whom he himself had saved from actual drowning in the waters of the Thames.

The characters of Mrs. Woodward's three daughters are also disclosed, primarily as they are confirmed in their natures or developed by their relationships to their respective lovers. Gertrude, paired with Alaric, acquires dignity and understanding in her misfortune, even if she loses her youthful gaiety; Linda, like Harry Norman, changes little. But Katie Woodward is transformed from "a happy, pretty, romping child" into a woman capable of sincere and mature love for the apparent reprobate, Charley Tudor. What happens to Gertrude is not presented in as much detail as the story of Katie; the reader is made aware of the difference only when Gertrude is seen through Harry Norman's eyes in what is almost her last appearance in the novel. Katie, on the other hand, is shown when her greatest joy was playing on an island in the river, dancing at her first ball, her love gradually (if predictably) deepening as she herself slowly, and yet suddenly, grows to womanhood. With all this, Trollope still has room for satire on the Civil Service, like Charley Tudor's examination (nobody in the Internal Navigation office will look at his carefully copied manuscript), and for gibes at political, social, economic, and literary life. Sir Gregory Hardlines (in whom Sir Charles Trevelyan was sketched), Mr. Chaffanbrass (the barrister), and Undy Scott (whose machinations result in Alaric Tudor's downfall) are among numerous other characters Trollope has room to present vividly.

Practically all critics express dissatisfaction with the ending of *The Mill on the Floss*. George Eliot herself, replying to Bulwer-Lytton's early criticism, admitted a disproportionate brevity in the third volume: "the tragedy is not adequately prepared. This is a defect which I felt even while writing the third volume. . . . The *'epische Breite'* into which I was beguiled by love of my subject in the two first volumes, caused a want of proportionate fullness in the treatment of the third, which I shall always regret."[58] From another point of view, that epic breadth allows Maggie Tulliver's character to unfold in the closely wrought texture of provincial life at Dorlcote Mill and St. Ogg's. The spaciousness of the three-decker form, as well as George Eliot's love for her subject, encouraged the detailed account of the influence of her environment on Maggie, an account which contributes much solidity and reality to that part of the work. The restrictions of the form may well have caused the rapidity with which events in the last volume (Books VI and VII) move. Nor, as such critics as Gordon Haight and Barbara Hardy have pointed out, would fuller treatment have guaranteed a more satisfactory conclusion. Although it might be urged that authors like Dickens and Thackeray, who did not habitually publish in three volumes, were also expansive, such treatment of character as that in *The Mill on the Floss* or *The Three Clerks* was encouraged by the prevalent form. The form was unquestionably a factor in marketing a novel and figured in the considerations of novelists.

Even when *The Three Clerks* was a new book, Walter

Bagehot felt that it had been too much affected by the triple volume requirement. Probably referring to Trollope's discussions of character, politics, and the civil service, he wrote, "I fear, it is written on the commercial method, whole dissertations and irrelevant reflections being inserted to make up the three volumes."[59] At times these "irrelevant reflections" took the form of asides which could have drawn the reader closer to the author in a kind of cozy little conspiracy. Although Henry James looked on these as "the betrayal of a sacred office," such a passage as that from *Barchester Towers* also helped to provide a unique relation between the author and his public, especially pronounced in serial publication, but evident in novels which appeared first in the conventional form as well.

Whether the three-decker fostered reflections as much as it did character depiction and a tripartite structure seems open to question today. Certainly it provided space for the author who could fill it if he chose with meditations. Wilkie Collins had no doubts whatever; he flatly accused the "vicious circulating library system" of compelling the novelist to garnish his story with "interminable descriptions, dull moralisings, or tedious conversations."[60] Bitter criticism of the prevailing system was also made by Charles Reade:

> What a mass of childish egotism, obtrusion of the Author's self, needless observations, descriptions, and irrelevancies of all sorts the Tri-Volumniors fling in to fill up the prescribed space as rubbish is thrown into a hole to fill it up—
>
> These are the acknowledged vices of all bad writers—but they exist nowhere upon a large scale now except in the Novel— they escape Criticism in a Novel but the disease kills the subject all the surer for not being attacked—[61]

If Reade remembered his words a few years later, he must have felt the keen irony when a reviewer accused him of one of those very offences. *The Times* charged that *White Lies* was "in dialogue and incident a translation from a drama called

Chateau Grantier, filled up into three volumes with the moral reflections of the distinguished appropriator." Reade at any rate felt called upon to defend himself. Since a three-volume novel was three times as long as a play, he argued in refutation, two-thirds of his novel must consist of moral reflections. Examining the novel, he discovered 1½ pages of political reflections, 1¼ pages on puppies, ½ page on Napoleon I, and some individual paragraphs on suicide and women. Of 768 pages, the "moral reflections" did not amount to more than 2 pages, he concluded, while all reflections, of whatever sort, probably amounted to 6.[62]

Dickens, too, apparently felt that the three-decker encouraged prolix meditations by the author. Discussing the triteness of many such novels, a writer in *All the Year Round* commented that "There were pages of reflection interspersed among other matters, the author pulling himself up when he had nothing more to add, stopping, quite abruptly, and saying, . . . 'But I am digressing.' "[63] Although the article is anonymous, the views probably corresponded with those held by Dickens, who was, as his colleagues agreed, an autocratic editor. He assured his readers less than a year later that "The statements and opinions of this Journal generally are, of course, to be received as the statements and opinions of its Conductor."[64] Whether the "dissertations and irrelevant reflections" amounted to a large or small percentage of the novel, however, it is important to remember that they were not just a Victorian characteristic belonging to an era more leisurely than ours, but were encouraged by a method of publication all but forgotten today.

Besides the "dull moralisings," Collins attributed "interminable descriptions" and "tedious conversations" to the "vicious circulating library system." Henry James made just these points in a review of *Far from the Madding Crowd*. Although he deemed the subject short and simple, he felt the work had been "distended to its rather formidable dimensions by the infusion of a large amount of conversational and descriptive padding and the use of an ingeniously verbose and redundant style. It is inordinately diffuse. . . . *Far from the Madding Crowd* gives us an uncomfortable sense of being a simple 'tale,' pulled and stretched to make the conventional three volumes."[65] While such charges are undoubtedly well founded, they are difficult to document specifically. Hardy's novel may well have been "pulled and stretched" although it actually reached only two volumes; James had apparently read the New York edition which did not indicate the English division. Whether a description or conversation was included for the sake of the nine hundred pages or for the author's own faith in its suitability is hard to determine. Contemporary critics laid the blame for this kind of tediousness squarely on the three-decker. When George Gissing intended to reprint *Workers in the Dawn*, he started to revise the novel, changing the phraseology slightly, but primarily shortening it. His alterations, carried through the first volume only, are indicated in Robert Shafer's edition of the novel.[66]

Since Gissing was acutely conscious of the three-decker requirement, what he removed may be partially due to that form; on the other hand, *Workers* was his first novel, and its subsequent abridgement may also be traced to his increasing skill as a writer. What he removed, however, corresponds to what contemporary critics attributed most precisely to the three-decker form: excessive dialogue, description, and authorial comment. He cut more dialogue than anything else, although much description and author's comments were excised, in accordance with his theory of the dramatic mode of presentation. Roughly twenty-two pages of dialogue (or soliloquy, as in Helen Norman's diary)—conversations between Arthur Golding and Mr. Norman, Arthur and Helen Norman, Arthur and Mr. Tolladay, for example—were pencilled for removal, as well as more than fourteen pages of description. Numerous sentences and paragraphs of narration were cut, and some of Gissing's comments, such as his reason for generalizing a conversation ("fear of being stigmatized as a 'realist' by the critical world"), were omitted. Some of the passages wandered so far from his tale that Gissing, like the writers castigated in *All the Year Round*, had resorted to awkward phrases like "But to return to our narration." Although exact passages must remain doubtful, it is clear that much of the original version may be traced to the librarian.

READERS, REACTIONS,
AND RESTRICTIONS

· Geraldine Jewsbury ·

MUDIE'S INFLUENCE—AND THAT OF THE THREE-DECKER—reached beyond the construction of the novel and the depiction of characters. Plots and attitudes, too, were affected by the New Oxford Street librarian. A rich source of information for studying these aspects of the fiction on Mudie's shelves lies in a series of reports to Bentley from Geraldine Jewsbury, who was one of the readers for the firm. These letters (mostly in the Bentley Collection in the British Museum, although some are at the University of Illinois) were written with quick vivacity and apparently great speed. They cover the years between 1860 and 1875, when the circulating libraries were flourishing. As a reader for a publisher who did a large business in three-deckers, she had the figure of Mudie constantly in the back of her mind as she read the manuscripts, approving, rejecting, or suggesting changes. Occasionally she notes that a book will fill a gap in a circulating library, or that "Mudie w^d. probably take a good many copies—and *general* circulating library readers w^d. take it and fancy it amusing."[1] These are not the novels she heartily recommends as worthy of the dignity of three volumes, but they are serviceable, saleable works on which Bentley will make his profit.

She is acutely conscious of Bentley's prestige (he was "publisher in ordinary to her Majesty the Queen") and is frequently anxious lest he take some unworthy novel, fit only to be issued by Mr. Newby or Mr. Reynolds (of *Reynolds's Miscellany*), whose names appear in her letters almost as epithets for purveyors of worthless, vulgar fiction. She describes a rejected manuscript as "what Mr. Newby might accept but nobody else," or she advises Bentley to "Leave it to Mr. Reynolds." Indeed, Reynolds's tall volumes with double columns of small type contrasted unfavorably with the wide margins of the dignified three-decker. Tinsley is also occasionally mentioned, again with a touch of contempt, although obviously of higher standing than Newby and Reynolds. Her judgments are sound, although (understandably) she tended to overestimate Bentley. Still he was undoubtedly at the top of the list of publishers specializing in three-volume fiction.

Even if she had not read for Bentley, Geraldine Jewsbury's letters would surely have provided many insights into the fiction of her day. Born in 1812, she lived her first twenty-nine years in obscurity. After this, however, she launched into the writing and reviewing that "gave her a familiarity with current fiction such as few women of her day could have equalled,"[2] and became, to Jane Welsh Carlyle, "the most intimate friend I have in the world." In the course of their rather tumultuous friendship, Jane Carlyle found her "a fine spirit in spite of all her vagaries," "a far more profound and daring speculator than even I had fancied," if "unpractical, like all women of genius."[3] It was Jane Carlyle who helped her find a publisher for her first three-decker, *Zoe*. Readers must have agreed with Jane Carlyle, who finished the first sketch "with a feeling little short of *terror*! So much power of genius rushing so recklessly into unknown space!" Later, she declared the manuscript "decidedly the *clever-est* English woman's book I ever remember to have read."[4] Bulwer-Lytton concurred, writing to Forster, as Michael Sadleir notes, one of his few favorable comments on novels by unknown writers, "There are . . . a strength and independence of thought which are sufficient to [? predict] a great and startling writer."[5] There was some helpful scandal about its indecency, and in 1845 Geraldine Jewsbury became a small lion of the circulating libraries. Critical opinion also endorsed her work. George Henry Lewes, who had, as Richard Stang observes, "almost uncanny ability as a critic to pick out the important novels from the chaff,"[6] noted a progressive improvement in her three novels, *Zoe*, *The Half Sisters*, and *Marian Withers*. What he termed her subtle and sometimes deep observations of morals and manners led him to expect still finer works from her.[7] A few years later, she was included in David Masson's list of British novelists of note since Scott.[8]

Within twelve years after the publication of *Zoe*, however, she was forced to stop novel-writing because of the illnesses suffered after the completion of each one. Although she could not continue to write fiction, she could still read it. "A voracious novel-reader by inclination,"[9] she was able to indulge her taste in her work as reviewer of the novels of the week in the *Athenaeum* and as reader for both Bentley and the firm of Hurst and Blackett. Her ideas about novels are firmly expressed, usually with abundant reasons, explanations, and even an occasional warning not to let an author see her report lest her handwriting be recognized.

How eagerly she performed her duties for Bentley is indicated first of all by the number of novels she read. Between January and May 1864, she reported on sixteen novels, three books of fiction shorter than novels, and six works of non-fiction— biographies, memoirs, and books of travels. Beyond the sheer amount, her impatience to read is revealed by such remarks or postscripts in her letters as this one, after an illness, "Yes! Please send *MS* as many as you will," or "Send me some more M.S."[10] Such avidity was hardly due to Bentley's lavish pay, which amounted to about a guinea for a three-decker. Finally, her pleasure in her work is apparent from even a quick glance through her reports, which reflect their author's personality as well as her judgments.

It was she who urged Bentley to accept *East Lynne*, which Meredith (at Chapman and Hall) and Smith, Elder had already rejected. Although she had "no hesitation" in advising him to publish it, she did warn him to "let the grammar and the composition be *thoroughly revised* by some competent person. The author is not qualified."[11] Bentley came to rely on her verdicts, and entrusted the revision of doubtful manuscripts to her pen. His main difficulty seems to have been her tendency to reject too much. Of the sixteen novels she read in the first four months of 1864, she advised the acceptance of only one, the conditional acceptance of two more (that is, Bentley should take it "if you pay nothing for it," or "if you need a novel," or "if you want to do the author a favor"), and the rejection of thirteen. Bentley apparently remonstrated, so she expressed regret, but changed no verdict, reaffirming that everything refused was rubbish.

As she recorded her judgments, the tastes, opinions, and preferences of that relatively small but significant group who subscribed to Mudie's become clear both by her words and by implication. Although her perceptions were sharper and her discrimination keener than those of the ordinary Mudie patron, her verdicts were not different in kind. *Under Two Flags* was "a very immoral book written on the pattern of French novels," although she correctly predicted it would sell; *Cometh Up as a Flower*, "coarse, vulgar and very objectionable"; a translation of *Emma Lyons* by Dumas would only bring scandal to Bentley's name. The quickness with which she rejects works she considered immoral is the more noticeable because of the furor that had been aroused by *Zoe*. Even before it was published, the author had arranged to cover the heroine with a more "liberal distribution of spotted muslin,"[12] at the insistence of Jane Carlyle. In spite of that, the reviewer in *John Bull*, like many others, felt the aim of the novel was to weaken the moral and destroy the religious feelings of the readers. "There *may* be such a person as Geraldine Endsor Jewsbury," the critic admits, but he doubts it because of the "language, sentiments, principles, situations, and characters."[13]

More than thirty years later the author herself used *Zoe's* case as the reason for the rejection of a manuscript; the suggestion of immorality had been found not in the material of the plot, but in its treatment. Chapman and Hall had accepted the novel on the basis of the report from their reader, who had seized on its intention and motive, and "overlooked its sins against good taste." When, however, it was printed and Chapman read it, "he *nearly had a fit of apoplexy* he was so shocked!—a work *he* had intended 'to circulate in the bosom of families' was not fit to be read—." He attempted to persuade her to write something else, but she refused, and with Carlyle's help, the book was published. "*I* had thought I had been writing a *Sermon*—well—sins against good *taste* are far more heavily visited than sins against morality."[14] Both her experiences as a writer, then, and her own inclinations as a reader of fiction, helped Geraldine Jewsbury in her estimation of what the Mudie reader wanted for his yearly one pound one.

She worked competently within the framework of the three-decker, noticing whether there were striking incidents in each volume, and whether the interest was strong enough to last until the third. She objected to that last resort of an author struggling to fill 900 pages: three separate stories jammed together in one novel (not uncommon in that era—Reade was accused of this feat with *Never Too Late*). Still, she refused to compromise by padding a story to fill volumes. She apparently cut so much from one manuscript Bentley asked her to revise that he wrote to protest. She held her ground that "the portions

I have taken out were *extraneous* to the main interest," and she refused to add material. "I *cannot* write any fresh matter—neither will I restore what I have erased—because it is all *bosh*." She is sorry for his dilemma, but cannot help except by suggesting that if "*1* volume w^d be so unprofitable, why not make *two* small dainty looking volumes. . . . you can *set a fashion*!" If his own invention cannot space out the manuscript, and if he refuses to print it as one volume, she cooly counsels him to "*sell* yr M.S. bodily."[15]

· *Some Typical Attitudes* ·

WHEN SHE LIKED A WORK, SHE WAS QUICK TO URGE ITS acceptance. What she liked soon becomes plain. In the first place, of course, she realized the eternal importance of love in the financial and popular success of a novel, and would have readily agreed with Trollope's statement, "It is admitted that a novel can hardly be made interesting or successful without love."[16] Trollope's productions bear testimony to his application of this principle. *Framley Parsonage*, as he explains in his *Autobiography*, was intended as a fragment in the life of an English clergyman who, although good, succumbs to temptations in the worldly life around him. Actually the plot is centered about Lord Lufton's wooing of the clergyman's sister, which was originally put in as a necessary adjunct because, as Trollope stated categorically, "there must be love in a novel."[17] An author as different from Trollope as Charles Reade noted in his preliminary sketch of *Foul Play*: "The Turnpike Road of Fiction. Since there can be no great success in fiction unless . . . the old, old story of love and passion, the thing to be done is to combine the wealthy materials in a story of the heart."

Love and marriage, with all the variations of secret weddings, bigamy, deserted sweethearts, unfaithful husbands, wicked brothers, and mistaken identities, form an unchanging theme in the fiction of that time, as in previous times, and in our own.

That novels of adventure and novels of religion, sensation novels and novels of character all had one common denominator, the love interest, is scarcely surprising, and is even less remarkable when it is remembered that the subscribers who stepped from their carriages in New Oxford Street were predominantly women whose primary interests and occupations remained in the home. It is in the attitudes towards the lovers and in the setting, in either space or ideas, of their emotions, that the qualities which distinguish the Victorian reader appear.

Details revealing location, occupations of characters, their religion, and their social standing loom large in Geraldine Jewsbury's considerations of fiction. Exotic and distant settings in foreign lands were not always happy choices. Exciting stories were necessary "to overcome the indolence of general readers who when they read a novel cannot be troubled to learn strange hard names and strange intricate geography."[18] Readers seeking amusement wanted to read something related to their own habits and sympathies. Tales of Anglo-Indian society had once provided just that, but by 1863 were already overdone, so that even a well written novel of English girls and gallant captains in Calcutta was rejected.

If general readers were already bored with tiger hunting, there was still a market in the colonies which was not forgotten by either Bentley or his reader, because Mudie's ironbound boxes traveled there regularly. Thus *Black and Gold*, with hairbreadth escapes, battles, and dangers would appeal especially to men in India, Miss Jewsbury wrote approvingly. One sure way to create interest in a foreign setting was to place an Englishman in it, and have him fall in love with a girl of the land. It might be difficult to get people to care about the Chinese, but they would like, according to Miss Jewsbury, and as Byron had earlier made clear, a story of an Englishman in Corsica who fell in love with a smuggler's daughter.

In the matter of occupations for the characters who peopled the three-deckers, the influence of the circulating library reader is clearly discernible. Those occupations in which Mudie's sub-scriber would be interested are noted again and again in Geraldine Jewsbury's reports. Colonial enterprise and emigration she approves; the anxieties and troubles of a merchant she rejects on the ground that people do not want to read about what they (or some member of their family) are facing daily. Such scenes are included in the novels of Dickens, but he took care that they would not be unpleasant. Although Geraldine Jewsbury and Mudie's patrons were averse to details of business in fiction, critics interested in theory were noting that its omission seriously narrowed the scope of fiction which was not just enter-tainment, but a portrayal of human life. William C. Roscoe criticized Thackeray because his characters had no external field of interest; they were shown generally only in their moments of "idleness or amusement." Roscoe attributed Thackeray's failure to deal with business (beyond his mere indications of occupations) or absorbing affairs external to the author's own nature, to his indifference to the active concerns of life.[19] A part of his reluctance, however, might be caused by the same sort of dislike felt by Geraldine Jewsbury. Of a book she found otherwise "clear, vivid, and truthful," she asked,

> Will fashionable fine ladies and gentlemen read of the painful anxieties of a broken merchant. . . ? Will ordinary female readers care to read of the gradations of business speculation? . . . Would men of business care to *read* what they have to face . . . six days in every week? Would a surgeon care to read a tale about dissection or morbid anatomy? W^d the general public?[20]

Geraldine Jewsbury enjoyed tales of a superior social class, or those in which members of the nobility might reasonably figure, for domestic novels. Sensational work like the "Newgate Novel," the materials for which were found in the Newgate Calendar, was of course published, popular, and accepted at the libraries. Still, although a fact in the literature of the day, she disapproved of them as a whole, a feeling in which many con-temporary critics concurred.[21]

In Dickens's work there was the saving grace of humor as well as the contrast and hope of higher stations, but Trollope was expressing a well established sentiment, not just Geraldine Jewsbury's, when he wrote, "The regions of absolute vice are foul and odious. The savour of them, till custom has hardened the palate and the nose, is disgusting."[22] Other things being equal, the novel that clearly revealed the author's knowledge of good society would be repeatedly requested at Mudie's, while the one with a "provincial" or low tone might gather dust in his catacombs. Thus Miss Jewsbury admired *Arcadia* as a work of real ability, ranking it much higher than even *East Lynne*. Still she hesitated to recommend it without qualification because it dealt with rural life as it actually was, with laborers, country squires, and farmers, and she wondered whether "*general* readers care for such company?"[23] To another novel she objected that "there are no refined cultivated *gentlefolk* as *standards*."[24]

In religious questions there was an obvious prepossession in favor of Protestantism, and hesitance about the propriety of incorporating scenes from the life of Christ in a novel. These attitudes should not be construed as hard and fast, of course, but as reflecting a general tendency. They would be overcome by a great novel, but in an average circulating library three-decker, might well tip the scales in favor of acceptance or rejection. In all fairness, however, a poor novel, with only the proper bias to recommend it, was not likely to find its way to Mudie's shelves through Geraldine Jewsbury. She advised the rejection of one such work against Catholics as no credit to Protestantism. Still, when a book dealing with Roman Catholics is recommended, as was Lady Georgiana Fullerton's *Too Strange Not to be True*, she felt it necessary to give her reasons in great detail. Although it did have the defect of being Roman Catholic, it would not prove disagreeable to the general reader, she began. In fact, she reasoned, although somewhat inaccurately, since it was set in Russia at the time of Peter the Great, it would have to be a Catholic novel to keep historical accuracy, because in those days all Russians were of either the Catholic or Greek Orthodox faiths. "The Catholic element will find favor with the Catholic reader," she concluded, and the author's name would attract the attention of all.

Another aspect of her attitude towards religion concerned the doubtful propriety of incorporating scenes from the life of Christ in fiction.[25] Even when there was simply a question of a character's glimpse of Jesus on the way to the Mount of Olives, she hesitated. There was no conversation, only "vigorous and striking" description. Although the treatment was admittedly "very reverent," Miss Jewsbury was troubled about whether "such an incident be admissible at all in a novel." Such attitudes testify to the continued existence of a shade of feeling that fiction, even though novels were widely read and though Mudie's was the very essence of respectability, did not stand high among the forms of literature, a feeling related to its popularity as a form of amusement as well as of instruction. A scruple similar to Miss Jewsbury's had been expressed earlier by a critic in the *Quarterly Review* who objected that the "awful truths of religion" had no place in a fictitious tale with its "due seasoning of sexual love." If they did not defeat the purpose of the novel by dullness, he concluded, they would be akin to blasphemy.[26] How much attitudes had changed in forty years is shown by George Meredith's recommendation that Chapman and Hall reject a novel, not because of the inclusion of religion, but because of its sustained attack on Christianity. In his capacity as reader for the firm, Meredith pointed out that although the book was well written, the attack would be offensive to circulating library readers—in 1886, still the significant group in the publishing success of a novel.[27]

Basically the subject matter of the plots of the novels on Mudie's shelves was not radically different from that which has always interested writers. Characteristic plots certainly dealt with love and frequently ended in marriage, but the variations on this theme were wide. Bigamy was a frequent device, as in

Lady Audley's Secret, Aurora Floyd, or *Recommended to Mercy.*
Sometimes the fault was intentional, sometimes not. In *Too
Strange Not to be True* a Russian noblewoman is ill-treated by
her husband. Through a series of events, he is believed dead.
She flees (fleeing, not always strictly necessary to the plot, was
very popular), and marries another, only to discover that her
first husband is actually alive. Lady Audley, in a somewhat
similar predicament, had acted quickly, pushing her first husband
down a well, but this was an extreme solution. The popularity
of the *Enoch Arden* theme extended beyond readers of poetry.

Next in popularity to bigamous marriages were those in
which one partner, who usually has been unwilling for one
reason or another, finds someone who can be truly loved. Such
was the case with *Zoe,* Geraldine Jewsbury's own first novel.
The heroine, daughter of an English officer and a beautiful
Greek girl, marries a man much older than herself because she
thinks this is the only way she can obtain her freedom. She
then meets a priest who falls in love and resigns his priesthood,
but also leaves Zoe to practice his new Protestantism among
miners. Zoe's husband and the converted priest die, leaving Zoe
alone to care for her two children.

Under the influence of her love for the priest, Zoe had
become a woman changed for the better, so that the final effect
was uplifting. This was important for Mudie's reader: matrimonial errors might form the material of the book, but its
message should be optimistic. Geraldine Jewsbury advised
rejection of a manuscript because there was "a total absence
of anything noble. . . . It wd *never* help a struggling person
but might injure by depressing their faith and . . . bewildering
their principle of right and wrong."[28] This is not the facile
optimism so often attributed to the Victorian age, but a deeper
and more complex attitude. In the first place, it results from a
sincere belief in the effectiveness of teaching as a way to help
people solve individual problems and to create a better world.

Secondly, it indicates the acceptance of the novel as a method of instruction. The Victorian reader would have agreed with Sidney that the final justification of literature lies in its ability to convey moral lessons. This was not apparent to all critics in the early days of the flourishing of three-deckers and circulating libraries, of course, and there was still prejudice carried over from "the old Minerva Press days," to which writers in mid-century occasionally referred with a shudder. A writer in the *Pall Mall Gazette* in 1869 thought novel-reading had been carried on until it constituted a serious interference with "more energetic and intellectual amusements," by which he meant, not Muscular Christianity, but playgoing and conversation. Although he admitted that some novels were works of art, as they should be, he went on to pronounce that "the reading of a novel is perhaps as near an approach to complete idleness of mind and body as can possibly be attained by a waking man."[29] Whether or not Fitzjames Stephen wrote the article,[30] he expressed a similar viewpoint in a letter to his wife the following year; he was "ashamed" to confess that he had had a strange fit of laziness, and had spent the day "in absolute idleness, reading novels."[31]

Even in 1869, however, such an attitude was becoming outmoded. A decade later, Trollope believed that although men commonly read novels as they ate "pastry after dinner—not without some inward conviction that the taste is vain if not vicious," the novel had become "the former of our morals, the code by which we rule ourselves, the mirror in which we dress ourselves."[32] Trollope's view expressed what came to be more and more representative of the belief of the Victorian reader after mid-century. If the lessons of the novel had been licentious and immoral in earlier days, Scott had redeemed it and put it on its true course. Trollope himself felt, as his *Autobiography* shows, "a profound conviction" of his responsibility as a teacher, a conviction which would not have been alien to Dickens, Thackeray, or George Eliot.

Trollope regarded the novel not only as didactic, but highly efficacious in its instruction. As an individual offering the lessons of a novel to a family, he would be laughed at or criticized, he believed; "but when I . . . come on the same errand with Mr. Mudie's ticket on my back, you admit me, and accept my teaching."[33] So effective, indeed, was the teaching of the novel that the representation of vice or immorality might well lead to emulation by the reader. This of course accounts for the imposition of a certain degree of reticence on the novelist to the end that virtue seem attractive and vice repulsive. At this point the novelist's task was difficult, since vice could be made far more entertaining than virtue with much less effort. Still, Trollope believed, and Mudie would have agreed, that "the novelist, if he have a conscience, must preach his sermons with the same purpose as the clergyman, and must have his own system of ethics." Furthermore, he must do it efficiently, "while he charms his readers instead of wearying them."[34] So Dickens did; Trollope noted with approval that no immodest girl is made alluring in all the novels of his contemporary.

In novels dealing with matrimonial tangles, it was imperative that virtue should triumph. Just how far it was necessary to go is explicitly indicated by some of Geraldine Jewsbury's notes for the revision of the third volume of *Struggle for Life*.[35] This book dealt with the familiar triangle: Elfrida, already a wife, falls in love with George Traherne, also married. She remains steadfast in her loyalty to her husband, however, and refuses to run away. This, Miss Jewsbury firmly maintained, is insufficient. The mere fact of her refusal to leave "is not enough to comprise a woman's virtue," she went on; in fact, it displays "a want of *reticence . . . quite incompatible* with any pretence of wifely duty or *womanly* self-respect." George Traherne, having no clear notions of right and wrong, might fall in love with his neighbor's wife, she admits, but reiterates the author's obligation to show her sympathy with virtue. "Elfrida must behave altogether differently," she directs;

she might instead of carressing [*sic*] G. Traherne and calling him "my George" tell him simply and gravely the circumstances that led her to commit the fatal folly of marrying her husband and her determination to hold on to the obligation . . . she need not deny that she *wd and cd* have cared for him but let her accept her lot and not . . . an unlawful love in her heart.

After Elfrida has sent George away, a more manly principle should begin to show itself in his life, and after the death of his wife he "might be moved to a sense of his own wasted life. . . . Let him go away and *do* something good and useful—head a government exploring party . . . a fresh life with some principle of *hard work* in it."

Miss Jewsbury, having provided George Traherne with a future reminiscent of that of the narrator of "Locksley Hall," went on to approve the reunion of Elfrida and her husband at the last. She made clear, however, that "the stern moral of the story should remain—that the *consequences* of our action *remain* and must be endured to the end."[36] This belief, which amounted almost to fear, in the power of the novel as a teacher obviously led to the creation of incidents that would be edifying and uplifting, even at the expense of probability, and the concomitant omission of any character or incident even faintly suggestive of sin or vice. When Trollope felt called upon to defend himself to Thackeray for a reference to illegitimate children, he brought to his defense Effie Deans, Beatrix Esmond, Jane Eyre, Hetty Sorrel, and even Dickens's *Oliver Twist*.[37] Still, Trollope unquestionably accepted Thackeray's rejection of his manuscript, acknowledging the necessity of "pure morals," especially in a periodical (the *Cornhill*). He further recognized the difficulties inherent in treating a subject such as adultery, and the consequent necessity of delicacy, but stuck to his ground that ignorance was not innocence, and that his presentation had never lent attraction to sin.

It was the "delicacy" with which writers like Trollope

approached such subjects that George Moore and other young writers towards the end of the century attacked as hypocrisy, but which its proponents would have defended on the basis that lessons should be offered for emulation. Morality in its broader sense, as Geraldine Jewsbury learned, depended not so much on the kind of incidents involved, as on the method of telling them. All Trollope's examples were aptly cited, but all had been handled with "delicacy," as Trollope felt his own were. Such delicacy amounted to "puerile conventionality" for the later writers like George Moore. "You can say what you like provided you speak according to rule," he charged, and used *Adam Bede* to illustrate an accepted method of seduction, in which Hetty and Arthur, after a flirtation, walk through a wood. Three months later Hetty is discovered to be pregnant. To destroy this "quibblery," he claimed he "was daring enough in my 'Mummer's Wife' to write that Dick dragged Kate into the room and that the door was slammed behind her."[38]

Such treatment was inacceptable to the Mudie subscriber; it was in fact on the basis of this passage that the libraries banned Moore's novel. It was at once too detailed and too violent. Like Trollope, Geraldine Jewsbury (who had learned the hard way with *Zoe*) objected, not to the existence of sin in a novel, but to the garments in which it was clothed. Eliza Lynn Linton's *Lizzie Norton*, for example, concerned a widower, remarried under the second part of his name, who was being blackmailed by a French swindler, the brother of his dead wife, who had convinced him that his first wife was still living. "The fault lies as much in the mode of *telling* . . . as in the materials of the story," she decided. As a whole, she found it *"disagreeable"*; but if it had been told by Miss Braddon "it wd have been *interesting* and *pleasant*."[39] Not the least of the qualities painful to Miss Jewsbury was the way in which the author held up the parents of the heroine to contempt. Methods of treatment were important to the Mudie reader not just in relation to love and the difficulties of marriage, but in all aspects of life.

CONTENTS.

The Collection of New and Choice Books in this Library is now by many Thousand Volumes the largest in the World, and is still further augmented and enriched, from day to day, by the addition of abundant supplies of all the principal New Works as they appear.

The purpose for which the Library was originally established—to create a more general taste for the higher Literature, and to meet the increased demand which has thus arisen—is still kept steadily in view, and great care continues to be taken that every work of merit and general interest shall be introduced as soon as published.

As the New Works added to the Library from time to time continue to exceed in value the whole amount of the Current Subscriptions, it is probable that the Stock of Books available for the use of Subscribers, deducting the number of copies sold or worn out while in circulation, will shortly exceed ONE MILLION VOLUMES.

Contents page of a Mudie Catalogue.

Over and over again works are censured because they are "disagreeable" or "unpleasant," qualities which Mr. Mudie's readers did not care to find in their novels. This was partly the result of an attitude very much like that which limited the scope of fiction as a teacher to those lessons obviously exhibiting virtue for emulation. Partly, too, it arose from the conviction that although the ultimate end of the novel was instruction, its more immediate goal, without which it could not hope to attain the farther one, was diversion. An extreme example of unpleasantness was found in *Black Moss*, about which Miss Jewsbury wrote,

> I don't think people wd care to read a story all about Fevers, Funerals, *and a wicked Undertaker*. It makes me feel as tho' one were assisting at one's *own funeral*—and there is a *broken drain* thro' wh the horrors of the *Churchyard* filter into the village Brook—Do you think *all that* pleasant reading??[40]

In any case, when disagreeable or unpleasant subjects were portrayed, credibility and preference required the inclusion of something to relieve the gloom. Alexander Macmillan wrote to Thomas Hardy about the manuscript of *The Poor Man and the Lady*, undoubtedly of three-decker length, "Your pictures of character among Londoners, and especially the upper classes, are sharp, clear, incisive, and in many respects true, but they are wholly dark—not a ray of light visible to relieve the darkness, and therefore exaggerated and untrue in their result."[41] In 1877, in rejecting a manuscript, Geraldine Jewsbury concluded that its great fault was "that it lacks any central *light*."[42]

Several years later George Gissing recorded in his diary a similar verdict from Smith, Elder about *Mrs. Grundy's Enemies*: " 'It exhibits a great deal of dramatic power, . . . but in our judgment it is too painful to please the ordinary novel reader and treats of scenes that can never attract the subscribers to Mr. Mudie's Library.' (!!)"[43] A later judgment confirmed that it was "sad almost beyond bearing."[44] Smith, Elder also thought

Gissing's *New Grub Street* " 'clever and original' but fear it is too gloomy."[45] Such pictures were not congenial to the prevalent attitudes toward fiction, nor would Mr. Mudie's subscribers have been properly enlightened by them, since the lessons were in the form of examples to be avoided rather than followed. The standard was set up by the needs of the audience, and the dangers of corruption by such pictures outweighed any lesson they might provide.

· *The British Matron and the Young Girl* ·

AS GERALDINE JEWSBURY POINTED OUT, *Black Moss* WOULD not have suited any of Mr. Mudie's readers, not the large body of women who daily trooped to his doors, nor their husbands and brothers, nor even the colonials who looked forward eagerly to the arrival of the ironclad boxes. These people, usually combined into what she called "general readers," were constantly in her mind as she read manuscripts, for their tastes, prejudices, and attitudes were determining factors in a book's success. As the Victorian family frequently read their books from Mudie's aloud, it was only natural that the standards were established for younger members of the audience, especially girls. Many writers accepted these standards; they were, however, increasingly galling to those who would have been in perfect accord with George Gissing's dictum about *Workers in the Dawn*: "It is *not* a book for women and children, but for thinking and struggling men." They would have readily agreed that "it is quite impossible to restrict one's literary activity with a view to the sensibilities of one's friends. Just that has brought English fiction to its present pass."[46]

The "young girl" standard was nothing new in Gissing's time, of course. Dickens and Thackeray had felt its restriction, and to authors who depended on the library for the original circulation of their novels, it was even more confining. One of these was Wilkie Collins, who refused to change a manuscript because "My story is *not* addressed to young people exclusively— it is addressed to readers in general. I do not accept young people as the ultimate court of appeal in English literature."[47] While denying that their writings would ever corrupt a soul, these authors, like Charles Reade, demanded freedom to choose subjects "fit for fiction of a higher order, though not adapted to the narrow minds of bread-and-butter misses, nor of the criti- casters who echo these young ladies' idea of fiction and its limits. . . ."[48] George Meredith, whose *Richard Feverel* had disappeared from Mudie's list, lamented, "If novels and poems are to be written for young women only, I must learn the art afresh."[49] An incidental convenience of the three-decker form, almost unsuspected today, was that it sometimes permitted Mudie to circulate just those parts of a novel suitable for young girls. Kate Stanley, who was to become the mother of Bertrand Russell, wrote of being allowed to read only the first two volumes of *The Mill on the Floss*, because Maggie "is so wicked" in the third.[50]

Although William Dean Howells, on the other side of the Atlantic, defended the standard as reflecting both the heightened stature of the author's profession and the increased decency of the people, Henry James found it made the English novel "rather shy." It was, he said, "a good thing for virgins and boys, and a bad thing for the novel itself, when the novel is . . . considered as a composition that treats of life at large and helps us to *know*."[51] George Moore, who had felt Mudie's ban, put it more bluntly: "Literature and young girls are irreconcilable elements, and the sooner we leave off trying to reconcile them the better. At this vain endeavour the circulating library has been at work for the last twenty years." The result had been the growth of a new school of criticism, he maintained, whose criterion was, "Would you or would you not give that book to your sister of sixteen to read?"[52]

In 1890 the *New Review* published a symposium by three authors, Walter Besant, Mrs. E. Lynn Linton, and Thomas

Hardy, on the question of "Candour in English Fiction."[53] Since they were all writers of three-deckers, and hence sensitive to circulating library requirements, their opinions provide a good cross section of the attitudes of novelists towards the "young girl" standard. Besant took the practical view that "he who works for pay must respect the prejudices of his customers." If a novelist "crosses certain boundaries," he will find that Mudie or Smith will not distribute his books, Besant asserted, and it becomes "a question of money—shall he restrict his pencil or shall he restrict his purse?"

Mrs. Linton could not accept such restrictions and proposed a compromise. Such restraints, she protested, cut off from fiction "one of the largest and most important areas of that human life we pretend to portray." If a novel is "written for the inclusion of the Young Person among its readers, it does not go beyond the schoolgirl standard." The solution she suggests is a "locked bookcase" for the volumes intended for thoughtful and mature readers.

In his part of the symposium, Hardy attacked magazines (which serialized novels) and the circulating libraries as responsible for the "indescribably unreal and meretricious" views found in fiction. When books are borrowed and not bought, Hardy pointed out, they are "made to wear a common livery in style and subject, enforced by their supposed necessities in addressing indiscriminately a general audience." To the circulating library he ascribes responsibility for lack of sincerity, since fiction "is conditioned by its surroundings like a river-stream." Authors had no responsibility for this stunting of their work, Hardy believed, because the arrogation of the dispensation of fiction is a circumstance "over which they, as representatives of Grub Street, have no control." Mudie and Smith stimulated not the advancement and improvement of fiction, not the growth of the novel which reflected and revealed life, but rather a vast increase in one type, a lateral but not an upward advance. Thus Besant accepted the circulating library and its young female subscriber and worked within its limitations; Mrs. Linton chafed at the restriction which excluded important segments of human life; but it was Hardy who struck out at a system which he felt was obstructing the growth of the novel as a form of art. Five years later, after the uproar over *Jude the Obscure*, he abandoned fiction altogether.

Not only was the young girl the standard, but the author was always to treat her with all the courtesy due a guest from the host. The attitude is epitomized in Thackeray's "Letter from the Editor to a Friend and Contributor" of the *Cornhill*. As a periodical, it had a policy, as Trollope had learned and as Hardy recognized later, even more restrictive than that of the libraries. Its writers he expected to "have good manners, a good education, and write in good English," adding that "we shall suppose the ladies and children always present."[54] So also Geraldine Jewsbury objected to the word *beggar* applied to a casual individual, remonstrating that

> in a book a certain amount of art and decorum is necessary. It is not the form in wh men wd speak before company and the author <u>must</u> . . . understand that the <u>reader</u> and the public <u>are</u> <u>company</u> and require a certain amount of ceremony and politeness to be observed before them.[55]

· The Circulating Censorship ·

Obviously, if Mr. Mudie's subscriber had to be treated as "company," and young and feminine "company" at that, the scope of the novel had to be strictly limited by the prevailing attitudes of the middle class. While these conditions existed, it was difficult for writers to discuss moral or religious questions in their work. The "British Matron," with whom Mudie soon was identified ("I would rather have Mudie and the British Matron with me than the whole army of the press,"[56] wrote George Meredith), seemed to many to shackle the imagination of creative novelists. Although the chains grew heavier as the years passed, protests against the powers of the librarian in newspapers and literary journals had elicited two public defenses even before Mudie opened his Great Hall.

One of the earliest of these indignant expostulations, in 1858, concerned Reade's *Cream*, a one-volume issue of two tales, "Jack of All Trades" and "The Autobiography of a Thief." The latter was originally planned as part of Chapter 7 of *It Is Never Too Late to Mend* but removed because abridgement was necessary to compress the work into three volumes. "A Subscriber both to the *Critic* and to Mudie's" complained that there were no copies of *Cream* in that library, in spite of its pledge that "all the principal new works" would be supplied.

Whether this or other murmurs against Mudie's selection were written by the injured author or at his instigation, or whether it represented the genuine dissatisfaction of an aggrieved subscriber, was hard to determine at the time, and is virtually impossible today. The *Critic* thought the case strong enough to defend it editorially, attacking Mudie's contention that the book was "too dear" (it was listed at 10*s.*) by maintaining that Reade's work fell into the category of "the principal new books" Mudie contracted to supply.[57] The founder himself replied to these charges in the columns of the *Critic*, reiterating his canon of furnishing "the principal new books," but adding only "under certain limitations, . . . clearly stated in all my prospectuses." *Cream* was excluded, "not simply on account of its price, but of its quality. . . . It appears to be . . . quite unworthy of Mr. Reade's high reputation, or of a place in any select library." He goes on to admit candidly that his estimation of the monetary worth of a book is determined by two considerations: circulation and subsequent sale. He concludes with assurances that if Reade would produce another work equal to *Christie Johnstone*, he would "cheerfully give a good round sum for the first edition."[58]

The *Critic* printed Mudie's letter but rejected his explanation, contending that he should furnish the books his customers wanted, not those he personally liked or disliked. As yet there was no question of censorship, or of excluding a work of questionable moral tendency.[59] Nevertheless, Mudie was on the defensive. His advertisement in the *Critic* of April 1, 1858, two weeks before the attack, had read, "An ample supply is provided of all the principal New Works as they appear"; on May 1, the same day his letter of explanation was printed, it had been changed to read, "The supplies of the *higher class* of works, for the circulation of which the Library was originally established, are also largely increased. . . ." Mudie's emphasis on *"higher class"* reveals the strategy used for the next three decades to repel charges against his selective policies. What it boiled down to was that Mudie's was a "select" library, and it was the librarian who selected. Actually, his was considered a more "liberal" library than W. H. Smith's, but even so he did not escape the deserved epithet of "censor."

If authors could not, in Besant's words, "respect the prejudices" of Mudie's customers, still they were not able to ignore the librarian as a distributor of books. Whether they expressed their indignation publicly in letters to the press, or privately in letters to friends, they were becoming more and more restive under the library's restrictions. When *Richard Feverel* vanished from Mudie's, the publisher Chapman demanded an explanation. Mudie replied, according to Meredith's account, "that he had advertised it as much and as long as he could, but that, in consequence of the urgent remonstrances of several respectable families who objected to it as dangerous and wicked and damnable, he was compelled to withdraw it." In another letter, also to Samuel Lucas, Meredith's indignation burst out:

> I find I have offended Mudie and the British Matron. He will not, or haply, dare not put me in his advertised catalogue. Because of the immoralities I depict! O canting Age! I predict a Deluge. Mudie is Metternich: and after him—Meantime I am tabooed from all drawing-room tables.[60]

Lucas, incited by his recent agreement to serialize Meredith's new novel in his respectable *Once a Week*, gave it a two-column, generally favorable review in *The Times*. Although the success of the novel was not materially changed by that notice (which was some four months late), authors continued to look hopefully to reviews for ammunition against Mudie. In 1877, Charles Reade wrote to Blackwood of *A Woman Hater*, "I am at present mortified and surprised at the dead silence of the London dailies and weeklies. Mudie's power and natural desire to take as few copies as possible of any deserving work needs the outward pressure of a few reviews to overpower it."[61]

In 1860, two years after his letter to the *Critic*, Mudie again publicly defended the policies of his library, this time in the columns of the influential and conservative *Athenaeum*. Answering an editorial attack in the *Literary Gazette*, Mudie had chosen the *Athenaeum* because of the abusive nature of its struggling rival's charges, which linked Mudie metaphorically with fire and plague and accused him of using his library to foster his own religious beliefs. As the great fire of London had started from Pudding Lane, so Mudie broke out upon the city from his little shop leading out of Holborn, began the *Gazette*, and went on to compare the spread of his influence to that of the plague. Admitting that he was "better known . . . than any man in England," the *Gazette* denied his necessity for the public he coaxed to pay one pound one a year. Rhetorically convicting Mudie of ruthlessness, the *Gazette* accused him of pulling "down his near neighbor's house" and indeed of absorbing a whole area to accommodate his expanding firm. Once in a position to dictate price, he obtained a guinea book from the publishers for 10*s.* and later resold the well-worn copy at the "greatly reduced price" of 7*s.*

Not content with attacking the policies of his library, the *Gazette* trained its guns on Mudie himself and his religious convictions: "He now began to feel that he was a monopolist; it was very delicious to such a man. . . . He can take or refuse whatever literature he likes, and, as a decided sectarian, we may be pretty sure to what it will lead. . . . Here we have a man exercising unlimited power, and making his own monopoly the means to achieve the success of his own sectarian opinions."

Because his reasons were either sectarian or simply ridiculous, the *Gazette* went on, he refused to acknowledge openly his reasons for declining to purchase or circulate a work. Instead, he simply instructed his assistants to say it had not yet been issued.[62] The *Gazette* ignored one cause: economic expediency. When a publisher would not allow the generous discounts Mudie demanded, the librarian countered by refusing to buy or by limiting the quantity. His delay with *Adam Bede*, reluctantly increasing his original order for 500 only by lots of 100 because Blackwood kept the price up, clearly indicates his practice. When assistants, trained by the enterprising Mudie, could not fill an order, for whatever reason, they frequently substituted another book, to the irritation of many subscribers. Trollope may well have heard of some of these difficulties from George Eliot and Lewes. In *The Eustace Diamonds* the formidable Lady Linlithgow explains, "I don't subscribe to Mudie's, because when I asked for 'Adam Bede,' they always sent me the 'Bandit Chief.' "

The castigation of the autocracy of the librarian was to continue for the next thirty-five years, but none of the accusations included Mudie's religion so specifically in denouncing the policies or monopoly of the library. Mudie's censorship was directed primarily against works which depicted violations of the established Victorian sexual code, a code which was generally accepted by members of the established church as well as by those of other denominations. Arthur Waugh of Chapman and Hall, who termed Mudie a "genius among librarians" as well as a "remarkable and cultivated man," did indeed call him "intensely religious," adding that he was one who "practised in private life the virtues he proclaimed on the Sabbath."[63] There is, however, no evidence to support the *Gazette's* charge that a work would be excluded because Mudie might say, "I am a Dissenter; I decline this book because it will do my cause a great deal of harm, and the Church a little good."

Nor did any succeeding attacks—not even the one by George Moore, who declared in print, "Mr. Mudie, to speak candidly, I hate you"[64]—exceed the virulent emotional quality of this one. The week after its appearance, the *Gazette* devoted almost a full page to correspondence elicited by its editorial. Two letters agreed with the charges against Mudie's policies; one, from "A London Publisher" who refrained from "making any comment on the style with which those opinions are expressed," contradicted the specific assertion that Mudie obtained his novels at no more than half price. The warmest remark in the brief letter is the conclusion, "I distinctly deny the truth of your statement." To this simple assertion of what was undoubtedly true for a few firms, or for exceptional novels (it has been shown that Blackwood, for example, held out for and got about 29*s.* for 3,000 copies of *The Mill on the Floss* in 1860), the *Gazette* replied with an editorial note terming it "uncourteous, passionate, and therefore, worthless contradiction."[65]

It is little wonder that Mudie chose to reply in another periodical, the dignified *Athenaeum*. Dismissing the personal accusations as impertinent or untrue, he reaffirmed his right to select books:

> The title under which my library was established nearly twenty years ago implies this:—the public know it and subscribe accordingly and increasingly. They are evidently willing to have a barrier of some kind between themselves and the lower floods of literature.

Of the two standards governing his selective policies—moral and commercial—he deemed the moral the more important, and he flatly denied any "sectarian or party bias."[66] The *Athenaeum*, although decrying the three-decker system and its price (pointing out that not even Mudie heeded it), nevertheless termed the charge against him "ridiculous." "Mr. Mudie has no more power to keep a book out of his library in the face of a strong demand than . . . to turn all the carriage traffic of New Oxford Street down the old channel of High Holborn."[67] As long as Mudie accurately reflected the tastes and attitudes of his readers, there was little likelihood of a strong demand for a work not to be found on his shelves.

The *Gazette* immediately condemned Mudie's reply as a "clumsy conglomeration of bald and irrelevant truisms." It had never, it maintained, "denied, or wished to abrogate" his right of selection.[68] A month later, however, it found that principle an "astounding proposition." "If he means," it then continued, "that no books shall enter the broad road which leads to his library, unless they meet with his approbation, we do not scruple to pronounce his assertion a piece of consummate arrogance."[69] Conceding that grossly immoral books should be excluded, the journal returned to name-calling and to charges of selection governed by "the narrow-minded prejudices of the Oxford Street sectarian." The *Gazette* further advanced its own "claims upon public gratitude" for its service in forcing Mudie to declare that his policy was selective—a declaration which, as Mudie had noted, was really unnecessary, since it had always been expressed in the name of the library.

Even an author named by the *Gazette* as having been injured by Mudie's capriciousness felt called upon to dissociate herself from the vitriolic attack. As an example of Mudie's "ridiculous" selection, the *Gazette* had cited his refusal to circulate *The Morals of Mayfair* "because *he* did not like the name." It is more probable that it was rejected because of its subject, the love affairs of actresses. At any rate, Mrs. Annie Edwards, the anonymous author, disclaimed in a letter to the *Athenaeum* "all share in the anonymous, personal attacks" against Mudie. "I think it right," she declared, "to say that my next work, 'Creeds,' was put into very large circulation through the agency of Mr. Mudie's Library."[70]

Although more personal and more concerned with religious bias (perhaps reflecting a desire to stimulate sales), the leaders in the *Gazette* and the correspondence they elicited contained charges which were little different from the ones which followed during the next thirty-five years: censure of the monopoly held by the librarian and suggestions for remedies. One letter, for instance, listed those who were being injured by the library: the publisher (who was paid only half price), the bookseller (who was undersold by Mudie's secondhand department), the author (by "worse than capricious" rejections), and the public (by an arbitrary censorship).[71] Although neatly put, the charges were hardly accurate. The publisher of the three-decker, as has been shown, was not being injured, but was actually profiting; authors who accepted the standards were virtually guaranteed at least a minimum audience; and as long as high prices for fiction continued, the public was reading at a bargain rate. On the other hand, authors who ventured outside Mudie's limits were severely handicapped, and the charge of arbitrary censorship was irrefutable.

The writer of this letter suggested that publishers should combine to keep prices up, although how forcing Mudie to pay 20s. or 25s. instead of 15s. a set would end the monopoly is not made clear, unless by limiting profits it simply put the library out of business. A combination of publishers could have been effective in breaking the library hold on first editions, not by raising prices, but rather by lowering them to a level at which large sales would have been possible. Another suggestion was also based on a union, this time of publishers and booksellers, which could operate a national circulating library, organized as a joint-stock company. Such suggestions did not take into consideration that Mudie's was already virtually a "national" library, and that publishers were unlikely to revolutionize a highly profitable system of issuing fiction without strong reasons. And, as a matter of fact, the Library Company Limited was about to provide an example of a joint-stock company's disastrous attempt to rival the Leviathan of New Oxford Street.

In spite of the *Athenaeum's* implication that the importance of the library was overrated, Mudie's power was great and steadily growing. The justification of his policies in the *Athenaeum* was the last he felt called upon to make publicly. Although it was made when Mudie's meant, in Mrs. Oliphant's words, "one very energetic, very brisk and enterprising man, attached to the Dissenting interest,"[72] the policies did not change with the formation of the limited company. Indeed, by 1868 he was honored by a series of "Mudie Classics" in Mary Elizabeth Braddon's *Belgravia*. The author of the highly sensational *Lady Audley's Secret* and *Aurora Floyd* chose the name "in compliment to the eponymous chief of the circulating library," and added that they were planned to reform the sensational element "devised by ignorant and reckless writers."[73] A few years later, Charles Reade, discouraged by his failure to sell *A Terrible Temptation*, noted in his diary, "I foresee that the librarians will all band against it, as usual; and at 57 years of age plenty of hot water coming."[74] Mudie's reputation for adherence to convention continued to increase during the 1870s, provoking Geraldine Jewsbury to observe that "Mudie wd hardly inspire *his* wife with the courage to venture to save his life when the rules of society were dubious!"[75]

· *George Moore's Role* ·

SUMMING UP THE CONTEMPORARY LITERARY SITUATION, George Moore, fresh from his observation of the new French naturalism, wrote Zola,

> Vous ne savez où nous sommes, vous ne savez pas les combinaisons que nous forcent d'être sentimental et faux, de faire sans cesse des romans plats et conventionelle et que nous interdi toute l'observation et analysis. . . . Il me faudrait des pages pour vous expliquer la situation—si se n'était que le public n'est pouvait abbatre les inflexible préjugés qui ont fait tomber le roman en Angleterre mais sont de librairies.[76]

Moore's expression of his thoughts was not confined to private letters; he denounced Mudie's in the press and through pamphlet and book. When his novels *A Modern Lover* (1883) and *A Mummer's Wife* (1885) were banned by Mudie's, Moore retaliated with "A New Censorship of Literature" in the *Pall Mall Gazette* (1884) and with a pamphlet, *Literature at Nurse, or Circulating Morals* (1885), directed against the policies of that institution. Nor did he stop when the three-decker was abolished; he continued to relate his part in breaking the library censorship until his death. His last work, *A Communication to My Friends*, contains one of the most detailed accounts.

Until the bonds represented by the circulating library were broken, he felt it would be impossible to formulate a "new aestheticism." Fuming over the banning of *A Modern Lover*, he pictured Mudie thus:

> At the head, therefore, of English literature sits a tradesman who considers himself qualified to decide the most delicate artistic question that may be raised, and who crushes out of sight any artistic aspiration he may deem pernicious. And yet with this vulture gnawing at their hearts writers gravely discuss the means of producing good work; let them break their bonds first. . . .[77]

Encouraged by Zola (to whom he had written, "Selon vos conseils, j'ai attaqué notre système de librairie"[78]), he had found a publisher, Vizetelly, to issue his second novel, *A Mummer's Wife*, in one volume at 6*s*. Moore rejoiced that "I shall now, therefore, for the future enjoy the liberty of speech granted to the journalist, the historian, and the biographer, rights unfortunately in the present day denied to the novelist. . . ."[79] This point was one Reade had advanced more than a decade before when he defended his "matter-of-fact" plots by citing the liberty allowed the journalist to report legal cases.

Although Moore's protest demonstrated more warm language than cool logic, it was important as drawing attention to library policies. The *Saturday Review*, for example, then picked up the case in an article called "A Circulating Censorship." Although it held no brief for Moore's particular merits, it did point out the danger of allowing two or three ladies in Bullocksmithy to determine the fate of a young author. If the ladies failed to understand a book, an excellent realistic novel might be "offered up a whole sacrifice to that British literary fetish, the drawing-room table in the parsonage." Meanwhile, the *Saturday* charged that the librarians, who had to make the scruples of the weakest their standard of admission or rejection, forced authors to water down their manuscripts "into dreariness and vapidity." The resulting "dropsical publications" were not worth buying, and so in turn strengthened the lending system. The remedy, the *Saturday* correctly inferred, lay in cheap books, but this was a remedy more easily perceived than accomplished. All the *Saturday* could do was note that France had been saved from England's fate by Michael Lévy with his cheap books, and wonder, "Who will save England?"[80]

George Moore evidently answered, "I will," and returned to the attack the year after his "New Censorship" with a preface to Zola's *Piping Hot!*: "We judge a pudding by the eating, and I judge Messrs. Mudie and Smith by what they have produced; for they . . . are the authors of our fiction," and they have "thrown English fiction into the abyss of nonsense in which it lies."[81] It was in *Literature at Nurse, or Circulating Morals*, however, that Moore marshalled all his points in an appeal to the public to withdraw support from libraries failing to supply the books it desired. By the time of its issue, *A Mummer's Wife*, in its fourth edition as a 6s. single-volume novel, had been refused by Mudie because of the passage in which Dick Lennox drags the married Kate Ede into a room late at night and closes the door. Citing this passage, he compares it to others from Mrs. Praed's *Nadine*, W. H. Mallock's *A Romance of the Nineteenth Century*, and Robert Buchanan's *Foxglove Manor*, all in circulation at Mudie's. After each citation, one of which displays the rationalization of a clergyman contemplating adultery, and all of which treat sensuality in tawdry and vulgar style, runs Moore's refrain,

It being well known that I am no judge of such things, tell me, Mr. Mudie, if there be not in this doll just a little too much bosom showing, if there be not just a little too much ankle appearing from under this skirt? Tell me, I beseech you.[82]

He goes on to indicate the nature of some other plots circulated by Mudie's: Ouida's *Puck* and *Moths* and Florence Marryat's *Phillida*, in which a young lady proposed to become the mistress of a young parson. The titillating qualities of women novelists had become a critical commonplace by this time, as a *Punch* cartoon of 1867 indicates. A man, inspecting a book at the counter of a bookstore (or circulating library), declares through his mutton-chop whiskers: "Ah! very Clever, I dare say. But I see it's Written by a Lady, and *I* want a Book that my *Daughters* may read. Give me Something else!"[83] Moore claimed that he wished not to censure the morality, but rather to prove the absurdity and futility of Mudie's censorship, which by that time overruled "the decisions of the entire English press." The librarian was castigated as pandering "to the intellectual sloth of today." The works on his shelves were termed "a motley and monstrous progeny, a callow, a whining, a puking brood of bastard bantlings," "rocked to an ignoble rest in the motherly arms of the librarian."[84]

Turning from vituperation to criticism, Moore attributed the poor quality of contemporary English fiction to the retardation of ideas and fresh thought by the library, seeing in this situation confirmation of Matthew Arnold's theory that for the creation of great literature, the power of the man must concur with the power of the moment. Forbidden to treat moral and religious feeling, no writer, Moore believed, could produce a work able to resist twenty years of criticism. "The librarian rules the roost; he crows, and every chanticleer pitches his note in the same key."[85]

Moore consistently attacked the librarian who had dared to ban his works, but not all authors agreed on this strategy.

Gissing's reaction has been noted; in a letter to the *Pall Mall Gazette* in 1887, George Bernard Shaw, who described himself as "a sufferer from that strange brain disease which drives its victims to write long stories that are not true, and to delight in them more than in any other literature," logically suggested that cheap editions by publishers would be of more value than declamations against the monopoly of the libraries.[86]

Actually Moore was answering Shaw's plea by publishing his novels in 6s. form, but he continued his intermittent fire on the libraries in *Confessions of a Young Man* (1888). In this he also pilloried Tinsley, describing him as conducting "his business as he dressed himself, sloppily; a dear kind soul, quite witless and quite h-less." The way to be published by Mr. B (as he refers to Tinsley) "was to straddle the counter and play with a black cat."[87] Later he was to write of Tinsley as a "literary cook," who had no confidence in Moore at all: "All the confidence he had was in his power to cajole two stubborn librarians to subscribe for a book that they did not like."[88] It was from Tinsley, according to Moore, that he had first learned about the censorship. As Moore told it, Tinsley felt the whole system was unjust, not only to authors but to publishers, and related "a long story of the persecution he had been subjected to."[89] Since Tinsley's success was founded on the three-decker, it would be astonishing if he actually felt a keen grievance against the library system. His own reminiscences reveal no such attitude.

Surprisingly, in the face of his previous colorful and vitriolic attacks, Moore presented in his *Confessions* artistic justification for the circulating library system. Its conservatism he judged well adapted to the natural conservatism of art. The library could lift the writer out of the "wild street of popular fancy" into a quiet place where there was less passion and more reflection. Both unknown and known writers could benefit from the certainty of a library sale: because of the relative security, the unknown is not forced to employ "vile and degrading methods of attracting attention"[90]; and the known is enabled to think more of his work and less of his market. The advantages of the library for the neophyte were frequently cited by proponents of the system, but it remained for one of Mudie's most bitter and vocal opponents to point out benefits to be derived by a famous writer. These were, however, only straw benefits, set up to be knocked down by the censorship, which Moore again stressed was ineffectual. Any purity that might have resulted from Mudie's policies had, in Moore's phraseology, been buried beneath the lava of fornication and adultery pouring from the previously slumbrous law courts.

Ironically, it was not Mudie's but Smith's which precipitated Moore's next outburst over censorship. According to William Faux, the head of Smith's library department, that firm banned *Esther Waters* because of "about twenty lines of pre-Raphaelitic nastiness." Furthermore, he felt the decision was justified: "Between Berwick-on-Tweed . . . and Penzance . . . we have 15,000 subscribers, and we have only received one complaint in the matter of not circulating 'Esther Waters.' "[91] In *A Communication to My Friends*, then, Moore turned the force of his invective from Mudie to Faux. Calling to inquire about the banning of *Esther Waters*, he writes he

> mounted a long concrete staircase to arrive . . . at lacklustre rooms in which I discovered a long, lean man, one of those men who have grown old without knowledge of life or literature in the dim shadows of their bookshelves. Mr. Faux was particularly attractive as a specimen. A tangle of dyed hair covered a bald skull, and as he . . . giggled, his false teeth threatened to jump out at me. His withered face betrayed amusement when he heard that I had called . . . to ask his reasons for excluding *Esther Waters*. . . . "You see," he answered, "we are a circulating library and our subscribers are not used to detailed descriptions of a lying-in hospital."[92]

Actually, Mr. Faux probably gauged his customers' reactions fairly. Feelings about such scenes were virtually unchanged from thirty years earlier, when Geraldine Jewsbury had indignantly rejected a manuscript thus: "I object absolutely to the indelicate prominence given the heroine's confinement of her first and only Baby; no author, unless a medical man writing for the faculty, ought to enter into so much detail . . . and the account of the new born baby is very disagreeable and painful."[93]

Mudie's circulation of Moore's novel had provoked some surprise in George Bentley, who commented to Maarten Maartens, "So Mudie's <u>Select</u> Library takes largely of Esther Moore [sic] which Smith rejects."[94] Unfortunately for Faux of Smith's, Gladstone read and approved Esther Waters. Moore himself called in an accountant who checked the sales and reported that Smith's had probably lost £1,500 by the ban. "It was after the publication of these figures that I had the satisfaction of hearing that the partners of the firm sent word to their librarian that it would be well in the future to avoid heavy losses by banning books, especially books that Mr. Gladstone was likely to read and to express his approval of in the Westminster Gazette," Moore exulted.[95]

According to Moore's report of his first conversation with Tinsley, the publisher had said that two or three successful novelists could, if they banded together, break the censorship of the libraries. Moore had, in fact, unsuccessfully tried to interest Henry James in the cause, sending him a copy of A Mummer's Wife and the letter he had contributed to the Pall Mall Gazette. Since James's reply was apparently limited to problems of presentation and proportion,[96] and since both Gissing and Shaw, who did contribute to the Gazette, urged reform through the artists themselves or through publishers, Moore carried on his fight alone, and eventually came to believe that in his final controversy over Esther Waters, he personally had broken the censorship. His blows certainly wounded, but the censorship fell victim to suicide rather than murder. Esther Waters came out in 1894, the same year in which the libraries had been forced to quash the three-volume system they had so long fostered. More than a method of publication fell; with it went the nineteenth-century circulating library itself, and a whole category of fiction floundered. The Mudie's that survived until 1937 and the Smith's in existence until 1961 were different libraries with a different public. Writing of Mudie's closing, Wyndham Lewis noted that the firm had been swamped by the "lending libraries which help forward Culture by broadcasting the very latest rubbish among that 90 per cent. of the populace mentally under the age of fourteen."[97] Such was not the case in Mudie's nineteenth-century hey-day; he accepted the young girl standard for the novels he circulated, but so did his solid middle- and upper-middle-class readers, whether men or women. Mudie's mirrored its subscribers, but also reflected ideas to them, although the reflected images never differed radically from the originals.

THE COLLAPSE

BECAUSE CENSORSHIP WAS PERSONALLY GALLING TO WRITERS it drew colorful charges, but it was not the only point of attack on the libraries. Critics also castigated the three-volume system itself; indeed, from the middle of the century, its doom had been prophesied. "The three-volume novel is clearly 'going out with the tide,' "[1] wrote a *Fraser's* critic in 1851. His thoughts were echoed at the end of the decade by a writer in the *British Quarterly Review*: "The costly three-volume novel, with its rivers of type and meadows of margin, is hastening to extinction."[2] After 1860, however, protests against both the form and the price multiplied in the journals. The price, as the point which the book buyer felt most keenly, often received the first barrage of the popular periodicals, even though it was clear that responsibility for this artificial convention lay with the circulating libraries. As early as 1852, when the first public library under Ewart's Act was opened at Manchester, the *Edinburgh Review* commented on the scarcity of purchasers in the face of greatly increased demand for books, and attributed this dearth of buyers to the circulating library.[3] Later the *Athenaeum*, while defending Mudie and his right to select books, also saw the situation clearly. Certain publishers, it pointed out, maintained their fancy prices and triple volumes for the libraries: "They lay themselves at the feet of Mr. Mudie, they publish at him, they are elated by his smile, and they tremble at his frown."[4] Interesting evidence of the strength Mudie's had acquired in its eighteen years of lending books is found in the *Athenaeum's* comment that this system of publishing "at Mr. Mudie" was no recent development, but a well established custom that had been "in active existence for some years." It further points out the fictitious quality of the price of 31*s*.6*d*. which almost nobody paid, since no individual would, and Mudie was accustomed to his generous discount.

Ten years later the objections had spread from the literary circles of the *Athenaeum* to the more popular press. The *Daily News*, while suggesting in a leader that "if we were to adopt the Continental or American fashion of issuing books . . . publishers, authors, and readers would be no worse off in England than they are elsewhere," nevertheless appeared resigned to the "canonical three volumes." Reluctant even to advocate trial publication of novels in one volume (because, among other reasons, "the conditions of publishing may be more costly in this than in other countries"), it contented itself with offering refinements of the existing system, recommending to the author, librarian, and publisher the practice of economy, patience, and a habit of expecting the worst. To the subscriber it advised an individual and discriminating selection of books.[5]

The *Saturday Review* more vigorously attacked the system as a monstrous anomaly. "The most crackbrained Communist never dreamed of a more painful dead level of depressing equality than that which actually exists in the realm of three-volume fiction."[6] To charge the same amounts for a novel by George Eliot and one that contains "only the crude nightmares of some spasmodic sensationalist or the sentimental maundering of some

blighted spinster" was like setting the same price on prime
sirloins and garbage, cried the *Saturday* bluntly. The point would
have applied to novels at any price, of course, but the inflated cost
of the three-decker obviously inflated the writer's resentment.

Not only was the price illogical, continued the *Saturday*, but
novelists suffered. "By exploding the tradition that makes three
volumes an inexorable conventionality, we should relieve many
a wretched author from the bed of Procrustes that cramps him
and tortures us." The only useful purpose served by the convention, the *Saturday* ironically concluded, was that of con-
vincing future generations (which would have abandoned it)
of their advancement beyond their fathers' intelligence. Apparently blithely unaware of all precedents, or choosing to ignore
them, the *Saturday* was certain that if only publishers would
revolt against the tyranny of the libraries, and publish novels
in single volumes at 5*s*. or 7*s*.6*d*., the public would support
them.

"An abomination and a curse," thundered a reviewer in
The Times the week after the *Saturday's* outburst. Castigating
the entire system, he maintained "It is the duty of every critic
to bring against it bell, book, and candle."[7] The question erupted
in the columns of *The Times* nine years later, provoked by Disraeli's *Endymion*, published in three volumes at 31*s*.6*d*. A publisher, James Griffin, had written to *The Times* attacking the
system on an always vulnerable point—profit. That newspaper,
in a Trollopian manner worthy of Tom Towers and the *Jupiter*,
analyzed the whole matter in a leader of December 17, 1880,
noting that the grievance was keenly felt because it was "aggra-
vated by the authorship of an ex-Prime Minister."[8] The worst
result, *The Times* felt, was that "the mass of English readers
have lost much wholesome literary nutriment," although Lord
Beaconsfield, too, had suffered, perhaps in pounds, shillings, and
pence, and certainly because of the bitterness felt by many
unable to afford his latest work.

Publishers probably had many good reasons for retaining

the fancy price, the leader continued, and went on to explain one: the small but fully guaranteed market provided by the libraries. However mercilessly the book might be handled by reviewers, however high the price, this select circle furnished reasonably sure buyers, thus enabling the publishers to "try the pulse of the reading public without risk of pecuniary loss." Nor was this unfair to readers who were "content to sip [books] . . . through . . . the library" while waiting for a cheaper edition, the leader went on, continuing its gustatory metaphors. Still, sales in the cheaper form would suffer because the time interval would have taken the edge off the public appetite.

Because the custom was so favorable to publishers and new authors, *The Times* saw little likelihood of changing it readily, although it had been in some respects "both suicidal and mischievous." The leader suggested, however, that even if the general custom seemed proper enough for most novels, it ought not to be applied indiscriminately to all, "without distinction of reputations and of persons" (a variant of the point made nine years earlier by the *Saturday Review*'s metaphor of prime sirloins and garbage). Finally, the leader urged the merits of appealing directly to the buying public, as opposed to the conventional system of stressing only "second-hand" purchase through the libraries—the principal merit being a reduction in the amount of trashy writing. Ironically, the novel which gave rise to these charges against three-deckers, their high prices, and by extension, circulating libraries, was one on which not Disraeli but Mudie lost money. Disraeli received £10,000 for his work, but within a few months of his order for 3,000 copies, Mudie was unsuccessfully offering the volumes for sale, and claimed that his premises were cluttered for years with stacks of the unwanted 9,000 volumes.

The correspondence in *The Times* in the days following the leader indicates interest and growing dissatisfaction. Within two years Edmund Gosse was labeling three-deckers as "those signs-manual of . . . dulness and crafty disdain for literature

. . . these sham resemblances of books."[9] As the years passed, casual references praised a novel that possessed "the advantage of being in two volumes instead of three."[10] Even if casual, the references came with sufficient regularity to lead writers as different as Gissing and H. Rider Haggard to believe that the shape of the novel was changing from three to two volumes. Revising his first novel *Dawn* under the direction of J. C. Jeaffreson, Haggard expressed views identical with Gissing's: "Would it not perhaps be well to compress the book into *two* volumes. I have noticed that reviewers seem to like two volumed books best and they take less time and labour."[11]

The problems of the production and distribution of "that ponderous item styled light literature"[12] warranted another leader in *The Times* in 1886. By this time an increasing number of protests against censorship were harassing the libraries. These complaints had been cropping up almost since the opening of Mudie's, but had received fresh impetus from George Moore. In the furor which followed *Literature at Nurse, or Circulating Morals*, *The Times* re-examined the monopoly in first editions held by the libraries. The writer, like the *Fraser's* critic thirty-five years before, thought that library bulwarks were "beginning to yield to the batteries . . . opened against them," and that the three-volume novel was doomed. Nor did *The Times* express regret. The price of a guinea and a half had prevented purchase until the re-issue, when not only had enthusiasm been lost, but the book itself might appear in a form too cheap to dignify the library book shelf. The leader reiterated the charge that because of the circulating libraries the best books shared the same hasty glance as the worst; there was no time for thoughtful perusal or quiet re-reading.

The leader conceded two points to the system: first, as long as the public was habituated to the three-volume novel, authors must accept that form or risk having a first edition mistaken for a re-issue. Second, a habitual novel-reader would in a period of weeks use up the price of his Mudie subscription buying even 3*s*. novels. *The Times* nevertheless took exception to the wastefulness of "a system which spends on printing and paper double or treble as much as is necessary, and is the admitted means of encumbering the book world with a load of stuff fit only for burning." If subscribers got more with the three-volume lending library system than with a one-volume distribution, what they got was "subsidized trash." If an unknown writer with talent had a better chance of publishing under the three-volume system, this advantage was counterbalanced by the avenue to publication it provided for the unknown writer with no talent at all. Eight years before the fall of the three-decker, this writer for *The Times* thus neatly summarized arguments which were to be restated and amplified many times with more verbosity than logic when the end came.

· *"The Cheapest Luxury"* ·

DEFENSES OF THE THREE-DECKER, AND HENCE NECESSARILY of the circulating library system, appeared during the last quarter of the century almost exclusively in the magazines owned by publishers (like *London Society*, one of Bentley's, and *Tinsleys' Magazine*) and in the trade journal, the *Publishers' Circular* (issued by Sampson Low). These shilling magazines existed primarily as cheap advertising for the firm's other publications; Tinsley justified his lack of profit on the magazine because "It advertises my name and publications and it keeps my authors together."[13] It is not surprising, therefore, to find glowing praise of the three-decker and of the library for everything from their usefulness to the public and their benefits for authors to their economic soundness, while other periodicals like *The Times*, *Athenaeum*, *Saturday Review*, and *Pall Mall Gazette* were labeling them "worse than worthless."

Libraries ranked with such modern blessings as gas, umbrellas, and hackney cabs, according to Hain Friswell, who suggested in 1871 that they might well be added to Sydney

Smith's list of the modern improvements achieved in his life-
time.[14] Cited to support this practicality of the three-decker
and the library was the apparently paradoxical argument of its
basic economy. Appealing to the Victorian regard for thrift,
advocates of the system called reading one of the cheapest
luxuries; *Tinsleys'* estimated that six to twelve members of a
household could, for two to three guineas, read in a year about
two hundred pounds' worth of books, three hundred pounds'
worth if they were assiduous in exchanges.[15] Thus the inde-
fatigable reader could have his fill of novels, and "decorate his
drawing-room table with an occasional volume of verse."[16]

In spite of the "tyranny" of fiction, poetry was generally
valued as a higher form of art; besides, it was more reasonably
priced. Still, no lack of justification for the inflated guinea and
a half was found. "Why *must* reviewers eternally prate about
the 'monstrous price' of works of fiction?"[17] asked a *Tinsleys'*
writer in exasperation. Probably because it would have been
difficult to defend the price logically, this writer followed a
general pattern in brushing it aside as irrelevant. In the first
place, it was a "well-known fact" that the English public would
not buy novels, so it made little difference whether three volumes
were 31*s*.6*d*., 21*s*., or even 12*s*. A corollary to this "well-known
fact" was that the public would not buy even one-volume novels.
A year before *Tinsleys'* defended the guinea and a half, a publisher had written, "The only conclusion . . . is that novel
readers will not buy novels in paying quantities; even at . . .
half a crown, they would still go to Mudie's and borrow the
volume, grumbling perhaps a little at the smallness of the
type."[18] The *Publishers' Circular* was taking a different tack on
the question of price: "How a cheap method is to clear the world
'of the rubbish that is published in three volumes' . . . it is
difficult to say."[19] In other words, cheapness alone was not
productive of worth.

In the second place, *Tinsleys'* continued, the library subscriber obtained a work irrespective of the published price.

In fact, the three-decker and the library were praised as a protection to the reader because he could determine exactly what was worth buying. Not only was he saved from littering his home with volumes of fiction that would soon be unwanted, but by the time he had decided what to purchase, a cheap edition, for which the three-decker was described as a kind of expedient dress rehearsal, was available. The English reader was then in the enviable position of being able to choose the form he preferred for his permanent library.

Taking into account the strained relations not uncommon then (and now) between authors and publishers, it is hardly surprising to find authors held up as recipients, with the public, of remarkable benefits from a method of publication that was undeniably extremely profitable for publishers. Although publishers like Tinsley and Bentley naturally denied that they were foisting worthless books by unknown authors on the libraries, and firmly maintained that the actual number of copies subscribed by the leviathans for a work by an unknown would not pay the expense of production, some of their other arguments contradict these assertions. For example, in 1872, the writer in *Tinsleys'* pointed out that the existing system allowed authors to get their first works produced, and thus promoted unknown writers. Publishers were indeed more likely to take a risk on a first novel with a definite library order waiting for the three-decker. A variation of this point concerned the necessity for perseverance; the author must not be disheartened by repeated failures, but must keep on publishing his work, through the facilities afforded by the circulating library, which was thus held up as the *sine qua non* for novelists, affording them both their first chance, and later the opportunity to develop a reputation. The admission by the publishers of thus being able to bring out doubtful three-deckers forms an amusing contrast with their denial that the library orders would pay the cost of production.

Unable to contradict the charge that the system was "cumbrous," the *Publishers' Circular* in 1872, with somewhat belated anti-Jacobinism, was defending it by drawing an analogy with the British Constitution: both were cumbrous, but both worked well. Shifting its figure, the *Circular* pointed out that with three-volume novels, rubbish fell through; good works survived to be reprinted at low prices. With one metaphor the *Circular* disposed of the "rubbish in three volumes" and devised support for its argument that the system was really responsible for the maintenance of high literary standards: it winnowed out those novels unworthy of being reprinted. The *Circular* stood on firm ground here; the books reprinted in single volumes had all passed a kind of "library test" and had proved at least their popularity. But the publishers' journal stopped short of the basically undeniable charge that the guaranteed market encouraged publishing houses to accept doubtful manuscripts.

Defenders of the status quo appealed also to the question of justice: did not the author (or the publisher) have a just right to produce his works in the form which would bring the best return? Furthermore, by producing a small edition at a large price the publisher was enabled to pay his author fairly and often handsomely, the *Publishers' Circular* maintained;[20] and *Tinsleys'* commented pointedly that if the orthodox system were abandoned, the author would be the greatest sufferer.[21] The circulating library took about the same number of copies whether the work was in one, two, or three volumes, the argument ran, while the cost of producing a book in one volume amounted to much more than one-third the cost of three volumes. Theoretically this makes a good case, but actually, for reasons already discussed, the circulating library would order, other things being equal, considerably fewer novels in one volume than in three. Although this point would have made an even better case for *Tinsleys'*, it would have shown the library in an unfavorably dictatorial position. Such a picture would hardly have been thought advisable by one whose business depended on Mudie's, his imitators, and his rivals. *Tinsleys'* did estimate that expenses for advertising would be the same for one volume as for three, although the profit would be at least forty-five percent less.[22]

Such were the arguments by which it was hoped to vindicate the three-decker and the circulating library from the charges leveled against them. Although the defenders of the system frequently urged that the public and even literature gained one of the cheapest luxuries because English publishers produced their books "in good readable type, on good paper, and in good handsome volumes," a corollary to that argument was advanced only rarely and seems really a last resort to the twentieth-century reader. Such type and paper not only formed admirable decoration for the ubiquitous table in the drawing-room of the home or in the library of the club, but brought the pleasures of literature within the scope of those with weakest sight, as *Tinsleys'* declared, with commendable humanitarianism. The large print of the three-decker would always ensure its market, at least for the many with poor eyesight, it was urged, perhaps unconsciously suggesting new opportunities for the manufacturers of spectacles. Others pointed out that the old or sick, who could just manage a light volume of the three-decker, would have to forego their entertainment if it were abolished.

Nor were defenses of the system confined to England. Although in 1874 Henry James had been pleased that Americans were "happily not subject, in this (as to minor matters) much-emancipated land, to the tyranny of the three volumes,"[23] not all of his fellow countrymen agreed. As late as 1890 the American playwright Oliver B. Bunce was suggesting in the *North American Review* that what the United States needed was "an extended and thorough circulating-library system"[24] on the Mudie pattern. Pointing out that it was impossible to make a valid comparison of the numbers of English and American readers on the basis of sales alone, Bunce estimated that each copy of an ordinary English novel found ten to twenty readers through the library. Since Mudie took most of the first edition of a three-decker, about 500 copies, readers there would total 5,000 or 10,000, or more than twice the number of readers of an American edition, whether bound in cloth or paper. Issued in hard covers, the American edition could not exceed 2,000 copies at $1.50, he calculated, although in paper it might run to 5,000. Bunce makes no numerical estimate of the readers, as distinguished from buyers, each copy of the American book would have.

The magnitude of Mudie's—much greater than that of the aggregate of libraries in the United States—he cited as proof "of a very large, alert, and eager book-reading community." Mudie alone took 1,500 copies of Trollope's *Autobiography* at $5.00, he continued, although he expressed doubt that the number could have been equaled in the United States at half the price.[25] Furthermore, Mudie's, "with its large body of alert and accessible readers, has been the means of building up an expansive and catholic literature," rendering possible the issue of many books that could not otherwise have been printed. Because prices to circulating libraries were high, "the profits are greatly beyond anything that we experience in America," to authors as well as to publishers. Readers in England obtained copies at a very small unit cost. At the same time, since no special outlay (that is, cash) was required for a particular book, it was more readily sought there than in the United States, where it would have to overcome the reluctance of the prospective reader to part with his money.

· *Impending Collapse* ·

IN THE SAME YEAR AS BUNCE'S GLOWING ACCOUNT THE *Spectator* observed that no better illustration of the inherent conservatism of the English could be found than the unwritten law decreeing that "the only strictly orthodox form of a novel is that of a work in three volumes."[26] Threatened customs, like threatened men, live long, the writer remarked, and credited the three-decker, which had certainly been threatened for many years, with a charmed life. The charm lasted for several more years. Commenting on "The Tyranny of the Novel" in the literary world of 1892, Edmund Gosse cited as the three most notable books published in London that season, the three "most widely discussed, most largely bought, most vehemently praised, most venomously attacked," *Tess of the D'Urbervilles*, *David Grieve*, and *The Little Minister*. Gosse chose those three to illustrate the tyranny of fiction over other literary genres: "If the poets in chorus had blown their silver trumpets, and the philosophers their bold bassoons, the result would have been the same: they would have won some respect and a little notice; . . . but the novelists would have carried away the money and the real human curiosity."[27] All three illustrate one further point: the continued domination of the novel itself by one form, the orthodox three volumes.

Even though the three-decker and the circulating library had been subject to intermittent but sharp attacks since mid-century, the form still seemed to most observers as "solid as Nelson's Column"[28] and as permanent as the British constitution, even setting a standard for emulation. The attacks in the seventies and eighties had met with apparently successful rebuttal, it is true, but signs of the approaching collapse of triple issue should have been evident enough to an alert observer. Most important was the growing dissatisfaction of the libraries themselves with the form. As early as March 1884 the *Pall Mall Gazette* quoted Mudie as saying that novels did not pay: "They are the fuel that drives the engine. They become ashes too soon." The *Gazette* writer himself used a different analogy:

> Novels are the gaudy butterflies of the trade, which live but a short day and perish. . . . The evil would at least be lessened if the three volumes could be compressed into one, and one ridiculous farce of the day abolished for ever. Any one who takes up three volumes of a novel, on looking at its big type, the broad margins, the wide spaces, the thick paper, and the gorgeous cover, will

see for himself that it is the papermaker, the printer, the ink manufacturer, the binder, and last, but not least, the publisher, who support the system.[29]

Mudie sent a copy of this article to George Bentley, marking it "to show you where I think my chief difficulty lies," and adding his own comment, "I would not much care . . if the 'butterflies' ~~would only live a little longer~~ were not quite so *ephemeral.*"[30] Within six months Mudie proposed a private meeting with George Bentley to discuss the problem of the three-volume novel:

> I will only say for the present and that in the strictest confidence (which I know you will kindly keep) that we find by careful analysis of figures extending over 2 or 3 years that not one in twelve of the 3 vol novels pays its way.
> We are not alone. Other libraries feel the difficulty arising from the over production and over pressure of this class of books.[31]

Mudie's discontent was caused by several changes in the literary marketplace, among them the widening gap between the increasing numbers of novels and a steadily shrinking market for used copies. Reprints at 6s. or lower were available a few months after the original issue, before the library edition had had its run and found its way to the secondhand catalogue. Then, too, free libraries were growing in the provinces. In the last two decades of the century the number of library authorities increased by more than three and a half times; the number of books in stock jumped even more spectacularly, numbering almost four and a half million by 1896.[32] These free libraries were limiting Mudie's used book sales. First of all they were taking many customers away from the Mudie agencies and small circulating libraries which had been accustomed to stock their shelves from Mudie's; and secondly, they did not buy Mudie's surplus copies readily. The New Oxford Street library disposed of books, once the demand slackened, in large lots at bargain prices. In November 1860, for example, Mudie advertised in the *Athenaeum* "Parcels of One Hundred Volumes each, at Five Pounds," and included *The Mill on the Floss* and *Castle Richmond* (both published that same year) among the three-deckers. The free libraries did not want to burden them-

The Catacombs, Mudie's storage cellars.

selves with the unnecessary expense of binding three volumes into one especially since reprints became available quickly.

Probably the main difficulty, however, was the shortening time gap between the original production and the popularly priced reprint. Although publishers acquiesced in Mudie's requirements in three-volume fiction because of his guaranteed market, they also sought the additional revenue to be derived from the reprint, for which there was a steadily increasing demand. Since Mudie's business depended not only on subscriptions but on the sale of books in his secondhand department once the first wave of readers had subsided, a quick reprint meant no market for the unwieldy three volumes and reduced profits for the librarian. A 1,000-copy order of a popular novel which was reprinted while the rush was still on at the subscription counters might well mean 3,000 volumes gathering dust in his catacombs later. Arthur O. Mudie, who succeeded his father as head of the firm,[33] claimed that Mrs. Humphry Ward issued a 6s. edition of *Marcella* only three months after the library had first received the original three volumes. Consequently he was left with 1,750 copies, or 5,250 volumes, of waste paper on his hands.[34]

The libraries' virtually guaranteed market for the three-decker had had the predictable result—quantities of the "gaudy butterflies." In 1891, the situation—present and future—was accurately sketched in *Lippincott's*: "The three-volume novel still lingers in England, a sad survival, by grace of Mudie. When the circulating library gives forth its long-delayed fiat, this cumbrous form will give way to American compactness."[35] By 1894 the situation had moved to a crisis. As Andrew W. Tuer of the Leadenhall Press put it, "There are too many books, and yea, verily, they are mostly bad."[36] Not only had the numbers of three-deckers increased, but quality had decreased, because publishers, confident of a small circulating-library sale, could afford to issue works which otherwise they might not have considered.

In response to a growing consciousness of form on the part of novelists, to a tendency to shorter novels, and to the publicity attending George Moore's outbursts against the libraries in the 1880s and his subsequent publication of novels in one volume, 6s. first editions were becoming increasingly popular. In 1894 a writer in the *Author* commented that "certain well-known writers have never produced a three-volume novel at all,"[37] thus testifying simultaneously to the strength of

the three-volume form, which made this accomplishment somewhat surprising, as well as to the greater number of single-
volume issues. Stevenson and Kipling were two the *Author*
could have mentioned who never published in the orthodox form,
while other novelists, like Gissing and Moore, were chafing
under its restrictions.

· *Action by the Libraries* ·

FINALLY, ON JUNE 27, 1894, THE LIBRARIES TOOK ACTION.
Indeed, from an economic standpoint, they had little choice.
Unwilling to raise subscription rates, they took the only alternative when they issued simultaneous circulars stipulating two
new terms for their purchases: the libraries would pay no more
than 4s. a volume for fiction (less the customary discounts),
and publishers would agree to wait a year before issuing cheaper
editions. Both the big firms concurred in principle, although
Mudie's expression was more direct than that of its rival:

> Owing to the constantly increasing number of novels and
> high-priced books, and of the rapid issue of the cheaper editions,
> the directors are compelled, in the interests of the business, to
> ask the publishers to consider the following suggestions:—
>   (i) That, after December 31, 1894, the charge to the library
> for works of fiction shall not be higher than 4s. per volume, less
> the discount now given, and with the odd copy as before.
>   (ii) That the publishers shall agree not to issue cheaper
> editions of novels and of other books which have been taken for
> library circulation, within twelve months from the date of publi-
> cation.
>   The directors have no wish to dictate to the publishers, but
> in making these suggestions they point out the only terms upon
> which it will be possible in the future to buy books in any quantity
> for library use.[38]

Mudie's circular had the advantage of stating the situation
and proposals concisely, with no apologies and no hypocrisy.
Smith's, on the other hand, added paragraphs of explanation,

apparently designed to absolve its library of any blame. In point of fact, the libraries were faltering under the burden they had themselves imposed. Smith's implied, however, with ornate phraseology, that it was the public which had created the demand for the three-decker, a demand which penalized the hapless library:

> For some time past we have noted with concern a great and increasing demand, on the part of the subscribers to our library, for novels in sets of two and three volumes.
> To meet their requisitions we are committed to an expenditure much out of proportion to the outlay for other kinds of literature.
> Most of the novels are ephemeral in their interest, and the few with an enduring character are published in cheap editions so soon after the first issue that the market we formerly had for the disposal of the surplus stock in sets is almost lost.
> You may conceive that this state of matters very seriously reduces the commercial value of a subscription library. We are, therefore, compelled to consider what means can be taken to improve this branch of our business.
> As a result of our deliberations, we would submit for your favourable consideration:—
> (i) That, after the 31st December next the price of novels in sets shall not be more than 4s. per volume, less the discount now given, and with the odd copy as before. You will please observe that the date we name for the alteration of terms is fixed at six months from the end of this current month, in order that your arrangements may not be affected by the suggested alterations.
> (ii) In respect to the issue of the cheaper editions and the loss to us of our market for the sale of the best and earlier editions of novels and other works, through their publication in a cheaper form before we have had an opportunity of selling the surplus stock, we propose that you be so good as to undertake that no work appear in a cheaper form from the original price until twelve months after the date of its first publication.

The smaller libraries both in London and throughout Britain followed the lead of Mudie's and Smith's. Joseph Gilburt, of Day's Library in Mount Street (one of the few which had survived the Mudie competition), explained his position in a letter to the *Publishers' Circular*. Since the libraries were caught in a squeeze between furious production and steadily decreasing consumption (of secondhand copies), Day's could see no other course for the libraries to take, unless a means could be devised for "supplying inhabitants of other worlds with three-volume novels."[39] The Douglas and Foulis library of Castle Street, Edinburgh, also joined the movement to pay only 4s. a volume. With the almost unnecessary support of the other libraries, there was no doubt, in spite of fond hopes by the *Publishers' Circular* to the contrary, that Mudie's and Smith's would have their way.

Besides the formal announcement, Arthur O. Mudie re-emphasized his convictions in private letters to publishers. On July 13, 1894, he was writing to George Bentley:

> My own feeling (ever since I have known our business) is directly against the three volume novel. It serves no useful purpose whatever in our business and I shall be heartily glad and much relieved if the gods (i.e. the publishers) will give us the one volume novel from the first. In every possible way it suits us better and I very long ago ventured to think that it would benefit English fiction.[40]

Arthur Mudie had been forced to decide between raising the famous guinea-a-year subscription rate, or lowering his expenses for fiction by killing the three-decker. He chose the latter. Clearly aware of the issues involved, he wrote to George Bentley ten days later that an increase in the subscription rate,

> even if it helped us in the present would certainly only make it more possible to "borrow" rubbish and "over produce" in the future.
>
> The 3 volume novel has in my opinion been a curse to us for many years. . . .

To Mudie, the future of the library lay not in fiction, but in "Select" books, and by "Select" he meant "history, travel, science, or belles-lettres," exactly the definition his wife cited for "Select" as a trade term when the library was founded.[41]

With one-volume novels, Mudie continued in his letter to Bentley, he could

> satisfy my subscribers much better, . . . & . . . give them also which I am most anxious to do a far better supply of literature of *all* sorts.
>   With £1.1. subscription I can read £100 worth of books and buy which I like best if I have the room to store them. . . .[42]

By the end of the year he felt called upon to reiterate his position much more firmly:

> My creed as to the One Volume novel is very easy to state— I don't believe in any other form of fiction for the Circulating Librarian & I never did at any time believe in any other! The Three Volume novel does not suit us *at any price* so well as the One Vol, and upon the old terms it is *no longer possible.*[43]

Thus Mudie defended his decision; his company's future depended on the outcome of it. Raising the time-honored subscription could have spelled the doom of the library as surely as the abolition of the three-decker did, and in any case other factors were influential as well. Business methods which were new and startling when Mudie sent off postcards to announce the swift arrival of fresh titles in his library, were no longer innovations near the turn of the century. Then, too, the centralization which in mid-century had so successfully replaced the small and scattered circulating libraries was itself now giving way to a new decentralization. The huge New Oxford Street Pantheon was obsolescent.

Mudie's letters do refute, however, if any refutation is needed, the *Nation's* charge that he acted to increase the prestige of the library edition, to "further hedge it about with dignity," and little dreamed that his circular would "shake literary England to its foundations" and start the downfall of the three-decker.[44] Nor did he fail to recognize the complexity of his position, as the *Westminster Gazette* assumed. That newspaper thought not only that Mudie wished to retain the three-decker form, but that authors, booksellers, and readers were the ones conspiring to abolish it, and that if they "should succeed, Messrs. Mudie may perhaps wish that they had not spoken!"[45] Mudie well knew what the repercussions from his circular would be, and having made his decision, he held to it firmly.

THE VANISHING THREE-DECKER

· Literary Upheaval: Early Reactions ·

THE APPARENTLY REVOLUTIONARY EDICT ISSUED BY MUDIE and Smith in June 1894 naturally caused a good deal of agitation, both public and private. Various associations held meetings to consider the action of the libraries, and private opinions filled columns of the *Publishers' Circular*. Echoing the interest emanating from St. Dunstan's House (home of the *Circular*) were the literary and other periodicals, whose pages repeated the discussion, both editorially and in letters from libraries, publishers, authors, and readers. Reactions varied from complete endorsement to consternation. T. Burleigh, of the London Booksellers' Society, declared on July 16 that his organization, predictably, was unanimously in favor of novels being issued in one volume at 6s.[1] While it disapproved of the stipulated twelve-month interval, this censure was academic since the purpose of the libraries, as is abundantly clear, was not to continue the three-decker under certain conditions, but to abolish it altogether. The point was not obvious, however, to many contemporary observers. The immediate reaction of the *Literary World* was that "It does not at all follow that the three-volume system is doomed because a lower price is demanded."[2]

The next group to consider the action of the libraries was the Society of Authors, which was trying, in the opinion of the *Pall Mall Gazette* at least, to avert "the extinction with which the libraries" were threatening novelists.[3] In spite of the *Gazette's* recommendation that they "insist on maintaining the present price," members endorsed the circular on July 23, a week after approval from the Booksellers:

> The Council, after taking the opinions of several prominent novelists and other members of the Society, and finding them almost unanimously opposed to the continuance of the three volume system, considers that the disadvantages of that system to authors and to the public, far outweigh its advantages; that, for the convenience of the public, as well as for the widest possible circulation of a novel, it is desirable that the artificial form of edition produced for a small body of readers only be now abandoned; and that the whole of the reading public should be placed at the outset in possession of the work at a moderate price.[4]

What the Society objected to most was that for the first six to twelve months of the existence of a novel, its author was shut off from all readers except the subscribers to a library, from all non-Mudieites not only in England, but in India, in Australia, in all the colonies. And what, it asked, was a circulation of perhaps 750 copies going slowly around the island compared with a possible circulation of thousands going around the empire?

Furthermore, the Society again pointed out that by the time a one-volume issue appeared, the library was selling the now unwanted three-decker at 2*s.*6*d.* or 3*s.* a set. More profit would accrue from a large single-volume first edition than from one in orthodox shape, and the writer's reputation would be enhanced, felt the *Author*, by his immediate appearance before the whole world, not simply the 60,000 library subscribers, amounting to perhaps 240,000 readers.[5] Today, some seventy-five years later, the Society is still perplexed by the complicated question of financial benefits to authors from novels bought by libraries—now, of course, one-volume works in the free libraries. The position of the less established novelist has, ironically, swung full circle. One point the proponents of the three-decker kept urging was basically sound: the writer who was not well known had a better chance of breaking into print and of acquiring an audience when a publisher could count on Mudie's to buy a minimum number of copies. Long after the downfall of Mudie's, and after the closing of Smith's library in 1961, *The Times* Book Club in 1962, and Boots in 1966, these relatively unknown novelists found they had indeed lost a substantial part of their sales, and began urging some method to insure financial return to authors (and perhaps publishers) from books loaned by public libraries. From suggestions that borrowers might pay 1*d.* a volume for copyrighted works, the idea has evolved to payment based on the number of books by an author in stock at libraries, a system similar to those already operating in Sweden and Denmark, and currently being studied by the British government.

Specific reactions from publishers show even more clearly than those from booksellers and authors the power of the libraries and the extent to which the three-decker had established itself in the publication of fiction. Publishers of novels might accept the ultimatum completely, defy it, or try to work out a compromise, but they certainly could not afford to ignore it. Before making any public pronouncements they conferred anxiously with one another about the best course of action. Among the most objective appraisals of the situation was William Blackwood's. Replying to the inquiries of Norton Longman, he revealed that he had been expecting the demands for some time, because of the "gaudy butterflies," "the deluge of trash that has been published during the last few years, . . .

to the serious detriment of good books." Although Blackwood had some reservations, on the whole he frankly approved:

I doubt if in future a novel by an unknown writer, however good, unless the journalists of the day choose to make a "boom" of it, will ever be as profitable to the publisher or author in the one vol. form as in the three vol., and if the circular helps to lessen the number of the indifferent and poor being published it will have done good and I shall not regret it.[6]

Blackwood was one of the few publishers who had actively resisted Mudie's dictatorial policies at the height of the library's power. He had steadfastly opposed the guarantee of an interval of a year between the three-decker and a cheaper edition, and he was one of the last to meet the librarian's discount requirements. In 1871 he had written to *The Times* expostulating about a review which implied Mudie had paid only 12*s.* for one of his Edinburgh firm's three-deckers. Actually Mudie paid the full guinea and a half for the 50 copies he took, Blackwood asserted.[7] While such a price was certainly unusually high, it could be explained by two circumstances: Blackwood's own reluctance to give the large library special discounts and the small number of copies Mudie took—deductions became progressively greater as the size of the order increased. Blackwood admitted to Bulwer-Lytton the next year that his firm had been obliged to grant an 18*s.* price; this was undoubtedly for the usual order running to approximately 500 copies, or sometimes more. As early as 1870, too, John Blackwood had said that the days of the three-volume novel were over, and the firm had experimented with various other methods of publication in the attempt to break the form and thus to escape dependence on Mudie.

Andrew Chatto, writing to George Bentley, agreed to go along with the library demands, although he added that he wished "to know exactly where I am in reducing the trade price to 4/- and not to leave the door open for further unrecognised reductions in the shape of 'the discount margin' and I intend to stick out for the 4/- nett. . . ."[8] Three days later he reaffirmed his decision to stand out for "4/- nett, 25 as 24," and conceded the twelve-month interval, although he stipulated that a cheaper edition could be issued at a shorter interval if it were so arranged at the time of the sale.

Chatto further declared to Bentley, "In the face of this declaration it seems to me that any combination of publishers (even if such a combination could be brought about which is doubtful) is powerless." Some such organization had in fact been urged two years previously by William Heinemann, in the *Athenaeum*. In the home market, according to his classical metaphor, publishers were oscillating between the Scylla of authors, printers, and binders and the Charybdis of the libraries and booksellers. Since bookselling by that time had become, in Heinemann's judgment, about as profitable as backing horses, with fewer chances but similar risks, the shops had been steadily reducing their orders for books in an attempt to minimize those risks. Consequently, an "enormous number" of books (about 75 percent of the total) were printed only in small editions, at high prices. This in turn led to the flourishing of the libraries, a flourishing for which he frankly admitted publishers had to accept much responsibility, since they encouraged it by means of discounts. Although the discount prices paid by the large libraries had originally been secret, the terms had

> soon leaked out, and we are now requested by every little library in the kingdom to supply it on the same terms as we supply the big libraries. I cannot say in how far publishers give way in this, and whether further inroads are likely to be made by the big libraries on the present prices. One thing is certain, viz., that if they do make further demands, they will all act together, with strength and determination, while we cut one another's throat![9]

In this accurate prediction that the libraries would "act together," while publishers adopted varied and contradictory policies, the young publisher shows an unusually clear understanding of the situation.

Printers and binders had their trades unions, he pointed out; authors had their Society (which, even if conducted with "purity

Sales Department.

of purpose" was directed against publishers); hence the historic houses should now take steps "speedily and energetically" to form a "brotherly band" among publishers. Approving his suggestion, the *Daily Graphic* pointed out that such a combination "might at least define the rights and privileges of the almighty library."[10] Nothing came of it at that time, but after the libraries' ultimatum, the *Publishers' Circular* picked up the idea, suggesting editorially that if such ancient rivals as Mudie's and Smith's could combine for their own interests, it was high time for the publishers to follow their example, not to mention the example previously set by the authors and booksellers. And, as a matter of fact, the furor created by the abolition of the "library edition" did soon result in the creation of the Publishers' Association.

Heinemann himself was quick to capitalize on the libraries' announcement, and probably reaped more profits by his prompt action than did other publishers who conferred with each other and then waited to see what others did. On July 5, 1894, the *Bookseller* carried the following advertisement: "Mr. Heinemann has much pleasure in announcing that Mr. Hall Caine's New Novel, 'The Manxman,' will be issued on July 15, in One Volume, crown 8vo, price 6s." Below it was a special notation, emphasized by three asterisks: "There will be no edition in three vols." This was not the first individual novel so published by Heinemann (Mrs. Grand's *Our Manifold Nature*, for example, had been issued in that way in March), but it was the first time an explicit disclaimer of a library edition had appeared.

While Arthur Mudie was privately attempting to convince Bentley of the wisdom of his library's action, and while publishers were evaluating their own positions, discussion in the periodicals continued unabated and is worth detailed examination. Comments ranged from lengthy analyses to such a simple note as one on the *Manxman*, which the *Academy* rather austerely deemed "interesting," in view of the recent discussion about circulating libraries.[11] The *Spectator*, on the other hand, while probing underlying motives and defining the type of novel most prevalent on library shelves, predicted continued success for Mudie and Smith, whatever the price of novels. The writer concluded that the Authors' Society, while ostensibly aiming at the three-volume system, was actually attacking the circulating libraries: "Novelists inflamed by stories from abroad . . . [believe] the libraries are their enemies, and that if they could only abolish those clearing-houses of fiction, the public would absorb an enormously larger number of their books."

The *Spectator* felt their efforts would prove futile. With more perception than is found in most of the contemporary opinions, the *Spectator* classified Mudie's novels as "sedatives," for which the circulating library was a necessity. Even if novels cost only 2s., the Mudie reader of this sort would soon spend £15 a year on novels, novels which he would not want on his shelves any more than "empty medicine bottles." Such a work as Meredith's *Lord Ormont* was so clever that it was stimulating. The sedative novel, conversely, was designed "to give rest to the mind," but was not "actively stupid," merely soothing. "As long as worry and overwork and nerves hold their place in the world," so long will the sedative novel be in demand, concluded the *Spectator*, and so long will "the circulating libraries flourish and abound."[12]

Some defenders of the system were found, of course, especially among publishers, but few logical arguments could be advanced. Ironically, the *Saturday Review*, which more than twenty years before had urged publishers to reform and end the tyranny of the libraries, now inferred from the action of the libraries and the current publishing situation, that such reform would mean "in short, down with three volumes, and cheap and nasty forever!"[13] In general, however, the conclusion reached by the *Author* was sound: the three-volume novel was "in the painful position of Mr. Pickwick in the Pound—of having no friends."[14] Indeed the three-decker seemed to have inherited the obloquy formerly directed against fiction. A few nostalgic appreciations appeared, recalling for example that the "mightiest" modern novels "which have wrestled with superstitions and propounded the Pure Woman have been in three volumes, and long volumes too." Perhaps, W. P. James hoped, like the Pipe-Plot Washington Irving's Knickerbocker described, the turmoil would end "in mere smoke."[15]

About the best most proponents of the three-volume system could predict, however, was a slow rather than sudden death. It remained for publishers, through their *Circular*, to buckle down to fight the proposed revolution. The *Circular*, in fact, registered almost the only systematic protest against the new library policy. Consternation had been immediately apparent in its pages. All the old arguments which had been wrangled over earlier were once more dredged to the surface of its columns. In an editorial printed the same day as the circulars, it termed the library proposals among the most sweeping and important for the trade in many years, and concluded that "if booksellers give unreasonable discounts and libraries accept unprofitable subscriptions, then it will soon cease to be worth while either to write or to publish books."[16] The best solution, the leader continued, would be for the libraries to raise the subscription rates. The *Circular* explored other aspects of the situation to make ominous but veiled predictions of ruin. Speculating about whether the three-volume novel was really doomed, it foresaw difficulties which it pretended to believe the libraries had perhaps not considered—that is, the desertion of the libraries by a public flocking to booksellers for cheap editions.

It also introduced a subject which was to be elaborated on by many of the three-decker defenders in the weeks to come: the plight of the author. R. B. Marston, of Sampson Low (the firm which issued the *Circular*), had emphasized the harmful effect on the struggling author in a letter to the *Pall Mall Gazette* the previous day: "I am afraid . . . the edict of the circulating libraries will . . . do more harm to the struggling author than to the publisher, because on the new terms the publisher will be obliged to decline books which left a small margin of profit for himself and the author on the present arrangement." Since what the novelist sold was reduced "at one stroke by 20 per cent.," Marston went on, it was simply lost, unless the *Pall Mall Gazette* and other papers would reduce their advertising rates, and literary agents would lower their charges "in the interest of the struggling author." Besides trying to picture the author as the greatest sufferer, Marston took care to point out to a public which might not understand the situation that the edict was virtual dictation from the libraries in spite of their denial.[17]

The *Circular* took much the same approach, playing a variation on the theme sounded by *Tinsleys'* more than a decade earlier, and maintaining that for the unknown author, the effect would be disastrous. Admitting that the really popular author would not be seriously affected, although at least one-third of the novelists "would be compelled to accept considerably lower terms," the *Circular* then directed its attention to the two-thirds without an assured circle of readers. Their occupations "would be destroyed at a blow," and there was a strong hint of injustice in their thus being deprived of a means of earning a living. William Heinemann concurred, fearing that there would be reduced "to destitution a considerable number of quite worthy and not unuseful writers."[18] There is no hint that either the *Circular* or Heinemann recalled *Bleak House*, published some forty years earlier. In that novel Conversation Kenge objected to changing Chancery law because of the effect on attorneys like Mr. Vholes: "Sir, that class of practitioners would be swept from the face of the earth" (Chap. XXXIX).

The *Circular* had obtained some preliminary reactions from a few publishers by July 7, although full-scale comments were promised for succeeding weeks. Chatto and Windus publicly (as Andrew Chatto had privately) declared its intention of following the directive, by issuing novels in three volumes at 6*s.* a volume, adding the hope that such action might tend to diminish the spectre of overproduction then haunting publishers, and might increase the circulation of "better" fiction. Chatto was the only firm to announce any positive course of action at that time; others simply voiced doubts or suggested alternatives; no one, predictably, expressed wholehearted approval. A. and D. Innes and Company naively repeated the frequent question of whether the three-decker could survive such a blow.

Marston, in the same letter to the *Pall Mall Gazette* mentioned above, proposed a possible solution which he and others actively but vainly advocated for the next few weeks: an increase of subscription rates instead of a decrease in the price of books. This, too, had been suggested at intervals ever since complaints about circulating libraries and three-deckers had started to multiply. Publishers especially were quick to advocate such an increase as the best or, in the words of an 1871 proposal, "the only way of meeting the wishes of the three parties [author, publisher, and public] concerned."[19] That such a plan had already been considered and rejected by the libraries should have been apparent, but with the undeniably tight squeeze felt by the libraries, it was really the last scheme which publishers could advocate. Since the libraries were asking a discount of 20 percent in the price of novels, Marston had suggested, with apparent logic, an increase of 20 percent in the subscription rate instead: "They have a monopoly, and are in as good a position to dictate to the public as to publishers."

His plan is interesting because it contains an indirect admission by a publisher that the prevailing price paid for library editions was 15s.: the 20 percent reduction, in other words, would bring the price down from 5s. to 4s. a volume. Although this price had been an open secret for some years, publishers had naturally been reluctant to disclose the exact amount of the trade discount unless they were in open rebellion against the system. The *Pall Mall Gazette*, which less than a decade before had rejoiced that the "hateful reign" of the three-decker with its evil influence must be nearly over,[20] now was quoted by the *Circular* as highly favoring Marston's idea: "The public as the consumers ought to pay a fair price for an article . . . now much in request."[21] William Heinemann was also cited in support of the plan, since he had written to the *Daily Chronicle* that a shilling or two a year would solve the whole difficulty. Since he adopted the 6s. form so quickly, his attitude in this is rather surprising. As a first reaction, perhaps he felt that even if 6s. editions were to become the rule, some compromise might be effected which would ease an inevitable transitional period. Heinemann further suggested the old idea of a price differential for books of different qualities—high prices for good books, low for bad—a plan which even the *Circular* was unable to back.

The *Circular*, which must have been aware of the growing discontent of novelists, nevertheless ignored it. Noticing that writers were considering what steps they should take in the crisis, the *Circular* blandly stated as its belief, "the general disposition of writers is to urge publishers to withstand the demands of the libraries."[22]

Meanwhile letters to journals other than the trade publications provided various interpretations of the situation. George Bentley thought that one written to the *Pall Mall Gazette* was worthy of pasting in his daybook, *After Business*. The writer, who signed himself only "X," and who claimed experience in all branches of printing and publishing, said he was old enough to remember when Mudie "was creating the organization his successors are now attempting to balance, tightrope fashion, between the publishers and the public." Terming the edict an essentially "cash-box conclusion" which had "nothing to do with brains either in relation to the commodity or the management of the libraries," the writer demanded to know why the libraries reversed the ordinary conditions of economic trading by announcing what they intended to pay. To one versed in publishing, such a question was obviously rhetorical: the libraries could enforce their own prices because of their monopoly.

"X" also broke down the figures of the "charmingly simple and supremely autocratic" circular; what it meant, he said, was that they would pay only 3s.8¼d. for a volume instead of 4s.7¼d. In other words, Mudie had ostensibly been paying 5s. a volume for fiction, but because of the trade practice of allowing 13 copies for the price of 12, he had actually paid 4s.7¼d. Thus, "X" pointed out, one volume cost the library 55d. the first year, about a penny a week, and nothing thereafter. The subscriber, on the other hand, was paying about 5d. for a week's use. While his figures do correctly indicate the principle by which Mudie made his profit, they are somewhat unfair, because a patron in London could, if he wished, exchange his volume daily if he went to New Oxford Street or one of the branches to do it. If he read five different volumes for 5d., he would be paying just what they had cost the librarian the first year, with no allowance for overhead or profits. Although such frequent exchanges were unlikely, they were possible. Furthermore, of course, allowance had to be made for "idle time," when volumes simply stood on the shelves.

"X" further accused the libraries of having bribed the publisher to put a fictitious price on his work; Charles Edward Mudie had "worked upon the principle of keeping up the price of books as the foundation of his position," knowing "what his successors fail to perceive, that with the advent of cheap books his *raison d'être* ceases." When the publisher became aware of this bribery, aware that he was being treated "as a blind and helpless child" by the library, "X" believed he would take the last plunge and start appealing directly to the public. "X" correctly predicted that "of course the result of all this will be the end of the three-volume novel and the circulating library together."

"X" then reiterated what Blackwood and Chatto had hoped, that if publishers had to rely on the public and not a half dozen library representatives for sales, there would be fewer of the "vast numbers of illiterate, ill-conceived works, that, but for the circulating libraries, would never see the colour of printing ink."[23] One of the earliest accounts of the financial situation of the libraries, this letter also contains one of the most complete and objective public analyses. If "X" seems overly optimistic in calling the elimination of the three-decker the solution to the great evil of contemporary literature, that is the enormous quantity of poor literature, it still must be admitted that its abolition did do away with the middleman and did allow fiction to appeal directly to readers. To an age in which many agreed with George Sand's 1875 prophecy that the widespread reading of second-rate literature would stimulate a desire for the first-rate, allowing readers to make their own choices must have seemed a real step forward.

Three weeks after the appearance of the circulars, when the smaller libraries, the Society of Booksellers, and the Society of Authors had all concurred, the *Publishers' Circular* saw the publisher as between the devil and the deep sea. Still, uneasy about so much open discussion of pounds, shillings and pence, it declared editorially that some degree of reticence about the trade prices of books should be observed. Since it was evident, to the *Circular* at least, that the libraries were giving subscribers "far too much for their money,"[24] that journal now suggested that, if increased rates would drive away subscribers, the libraries should agree to reduce the number of books lent for each subscription, a proposal even more futile than its first one. Nor did the *Circular* specify how the famous one exchangeable volume could be reduced in number. If the subscriber could exchange his volume only once a week or a specified number of times a year, the expense of bookkeeping and checking might have cancelled out any profit. The possibility of arguing with a subscriber about the number of times the volume had been exchanged would undoubtedly have been distasteful to a library like Mudie's, with an established reputation for courtesy and service.

Meanwhile, *The Times* noted the situation in an editorial, in the course of which it termed the resolution by the Authors' Society "a sort of Ernulphus's curse against the three-volume novel."[25] That newspaper held no brief for the three-decker, nor for the Society, which it termed a "recently-formed trade union." It did feel, however, that circulating libraries must maintain the form for solid reasons, such as the wider range of choice thereby given subscribers, and added that the Society would have as much difficulty persuading Mudie and Smith and Cawthorn and Hutt that they did not know their business as in persuading publishers that they did not know theirs. *The Times* also perceived that either the downfall of the circulating library system, or a radical change in its method, must attend the sinking of the three-decker.

Furthermore, it indirectly chided the Society of Authors for intruding in what *The Times* believed was properly the business of libraries and publishers. In fact, writers should consider the system a privilege rather than a grievance, felt *The Times*, citing again the avenue to publication provided by the three-decker for many shallow and worthless authors. The successful novelist, continued the leader, had no reason to complain of a barrier between himself and the public, because he could insist on an immediate single-volume edition. Indeed the kind of novel determined the form. Novelists of adventure (i.e., Stevenson, Kipling, Haggard) preferred single volumes because they were suited to the shorter theme, although here the writer overlooked Haggard's first two novels, issued in orthodox library editions. On the other hand, *The Times* concluded, novelists dealing with "society" (i.e., Mrs. Humphry Ward, Hardy, Meredith) favored the three-decker. Actually, although the last three novelists had used the form, all three were dissatisfied with it or with Mudie's. Failing to foresee how completely the three-decker was to disappear, and failing to recall some of the arguments against it in its own columns, *The Times* inaccurately predicted, "Whatever the future may have in store, it will never bring publishers to issue in one volume a society novel which fits naturally into three."

To this conclusion H. Rider Haggard immediately took exception. Individual authors had thus far issued few statements; interviewed by the *Daily Chronicle*, Hall Caine had expressed his approval of the doom of the three-decker; Walter Besant, on the contrary, had felt it was merely suffering from the prevailing depression in the trade. Haggard agreed with Caine, and supported his belief by a letter he had received from one of the largest London publishing houses which remarked that except for the books then in press it would print no more three-volume novels. Haggard also believed that the crux of the matter lay in overproduction, which he deplored from the author's viewpoint. He cited particularly payment by aspiring authors to cover or contribute to the cost of the novel, which the publisher could then supply to the library at a low price while retaining a wide margin of profit (the custom satirized in *Confessions of a Publisher*).

Every copy of a novel bought by a library stopped the sale of two other copies, wrote Haggard, who, with one exception, had abandoned the orthodox form after his first two novels, and who had achieved extraordinarily high sales, even at the libraries, with one-volume fiction. With the keen competition then existing in the market, he felt even budding authors should be able to find publishers. If the three-decker were destroyed, he concluded, and the whole tone of his letter reflects his satisfaction, it would be regarded as an unmixed evil only by those firms in debt to paper-makers, printers, and binders, and therefore "forced to go on publishing remorselessly to avoid foreclosure."[26]

Still other opinions were being voiced through the columns of the periodicals. The *Literary World* proposed on July 27 that the publishers form a syndicate to organize an opposition circulating library, a suggestion reminiscent of the proposal by the *Literary Gazette* in 1860 of a "national circulating library" to be operated by publishers and booksellers. "Did not something of this sort happen when Mr. Mudie started his?"[27] asked the *World*, apparently confusing the leviathan with its ill-fated rival, the Library Company Limited. From *Atlas* came the exhortation for "novel-readers with one accord" to "raise the voice of indignant protest" against losing their favorite in this "latter-day Battle of the Books."[28] The *Saturday Review* admitted, with heavy-handed sarcasm, that the three-volume system was indeed "quite useless" for those who read only on trains, or for those "whose literary tastes do not soar to the average level of the British novelist."[29] As far as advantages were concerned, the *Saturday* apparently could think of only two: the luxury of the large type and good paper, and then the crowning luxury of its being removed when the reader finished. However, it doubted that the form could survive: "It is almost an axiom of economics that the cheap and nasty not only outsells, but exterminates, the choice and expensive." The result, it felt, returning to attack the resolution of the Society of Authors, would be to kill about three-quarters of the novelists. The *Publishers' Circular* also kept sniping at that resolution, which it probably regarded as tantamount to treason, and reiterated its warning to authors that with cheap editions free libraries would acquire novels, and the predicament of writers would be worse than before.[30]

With so much criticism, the Society of Authors felt called upon to defend its resolution in its journal, the *Author*. It countered the repeated argument that the three-decker afforded the best chance for beginners by mentioning abuses also made possible. For example, although a manuscript might be accepted easily, its author might be hurt; with his profit secure, the publisher would lack incentive to advertise or to go on to a new edition. The author would thus be limited to the rewards provided by the circulating library alone, rather than reaping whatever benefits might accrue from the publisher's announcements or a large sale in a cheap edition. Nor was the *Author* alarmed by the dire predictions of a great eradication of writers; in the long run, the author would be careful with his work and, in a kind of social Darwinism, the fittest would survive.

Looking at the probable market among the general public, the *Author* predicted ready sales for favorite authors, although it overstated its case by asserting that a book by an unknown would not sell any more readily at 6s. than at five times that amount. To the objection by publishers that they should be able to do what they liked with what they had bought, the

Author agreed, but noted that most did not buy manuscripts outright, but published on a royalty system. In spite of these defenses, it prophesied that the three-decker would not disappear suddenly, feeling there would always be some demand for it, especially among the sick.[31] Here the *Author* was undoubtedly influenced by the charitable contention of proponents of the three-decker that the light volumes of the triple issue, with their large type, provided for the infirm an entertainment which would be lost with single volumes. About the same time "An Old Library Subscriber" epitomized this argument in a letter to the *Publishers' Circular*. He based his case for the three-decker on the physical condition of the majority of patrons who, he said, having "passed their grand climacteric," may lack their original eyesight, but who have leisure and hence like to borrow "legible and handy" books. For this privilege they willingly pay annual tribute to Mudie or Smith. If the three-decker were abandoned, the libraries would lose much business, he predicted; a large contingent of subscribers would be forced to flock to the free libraries where the 6s. novels might be borrowed by rate-payers who had to pay rates, but were not compelled to pay subscriptions.

Even though the circulars had stipulated January 1, 1895 as the date on which the new regulations would take effect, the libraries started cutting their orders on multi-volume works almost immediately. George Bentley wrote Maarten Maartens that

> Mudie has severely shut his door against 'An Interloper', which is really a good story. Of Miss Peard's stories he generally uses about 300—100 he makes to answer him of Interloper but I am told some of his subscribers are so savage that they are transferring themselves to Smith & Son's.[32]

Bentley must have been aware of the wishful character of his last remark; by this time the policies of the two big libraries were so similar that the publisher could expect no more leniency about the three-decker from one than from the other.

· *The New Season* ·

Bentley was still speculating about the best course to take, but by August 1, 1894 he had conceded the main point, telling Maartens, "We shall drift on until the end of the year & then shall probably alter the 3 volume form, into a pretty 2 vol. differently shaped novel, or into 6/- at once," preferring the latter alternative for authors of reputation. The idea of a two-volume transitional phase was not new. In 1859, John Blackwood had written George Eliot of *Adam Bede* that "with the aid of the insatiable Mudie" so many copies of the first edition had been sold that a second was inevitable. The question was the form: should it be in the orthodox shape at 31s.6d. like the first, or in two volumes, small octavo, at 12s. "The two vol. 12/- must be the form one day even as intermediate to a people's edition, for which I have a strong inclination," Blackwood had commented.[33]

Bentley was not the only one to admit defeat among publishers fighting to retain the three-decker. Sampson Low, which had provided, through the *Publishers' Circular*, most of the publicity for its continuance, abandoned the form in just two months. Taking the last page of the *Circular* early in August, Low announced its new policy in large black type, and attributed it specifically to the edict issued by the libraries:

The New Departure in Publishing Novels
Special Notice to the Trade

Messrs. Sampson Low, Marston and Company beg to announce that in consequence of the CIRCULAR issued by the principal Librarians, . . . they have decided in future (except in occasional special cases) to avoid the publication of novels in THREE VOLUMES, and to produce ORIGINAL NOVELS AT ONCE in the popular one-volume form.

Although this decision is not quite in accord with the proposal contained in the CIRCULAR above referred to, seeing that ORIGINAL NOVELS will thus be available for SALE TO THE PUBLIC AT THE SAME TIME THAT THEY WILL BE

ISSUED TO THEIR SUBSCRIBERS BY THE LENDING LIBRARIES, they have yet good reason to know that this method entirely meets with the approval of the LIBRARIANS.[34]

Low was the only publisher to draw attention publicly to what was the actual reason for the change, as well as to what was implicit in the declaration from the libraries—that is, the extinction of the three-decker, not its preservation at a reduced price. What the libraries wanted was the 6s. novel, as Low had "good reason to know."

The first novel thus issued by Low was Richard D. Blackmore's *Perlycross*, which appeared simultaneously in "one very handsome volume" at 6s. and in the previously customary three. Low explained that the three-decker "had been printed before the Librarians' Circular appeared." Apparently still clinging to a faint hope for the preservation of the three volumes, Low looked on the dual issue as a kind of experiment. "Readers will therefore be able to make their choice of borrowing the Three Volumes, or of buying or borrowing the One Volume," the advertisement noted.

The quick appearance of cheap reprints had been one of the crucial points in the decision by the libraries, and it is interesting that Low carried over this consideration with the issue of one volume, listed at less than twenty percent of the three-decker's cost. "It will be obvious that in order to be successful the PRICE OF SIX SHILLINGS A VOLUME must be maintained; therefore no Cheaper Edition will be published for at least eighteen months or two years," the advertisement concluded. Low's guarantee was addressed primarily to the libraries, who were still important in determining publishing practices, but it also served to reassure prospective individual purchasers who might feel some timidity in buying after years of borrowing.

Although Sampson Low, Marston and Company had yielded as a publisher to the library demands, its *Publishers' Circular* kept up the struggle to preserve the "dignified" form. On

August 4, the same day that Low announced its capitulation, the *Circular* renewed its attack on the Authors' Society; it did not admit that the resolution represented the opinion of writers in general, or even of a majority of the Society's members. Nevertheless it proposed to consider the whole question solely on its merit. If the triple volumes were artificial, so was fiction itself, and so were the libraries. Using the hoary argument of the traditionalist, the *Circular* continued that the very existence of the system proved that its advantages must outweigh its disadvantages. Abandonment, the *Circular* never tired of repeating, "would deprive three-quarters of . . . its [the Authors'] Society of their occupation and means of living."[35] It was only fair, the *Circular* cried, that the struggling beginner or courageous man or woman fighting on in the face of repeated failure should be given a chance, implying, of course, that a one-volume juggernaut would ruthlessly crush worthy authors. The *Circular* finally attributed the crisis not to any unsuitability of the form, but to a general economic depression, and cautioned against any kind of hasty action.

While the *Circular* was desperately searching for reasons to continue the three-decker, the *Bookseller* had few comments, beyond noting the "bold step" taken by Chatto and Windus in announcing new library novels at 5s. a volume (off 1s. from what the firm had originally proposed). This step might cause the latest novels to reappear on the shelves of bookstores, where works by even the most famous authors were "rarely or never ordered until a customer asks for them."[36] At the beginning of September, a month after Sampson Low's announcement, Chatto advertised his new format, prefaced by this explanation:

New Library Novels

[Believing that the conventional price of Half-a-Guinea a Volume, at which New Library Novels in two and three Volumes have hitherto been issued, no longer meets the requirements of the times, we have decided for the future to issue our new Library Novels at the uniform rate of 5s. net per volume. This reduced price will, we hope, greatly extend the demand for the first issues of works of fiction, and secure to stories of merit a lasting and increasing value.—The terms to the Trade may be learned upon inquiry.][37]

In August, Mudie's advertisements for the first time had headlined "Novels in One Volume," and the columns of the *Circular* contained more and more notices that new novels would appear in one volume, or that a one-volume edition had been sold out and another was being prepared. The announcements of Sampson Low, for example, called attention to "the marked and very gratifying success which has attended their first effort to approach the Public direct . . . with a One-Volume issue of an Original Novel."[38] Nevertheless, at the end of the month, the *Circular* was stubbornly maintaining that it was still impossible to forecast the fate of the three-decker with any degree of certainty. The most it would admit from a scrutiny of the lists for the new season was that it might be going, but it was by no means gone. It was impossible to deny that most of the fiction already issued was in one volume, but the *Circular* looked hopefully to what it termed the "many" announced in the so-called "established" fashion as proof that the life of the three-decker might be longer and happier than some supposed. An indication that the *Circular* was gradually yielding to the obvious came from its concession that sooner or later the form would probably die, "if only from the tendency of stories to become shorter."[39]

As the new season really got under way in October, more advertisements, comments, attacks, defenses, and explanations appeared on both sides of the Atlantic. Methuen tried to hedge against all possible contingencies, announcing among its new novels a one-volume, 6s. thriller by Conan Doyle, a two-volume work by Anthony Hope, and a three-decker by Sabine Baring-Gould. W. P. James's "New Pipe-Plot" in *Macmillan's* surveyed most of the arguments used to defend the three-decker with something of "a sanguine faith that good things linger and last or reappear." In addition to the familiar aspects, James presented two fresh views of the reader and the author of the three-decker. The great devourers of three volumes, he maintained, were not, contrary to frequently expressed opinion, the feeble in body and mind, but "the keen politician, the shrewd lawyer, the self-sacrificing physician, the hard-working man of business," who received from the three-decker the beneficent function of entertainment. How this function was better performed in three volumes than in one James did not make clear. Attacking the problem of length and padding, he suggested that the true artist made his condition subserve his art, as Michelangelo took the block as he found it to carve his David. If the second volume was generally heavy-going, he attributed it to the author's being a dilettante or amateur rather than a true artist.

Exactly the opposite view was presented in the October *New Review* by Arthur Waugh, then one of the editors and later the managing director of Chapman and Hall: "At last the storm has burst. It was supposed that publishers would . . . revolt against the libraries; but the miracle of miracles has happened—the libraries have revolted against the publishers." The full significance of all that the suppression of the three-decker would mean for literature had hardly yet been grasped, Waugh felt. The number of novelists who "in the course of justice" would "go to the wall," was very large, but their loss he considered a benefit to literature. The result of the circulars, Waugh predicted, would be that fiction would probably undergo, during the succeeding months, as wholesome a weeding-out and rearrangement as it had ever experienced.[40]

While Waugh was rejoicing over the fall of the three-decker in England, Walter Besant was explaining "the rise, the growth, the greatness, and the fall of that mysterious institution, the Three Volume Novel" to American readers of the *Dial*. In general his points reflected views already expressed in the *Author*, of which he was editor, with more detailed interpretations.

It was necessary to point out, for example, that the English brought out first editions exclusively for the libraries; that a home population of thirty-seven million and a colonial population of fifteen million were kept waiting until the lucky quarter of a million Mudie and Smith readers had had their nine-month run. By this time Besant had of course modified his earlier opinion that the day of the three-decker was not yet over; now he recognized that it had received a mortal blow, and that even if it did recover partially, it would never again flourish.[41]

Comments in the *Publishers' Circular* during this month were noticeably fewer, mainly confined to disagreeing with Waugh's assumption that the three-volume novel had been suppressed, and to routine announcements. The *Circular* admitted, however that "indeed the run on one-volume novels is altogether exceptional," but hastened to add, "Several novels lately issued in two and three volumes apiece are also doing well at the libraries."[42]

In November of 1894 another symposium of publishers— Chatto, Marston, and Murray—commented on the three-decker, generally approving the form, but expressing increasing doubt about its continuance. Chatto, who had promptly and literally followed the libraries' directive, nevertheless regarded the matter as unsettled. "My view is," he stated, "that the luxurious form . . . is an absolute necessity as things go. It suits a class of people who like to have a book in a convenient form." He pertinently asked why, if they were ready to pay, they should not have it. The point, of course, as Chatto realized, was that no individuals were ready to pay, only the libraries, and they had just declared their unwillingness. Publishers, while pocketing their safe three-decker profits, had always been chary about public admittance of any gain from the system, and even went so far as to declare it harmful to their profession. "The misfortune is that it is unprofitable on the whole both to author and publisher,"[43] they were likely to maintain.

Although not brought up as frequently as other points, the

idea of triple issue as providing prestige had been present since mid-century. Forty years before the library circular, *The Times*, while explicitly disclaiming any intention of eliminating "costly literature for the luxurious and the rich," had proposed "that the old and vicious method of proceeding . . . be reversed." Instead of starting with expensive editions "for those who buy their books as they do their plate—by way of ornament and luxury," and then gradually coming down during the course of years to cheaper ones, *The Times* felt that on their first appearance all good books should "appeal to the needy multitude, while the requirements of the fortunate and lazier few are postponed to a more convenient season."[44] About twenty years later, a writer to the *Daily News* observed that novel-readers showed "no disposition" to part with the luxuries "of fine paper, large type, and circulating libraries."[45]

Besides its suitability for the luxury trade, the three-decker carried profits not to be realized with single volumes. Citing the sales of *Endymion* as 15,000 at 31*s*.6*d*., Chatto asked whether Disraeli could have received such great profits from a single-volume issue, which at 6*s*., he estimated would have had to achieve sales of 100,000 copies to get the same result.[46] Although *Endymion* was thus apparently a good case in point, Longman's had actually had trouble getting out of the red with that novel, achieving it only with the publication of the reprint. In 1870 the firm had brought out *Lothair* on a royalty basis; Disraeli received 10*s*. on the pound on all copies sold. Its brilliant success encouraged Longman's to offer the former prime minister the staggering sum of £10,000 for *Endymion*. When it became evident, a few months after the library edition had been published on November 26, 1880, that it was not a financial success, Disraeli volunteered to cancel the agreement and substitute the terms he had obtained for *Lothair*; Longman, in refusing, judged that his offer amounted to presenting the firm with £3,000. What Longman did do was to bring out a 6*s*. edition quickly, and its success had paid off the debt on the book by early in April 1881; ultimately a modest profit was achieved.[47] *Endymion* thus provided almost a better case for the 6*s*. book than for the one at 31*s*.6*d*.

Chatto, however, was firmly, perhaps sentimentally, attached to the three-decker. "I have a most hearty appreciation of the three-volume novel," he admitted in the symposium; "take the great works of fiction in the past; it seems to me unquestionable that they have benefited by being published in the more luxurious form." Marston found the situation "perplexing," since the libraries, he felt, were now dead against the three-volume system, "even when the books are offered to them on their own terms." The libraries wanted one volume, he summarized; most reviewers preferred three (one reason was that the value of the three-decker in the secondhand market had provided a valuable extra compensation); and buyers wanted cheap editions.

Murray, the third of the publishers in the symposium, expressed no emphatic opinion, although he did acknowledge that there were novels which were better in three volumes than in one. Murray's had banned fiction earlier in the century, but in the 1890s was issuing three-deckers. At the Copyright Commission hearings of 1876–1878, while denying that books were dear at all, Murray had paradoxically argued that it was for the best that the general public had to wait for cheap editions. He drew an analogy between books and the latest fashions, which were also not reduced for a year or two. The firm's sympathies, at any rate, were apparently with Chatto and Bentley in 1894, even if there was caution about their explicit expression.

As the year ended and the time came when the libraries' edict was to take effect, the publishers, although generally reluctant, were complying with its provisions. By the end of November the *Literary World* was referring almost nostalgically to "the full tide of the old three-volume days."[48] The disapproval of the publishers is epitomized in a note from the *Principal Publications Issued from New Burlington Street*. These volumes were compiled by Richard Bentley II and F. E. Williams and privately printed. They detail Bentley's operations from 1829–1898. Under "Notes upon the Year" for 1894 (dated 1920) is this single comment: "In the course of this year the Directors of the various Libraries were in consultation with the Society of Authors with a view to the extinction of 'the three-volume novel,' and the substitution of a one-volume issue at a low price and in very small type in its place."[49]

· *The Crisis?* ·

EIGHTEEN NINETY-FIVE BROUGHT THE INEVITABLE SHIFT from three volumes to one, accompanied by continued pronouncements from publishers and authors. The *Bookseller* predicted in January that as the circular took effect more prominent novelists would follow the lead of Caine and Blackmore, issuing their works in one volume, while those of lesser importance would probably publish both in one and in three volumes, at a reduced price. If the new order would indeed be hard on young and untried authors, the *Bookseller* saw, as Waugh had earlier, some compensations, specifically the increased chances for recognition which would follow from the diminished quantity of inferior fiction.[50]

Heinemann had quickly capitalized on the edict with the issue of Caine's *Manxman*. Early in the year he stated flatly, and in the *Publishers' Circular* at that: "I believe greatly in the single-volume form of publication for popular fiction, and since the circular . . . I have not published any novels in three volumes," adding that "six-shilling volumes of fiction are . . . selling remarkably well."[51] Heinemann was then benefiting from the advice of Sidney Pawling, a nephew of Mudie, and previously one of the managers of the library. Heinemann had consulted him about the advisability of publishing several doubtful works, among them the highly successful *Heavenly Twins*, which had been rejected by Meredith at Chapman and Hall before it came to Heinemann. When Pawling's recommendations proved sound, Heinemann chose him as a permanent partner in 1893. In spite of his professedly firm belief in single volumes, however, Heinemann was prudently hedging. He admitted to the *Circular* that he was planning to publish Mrs. Linton's new novel in the triple form soon, and her *In Haste and at Leisure* appeared in that shape in March, at 31s.6d.

In February Ouida attacked the English book trade and the circulating library system in the *North American Review*. Apparently wanting to preserve the three-decker without openly championing the form, she charged that the recent demand by the libraries to be allowed to dictate prices had not excited the attention it should, and had caused much nonsense to be written about the three-decker. In addition to price-fixing, the libraries were guilty of censorship, she continued; being merely middlemen and not police officers, they should provide books freely. Her sensitivity on the latter point was, of course, understandable, because of the sensational nature of her novels. Nor could she accept a general depression as a reason for the libraries' action; why, she inquired, should the book trade be affected, if so few books were actually bought?[52]

On February 9, 1895, seven months after the edict, the *Publishers' Circular* finally admitted for the first time that "It is now generally recognized that the three-volume novel is doomed."[53] Publishers and others were still writing to periodicals deploring the results on elderly readers and young authors, but almost all had actually given in. "You see that we are trying one volume novels," George Bentley told Maarten Maartens as early as February 12, although he added, "But the advertizing!" Advertising or not, Bentley's hand was forced and he knew it. No longer toying with hopes for two-volume editions, he wrote

Maartens at the end of March concerning that writer's next work, "By the end of this week we ought to know how they [Mudie's] will serve us if we come out in 3 vols. If they mean to boycott us, we must go in for 6/- and 1/- royalty to you. . . ."[54]

Nevertheless, some publishers were reluctant to give up their guaranteed market and were still advocating the three-decker. One was Hutchinson, who declared in an interview that apart from financial considerations, there was much to be said for the first issue of a novel in three volumes. All he could muster to say, however, was simply the old argument involving prestige, the appeal the triple form made to the "better and wealthier class of readers." "The three-volume novel is not dead," he declared firmly; his own company had several in the hands of the printers, as well as some two- and one-volume works. The *Circular's* feelings about the desirability of the form naturally coincided with Hutchinson's, but logically it was forced to concede that even library subscribers, on whom three-decker adherents had pinned high hopes during these months, apparently preferred the one-volume form.[55]

The next six months passed quietly enough, and then in September the event which the *Circular* marked as "the crisis in the fate of the three-volume novel" occurred. Simpkin, Marshall, Hamilton, Kent and Company published Mary Elizabeth Braddon's *Sons of Fire* at the old price of a guinea and a half, probably making a deliberate last-ditch stand against the libraries. Earlier in the year, undoubtedly aware of his firm's plans, one of the managing directors of Simpkin's bookshop had been wary of commenting on the shift to one-volume issue. Although he admitted it had occasioned good sales for novels that had appeared while the change was being discussed, this bookseller, who stood to gain much from the shift, had declared it was a change that principally affected the libraries, and "not being a prophet," he had expressed "no opinion" about any permanent increase in sales as a result.[56] Knowledge that his firm was going to try to maintain the form and compel the libraries to accept it would account for this hedging about one-volume sales.

When Mudie's immediately banned the book, it issued this circular to patrons requesting it: "The publishers having decided to publish this book in three volumes, at a prohibitive price, the directors are compelled to wait for the production of the one-volume edition, which (judging from past experience) will be in a very few weeks."[57] Simpkin's immediately announced in its advertisements that there would be no cheaper edition until August 1896, and Miss Braddon herself reaffirmed this to the press. No longer as respectful as in the days when she had named her deliberately "anti-sensational" series in honor of the "eponymous chief of the circulating library," she pointed out to the *Daily Telegraph* that the "prohibitive price" was the one paid by Mudie for every one of her novels during her thirty-three year career. She was "happy to assure the West-end, suburban, and provincial librarians, who are freely circulating my new book, that no other or cheaper edition" would appear until August 1896.

While *Sons of Fire* did not, as the *Circular* believed, mark the crisis in the fate of the three-volume novel—that crisis had occurred on June 27 when the decision of Mudie and Smith had been announced—it did emphasize two phases of its fate. As the only important resistance to the libraries' decree, it showed how complete their power was in this respect. Other firms had regretted the change, and there had been much discussion in the trade about possible methods of opposing the libraries, but nothing had come of it. *Sons of Fire* provided a matchless example of the futility of such resistance. In the thirty-three years between her extraordinarily successful *Lady Audley's Secret* and the libraries' ultimatum, its author had produced forty-seven three-deckers; *Sons of Fire* was her last novel in that form. Her success may have led her to believe she could force the libraries' hand, but actually all it indicated was her own dependence on the method of publication they had just quashed. If anyone could have sold novels in that essentially unsaleable form, this "Queen of the Circulating Libraries," as her publisher termed her, should have been able to do it.

In the second place, *Sons of Fire* provided the final flare-up of publicity about the fall of the three-decker. Miss Braddon wrote a detailed defense of the form in the *Westminster Gazette*, and Walter Besant, who had now realistically accepted the decree, answered in the *Author*. If Mudie's subscribers, she observed with heavy irony, preferred small type and crowded pages, the matter was settled. She, however, found that difficult to believe, basing her conclusion on a half dozen points. First, she maintained that three volumes were the handiest and best looking form, not to mention the healthiest—for the eyes at least. Whether circulating library books were indeed healthful was a question that cropped up frequently in discussion. Some took Miss Braddon's position; the opposite was upheld by others who would have agreed with Ruskin that "We are filthy and foolish enough to thumb each other's books out of circulating libraries!"

Miss Braddon varied the familiar theme that the libraries and their three-deckers provided choice opportunities for beginners by suggesting that they also furnished a market and readers for novelists who wrote over the head of the average book buyer, and for novels like *John Inglesant*. "Will not this insistence upon cheapness rather encourage the production of the flashiest, most audacious, and ephemeral of books?" she inquired. The prestige and expense of the form had led many another staunch three-deckerite like Miss Braddon thus to equate price and worth.

Reiterating that cheapness would weaken the influence of the libraries, she observed that in time the circulating library might "cease to be one of the needs of civilized life." As the appearance of novels in expensive, multi-volume form had influenced the production of other kinds of books, so their reduction to inexpensive, single volumes would have effects, and "all that is tasteful and costly in modern literature will disappear," she warned, echoing the *Saturday Review*'s earlier cry of "cheap and nasty forever!"

Excellence, she concluded, was not to be obtained by a mandate from the libraries. Any writer who was diffuse in three volumes could be diffuse in one.[58] As far as they went, these final arguments were sound, but they were essentially irrelevant, in that the libraries were admittedly concerned with solvency rather than with literary excellence. By this time, too, it was generally recognized that the three-decker and one-volume editions had just about the same upper limitations on length, but again, the libraries were not trying to change the structure of the novel.

Besant's reply in the *Author* for the following month contained little new in refutation: the possible weakening of the power of the libraries was a danger to be considered by those firms and not by authors; ephemeral stories were encouraged, not discouraged, by the system; the new form would be much better for literature. The strange anomaly by which the English published a book twice, once for library patrons and once for the general public, and delayed its reception by that public for a year, should be removed, he concluded.

A few two-volume works were still appearing: Constable brought out Meredith's *The Amazing Marriage* that way in November, although at the reduced price of 12*s*. Bentley was still advertising one two-decker at the end of that month. Even as late as December Chatto issued a new three-decker, but actually the form was dead, and henceforward it was to be even more difficult to break the one-volume rule than it had been to vary the three-decker form.

In 1896 the controversy about the "mandate" died away in the press. Robert Buchanan, that perennial protester, brought it up in his *Is Barabbas a Necessity?* but only as a subsidiary point. Bitter against both publishers and libraries, Buchanan spoke of the "humility" with which the trade had received the ultimatum from the libraries, and described, much as George

Moore had more than a decade earlier, "our beautiful Library system, which allows an irresponsible tradesman to be an autocratic *censor morum*." In the furor created by the demand for a price reduction, the only person who had any right to say at what price his wares should be sold, the author, was not consulted. Consequently, only the author was a loser by the timidity of publishers in the matter, Buchanan noted. Buchanan, who incidentally was the author of one of the titillating novels Moore castigated in *Literature at Nurse*, did not aim his attack primarily at the libraries, but at the publishers, whom he termed robbers with but one interest—plunder, robbers "whose heirs are rich men, when the descendants of the Author are being carried to the workhouse."[59]

The striking effects of the firm stand taken by the libraries against the three-decker can be seen in this table compiled by Joseph Shaylor:

Year	Number of three-volume novels issued
1884	193
1885	193
1886	184
1887	184
1888	165
1889	169
1890	160
1891	162
1892	156
1893	168
1894	184
1895	52
1896	25
1897	4[60]

So complete and thorough was the disappearance that within seven years of the library edict, the *Spectator* was citing the abolition of the three-volume novel as one of the reasons for the enormous expansion of the reading public.[61]

· *Who Killed the Three-Decker?* ·

WHEN THE FATE OF THE THREE-DECKER WAS NO LONGER in any doubt, some discussion arose about just who had really killed it, with some rather ironic attributions. The honor was claimed for both publishers and authors. George Moore, of course, who virtually never stopped talking about his part, wrote after *Esther Waters* that "The censorship of the libraries has come to an end, I said to myself, and I boasted that I had served the cause of humanity."[62] Moore's publisher, Henry Vizetelly, had also "served the cause." According to Ernest A. Vizetelly, it was Henry Vizetelly who abandoned the three-volume form altogether when he issued *A Mummer's Wife* at 6s. in 1885. The firm had a whole series of novels at the popular price and, continued Vizetelly, "it may fairly be claimed that Mr. George Moore and Henry Vizetelly were its pioneers."[63]

H. Rider Haggard somewhat diffidently noted in his auto-biography that *She* (1886) was one of the first novels published in one volume at 6s., and commented that the sales and orders of 30,000 copies were considered large, since people were then accustomed not to buying novels in one volume, but to borrowing them from the library in three.[64] Janet Trevelyan rather grandly attributed not just the end of the three-decker but the resulting brevity of modern novels largely "to the flaming up of an old quarrel between librarians on the one side and publishers and authors on the other," exemplified by the one between Mudie's and Mrs. Humphry Ward. Since the publication of *David Grieve* in 1892, Mrs. Ward had objected to the way the big libraries were "starving their subscribers," that is, buying too few copies to meet the demand. After *Marcella* came out, she reported to George Smith that "Sir Henry Cunningham . . . had made a tremendous protest to Mudie's against their behaviour . . . which he seems to have told them he regarded as a fraud on the public, or rather on their subscribers, whom they were bound to supply with new books!"[65] This feud, coupled with an offer to serialize her next novel providing it were only half the length of *Marcella*, induced her to consider writing shorter books. With her decision the end of the three-decker was determined, her biographer decided, for other novelists soon followed her example.

To the *Bookseller* it appeared that Hall Caine and Richard D. Blackmore had taken the lead in issuing works in one volume, and that others were likely to follow them.[66] Apparently the library edition of the latter's *Perlycross*, the twelfth in his almost unbroken series of three-deckers, had been so obscured by the one-volume edition that the *Bookseller* overlooked it. Hall Caine's *Manxman* had, of course, been given wide publicity, which Caine himself encouraged. His *Who's Who* entry asserts that he had "had a good deal to do, 1894, with the breakdown of the three-volume novel."

If Vizetelly among the publishers had been the pioneer, Heinemann had received the full flood of public attention for single-volume fiction with *The Manxman* and its accompanying proclamation of a revolution in publishing. Nevertheless other firms received credit for the killing of the triple form, among them two that had most wanted to preserve it. The historian of Cassell's, which had just entered the three-decker field, noted the Chatto and Windus advertisements, and felt that this firm, which, ironically, had first acceded to the library demands, led the way to cheaper novels.[67] Its novels indeed sold at less than half the customary price, but with their archaic form, were still twice as expensive as single volumes. Even a most stalwart defender of the three-decker, Simpkin's, was credited with taking the initiative to destroy the form when that firm capitulated to the edict by issuing as a single volume *London Pride*, written by Mary Elizabeth Braddon, the one author who had tried almost single-handedly to preserve triple volumes.

Actually no one person or firm destroyed the form. Even the libraries, which alone could sustain it, combined forces only after years of economic pressure. Publishers and authors had vainly protested by word and acts for many years, but it is unlikely that they would have been much more successful if the libraries had continued to buy. What is remarkable about the end of the three-volume form is the completeness and rapidity of its disappearance. Even its opponents had felt it was so firmly entrenched that it would be dislodged only gradually. Of the popular novelists, Miss Braddon alone attempted to defy the edict, and her conspicuous failure is accentuated by the quiet appearance of her next work in one volume.

If Miss Braddon almost alone expressed her condemnation of the libraries' move, on the other side, outspoken approval was similarly voiced by few authors, and those mainly writers whose works were widely popular at the time. Serious novelists were generally silent, even one like Henry James; although he recognized and used the form, he did not rely on the libraries as the popular writers did. Others, like Gissing and Moore, had already been using cheap editions to sell directly to their readers, so that the actual eradication of the form must have appeared anticlimactic. A very few novelists, of whom William De Morgan is the best known, later quietly tried to maintain a multi-volume form. De Morgan, an associate of William Morris, not only had a natural tendency toward long novels, but felt an aesthetic appreciation for the large type, wide margins, and heavy paper of the traditional three-decker. Furthermore he looked on the one-volume form as many earlier writers had seen the three-decker: a rigid form into which novelists had to force their works at any cost, and to De Morgan, the cost was superficiality. Ironically, his publisher was Heinemann, one of the earliest and most successful issuers of the 6s. single volumes. Although Heinemann kept urging compression, De Morgan prevailed on him, some fifteen years after the boycott, to allow a work coincidentally titled *It Never Can Happen Again* to appear in two volumes. The libraries of course did not buy, and De Morgan sadly acknowledged, "It is the old cry for cheapness;

comfort and luxury—even the quality of the contents do not weigh in the balance."[68] Four years later, when De Morgan was still insisting on two volumes, Heinemann compromised. He issued *When Ghost Meets Ghost* in one volume, and also printed a two-volume edition to satisfy his author—but this time at his author's expense. Multi-volume issue of novels had become a whim for the indulgence of novelists who could afford it.

Some publishers too still looked back with nostalgia to the three-decker, but they did not allow sentiment to affect their business practices. The year after Heinemann unsuccessfully risked two volumes, Joseph Shaylor made a plea for multi-volume issue, implying it should be used for fiction which was written not simply to amuse, but "from a still higher literary standpoint." The former could retain what he described as "its present ephemeral condition," while the latter might be produced in one-, three-, or even ten-volume forms. "This hope may be Utopian, but there is much of today's fiction which should be issued in a more expensive form, and for which the author should receive larger royalties, the publisher and distributor much larger profits, and which deserves production in a more permanent form than the ordinary one-volume novel,"[69] he argued. Shaylor, however, had no faith in realizing such a scheme. Almost twenty years later, the Society of Bookmen wishfully expressed the belief that the libraries, which it felt could scarcely be blamed for the destruction of the three-decker, would enthusiastically embrace any revival of it, even in a less pronounced form.[70] Whether "less pronounced" referred to fewer volumes or to a lower price the Bookmen did not specify, and there appears no evidence that the libraries themselves wanted any part of such a revival.

THE END OF AN ERA

· *The Influence of the Librarian* ·

THE HALF-CENTURY "AGE OF MUDIE" HAD COME TO AN end. As some critics had predicted, the extinction of the three-decker and the advent of cheap books marked the downfall of the huge library; it lingered for another forty-three years in form but not in power. During its era it had revolutionized the English book trade, maintained an artificial form for publishing fiction, and established what amounted almost to a monopoly in the distribution of novels.

The small bookshop in Southampton Row where Charles Edward Mudie had started to lend books in 1842 had been a portentous sign of the times. "Within an incredibly short space of time he had entirely metamorphosed the system of distributing fiction throughout the country," Arthur Waugh put it.[1] Once established in New Oxford Street, he strengthened the centralization of book lending, driving out of business or swallowing many smaller libraries in London and the provinces. Fifteen years later he was important enough to be attacked for his policies in the *Critic*, the *Literary Gazette*, and the *Athenaeum*, although sufficiently insecure to defend them publicly. Readers had grown to depend on the library; in fact, a writer for the penny weekly *Leisure Hour* wondered, "After having Mudie in the house for the last ten years—often the last guest at night, and frequently the first in the morning—by the fireside in winter, by the open garden window in summer . . . what should we do without him?"[2] The streams of customers into the "emporium of books" in New Oxford Street regarded it more like the Pantheon than a circulating library. About this period the firm reached its zenith in size and importance, and then adopted an Olympian aloofness to the intermittent sniping attacks.

By the eighties, however, when George Moore opened his barrage, a combination of circumstances had made the library peculiarly vulnerable. Some of the practices by which Mudie kept up dividend payments to stockholders in the limited company were openly criticized. Allowing for exaggeration by aggrieved authors, who were the readiest to publicize his practices, it is clear that the contemporary fate of books and the reputation of writers were largely influenced by the number of copies Mudie subscribed. Hence, sales that did not come up to the author's or publisher's expectations might be the result of Mudie's purchasing insufficient copies to meet the demand, not of lack of interest on the part of readers. Thus Browning wrote to George Eliot expressing his regret at not finishing *Romola*, and to Isabella Blagden his exasperation at the reason: "I cannot get Romola—spite of my repeated applications at Mudie's— and shall give up subscribing to him in consequence; his humbug is too much."[3]

Another sore point with authors was, of course, Mudie's policy of selecting his stock. If he did not actually ban a book from his shelves (as he did Reade's *Cream*, Mrs. Edwards's *Morals of Mayfair*, and Moore's early novels), he might make only token purchases, remove it from his advertised lists, or see that his assistants advised against it. Frances Power Cobbe, that early feminist and philanthropist, mentioned such a case to Bentley in 1894:

> the days are past when Mudie tabooed me on account of my heresies! I have heard thirty years ago, of more than one lady asking for my books at his counter and being answered by the Assistant "Do you know what sort of books they were, Madam," with dark hints which caused the inquirer to retreat horrified under the impression that she had asked for something quite improper![4]

Miss Cobbe's comment testifies to still another reason contributing to Mudie's fall from power: the changing tastes and attitudes of the nineties. In mid-century Mudie's growth and strength sufficiently indicate the degree to which he responded to the desires of his subscribers, who felt "it rather a good thing that some one should exercise a certain restraint of this kind," as Margaret Oliphant recalled. She herself felt in the nineties that "such a restraint is always injudicious"[5] and might be wrong and dangerous. Rather than a dictatorship, of which he was often accused, Mudie had set up a protectorate over books. He looked on his subscribers as his responsibilities, and they, in turn, placed their confidence in him; they admired him for risking the success of his business by "excluding anything that would corrupt the public mind."[6] Wyndham Lewis, from the vantage point of the 1930s, appraised the situation briefly and fairly: "Mr. Mudie saw to it that his customers never read anything likely to shock them; in one way a good thing, if you cared at all for decency and fundamentals, in another a bad thing, since they were probably equally debarred from enlarging their experience in ways that matter."[7]

In the mid-eighties, when George Moore held out the hand of welcome to all who attacked the sovereignty of the libraries, he found few to take it on the grounds of censorship. Far more undesirable, in the view of Mudie's contemporaries, were his maintenance of the three-decker and with it the artificially high price of fiction. To readers growing both in numbers and in democratic tendencies, the restriction of the market for novels to a limited, "select" audience of Mudie subscribers appeared increasingly objectionable. Gladstone had told the Commons in 1852, "I don't believe there is any article for which the public

Subscribers at the counter of Great Hall at Mudie's in New Oxford Street.

are called on to pay a price so high, in comparison with the actual cost of production, as books, . . ." and explained how "the natural healthy play which ought to regulate the price" was "totally intercepted" because book societies and circulating libraries were "not sensibly affected by the price of the book being more or less."[8]

The Times in 1854 contrasted the 70,000 persons who in one day thronged the glasshouse of the Great Exhibition searching for information and instruction with the 500 to 1500 copies comprising an average edition by the principal publishers, adducing from the former that new and cheap books could find a market, in spite of publishers' protests to the contrary.[9] That in spite of such public feeling the price of first editions of fiction, and through their influence, the price of other works, generally remained at the same high level for almost half a century, simply underscores the power of the libraries. Cut off from new books if they could not afford a subscription to Mudie's, readers certainly could not afford the works themselves. It was to this market that such writers as Dickens and Thackeray appealed through part-issue; its installment plan of spreading the cost of a pound over a period of months represented the one substantial challenge to the three-decker. It was, however, a form chiefly for established authors with assured popularity, because of the large printing necessary for profit. By the seventies, it had been largely replaced by the magazine serial which frequently preceded, as part-issue did not, issue in the orthodox three volumes.

Mudie's ability to foster three-deckers so long arose in part from the basic enjoyment the middle-class Victorian found in prose fiction. Arthur Hugh Clough attributed this preference for the novel over poetry to its material—"general wants, ordinary feelings, the obvious rather than the rare facts of human nature," and "the actual, palpable things with which our everyday life is concerned." While the poet is "talking of what may be better elsewhere," the novelist, dealing "with what *is* here," tells a plain tale, Clough pointed out, and that tale obtains one reading at any rate. Even if the novel were thrown away (or returned to Mudie's, he might have said, with equal applicability), it was read once, thus achieving one of the aims of literature often missed by poetry.[10] Charles Reade's vast collection of clippings sufficiently testifies to his theory of incorporating such actual, palpable things of everyday life "in the gay colors of fiction."[11] Undoubtedly this sense that the novel was dealing with positive matters of fact which ordinary people, as opposed to verse-writers, were obliged to be concerned with, contributed to Fitzjames Stephen's preference for prose. To the younger Lytton he expressed an aspect of the popular feeling: "It always appears to my abominable coarse mind that if one has anything to say it is so much more satisfactory on all possible accounts to say it in prose in so many words."[12] No disrespect to poetry was implied; on the contrary, it was regarded with esteem and admiration, but esteem and admiration for something on a different level from actual life. Prose was everyday, matter-of-fact, and above all, understandable.

With purchase of new fiction virtually precluded—Edmund Gosse testified that he made no effort to possess first editions, even of George Meredith, preferring "the decency of a single volume"[13]—the libraries were also stimulating a meretricious demand, meretricious in the sense that works of doubtful value could find a place on Mudie's shelves simply through their form. Throughout these years when the numbers of novel-readers were increasing with dramatic rapidity, and when the novelist was emerging as the writer with possibilities for earning a good living from his pen, Charles Edward Mudie stood as a barrier between the author and his public. Readers exercised little direct influence on publishers, and through them on writers. It was rather Mudie's opinions which were sought; it was rather speculations about the number of copies Mudie might buy which determined many publication policies.

The charge of his critics that he recognized only a single quality, and that one rather more a quantity than a quality, is not quite fair. Still he did accustom his subscribers—the "Colburn caryatides" as Lewes termed them—to bulk for their yearly guinea. The Victorian preference for length in fiction—for a meal, not a morsel; for a square dinner, not a snack[14]—was fostered by Mudie's insistence on three volumes. The Emmanuel Professor at Cambridge expressed to Mrs. Humphry Ward his satisfaction with the long novel, with seeing "an entire slice of life . . . the mutual interaction of a number of characters."

Her *Miss Bretherton* he considered "dainty." Ideas, like characters, he felt, should be presented in both depth and variety
to "touch the great springs of life."[15] Those readers who did
not analyze their taste so carefully still "delighted in voluminous
works . . . in that sort of detail which permits so intimate
a familiarity with the subjects of which it treats," as Mary
Russell Mitford described her own feelings.[16] Conversely Mudie
encouraged the attitude that one-volume fiction (always excluding religious and juvenile works and novels of adventure)
probably fell into one of two categories: the cheap reprint or a
work which was a "mere chip" of a long novel.[17]

It was length, however, that probably influenced the increasing critical agreement, after the popularity of the Waverley
novels, with Fielding's identification of the novel and the epic.
This conception of the novel as "an accommodation of the
ancient epic to the average capacity of the numberless readers
of modern times"[18] gained strength as the century advanced
and the number of novels increased. Mudie fostered this general
equation of greatness with length. As it was expressed by a
lecturer on novelists in 1888, Stevenson had as yet produced
no great book, possibly because of weak health, or "because he
cannot always be writing his dreams into several volumes."[19]

The attempt to meet Mudie's demands might cause an author
to turn a vignette into a shapeless monster of a book, Gosse had
pointed out. How far a novelist was influenced by Mudie depended on many considerations, but not one remained untouched
by his power. At one extreme stood a novelist like Walter
Besant, who spun his yarns to the length "wisely fore-ordained
by Mr. Mudie,"[20] as a *Pall Mall Gazette* reviewer put it. At the
other were writers like Dickens and Thackeray, who circum-
vented the libraries with part-issues, or those like George Eliot
and Trollope, who refused for artistic reasons to alter manuscripts even when their publishers were concerned about probable effects on circulating library sales. Between the two
extremes were writers with a keen eye on Mudie's lists. Into

the nine hundred pages he preferred, they fitted first of all the romantic interest, Reade's "Turnpike" to success. Beyond that, the novels differed widely. Some depended heavily on incidents, organizing them, with varying degrees of success, by multiple or parallel plots, and relieving them with large segments of description or dialogue. Those who wished had room to indulge a penchant for the informal essay or for casual chats with the reader. Mudie's encouraged all these characteristics as well as the tripartite construction so suitable for the three-decker. In revealing character or in showing development and change in individuals through time or environment, as authors as varied as Thackeray, Trollope, and George Eliot did, length was a decided advantage.

Length, then, and appeal to a wide audience, comprised two similarities between the novel and the epic. Again and again in reviews and criticism of fiction another recurs: the novel at its highest was a prose epic with capabilities similar to those of poetry.[21] What epics taught the ancient Greeks, novels taught Victoria's subjects. "In one shape or another, they enter into the education of us all," Fitzjames Stephen put it, and furthermore "constitute very nearly the whole of the book-education of the unenergetic and listless."[22]

As works of imagination, novels were seen as conforming to pragmatic theories, with the power to move their readers along the paths of virtue. As the century advanced, and the conviction grew that scientific discoveries were about to create a new world, novels were regarded more specifically as a means of preparing people for their new roles. From being regarded as a "vain if not vicious" idle amusement, novel-reading had come to occupy an established place in daily life, a place Mudie had done much to establish. J. Hain Friswell was expressing what was almost a truism when he implored his readers in *London Society* in 1871 "to look the matter boldly in the face, and to remember that the education of novel reading is the only kind of education that many even of the higher and middle classes can be said to have."[23] Fortunately, Friswell noted, the novels, though romantic, were "noble and pure." How far the standard of morality had shifted in a little over a century is revealed by his incredulity over Lady Mary Wortley Montagu's criticism of the contents of a box from an old-fashioned, pre-Mudie library. What Lady Mary objected to was not what Friswell considered the "vice and immorality" of the eighteenth-century works, but rather the false views of life they were inculcating, the great expectations they aroused. It was incomprehensible to Friswell that she could think "any simple English love story in prose, of which there are many, thank God—which tells you 'Love is lord of all,' and makes a peasant girl fit wife for the Lord of Burghley, is pernicious nonsense more harmful than 'Don Juan!' "[24]

Mudie was the guardian of the changed standard, deriving his power from his subscribers, who believed in fiction as a teacher of the young, but a teacher providing lessons by furnishing examples rather than by offering precepts or portraying what was to be avoided. There was strong feeling that vice, graphically depicted, would pollute rather than deter the young.[25] Thus Mudie performed a valuable service to the Victorian reader as a purveyor of respectability and education in three volumes.

Mudie's subscriber was keenly interested in ideas, and enjoyed the disquisitions which nine hundred pages allowed authors. The ideas in the novels, however, he expected not to differ radically from his own firmly established beliefs. He was interested in religion, for example, but he liked to see the Catholic or the atheist in his novel converted to Protestantism, and he was pleased to find the reformed rake hard at work in the colonies bringing his religion to others.[26] His wife and daughters were more interested in the romantic plots perhaps, but he had no fears that Mudie would circulate any book which might be harmful or even embarrassing to read aloud in the family circle.

Other attributes of the novel encouraged by Mudie included

a preference for agreeable scenes, culminating in a conclusion inspiring hope or admiration. Of the numerous examples, one of the best known is Dickens's alteration of the conclusion of *Great Expectations*. He changed his original melancholy ending at the instigation of Bulwer-Lytton, who was noted for his ability to shift with the winds of public taste. Trollope's Loiter, in *The Way We Live Now*, had urged his budding novelist, "Don't let it end unhappily, Lady Carbury . . . because though people like it in a play, they hate it in a book" (Chap. LXXXIX). Rider Haggard acknowledged J. C. Jeaffreson's suggestion about his first novel, *Dawn*, that a "happy ending is so needful for a storys success." Although he reluctantly acquiesced, Haggard confessed, "it does go against the grain."[27] Mrs. Oliphant objected to any affliction, such as hereditary insanity, as the central subject of a novel, because no satisfactory result could come of it.[28] George Meredith, too, doubted that hereditary insanity could successfully be handled in a novel, and agreed that the novelist should not give undue prominence to the painful.[29] Partly, of course, this attitude reflected the general optimism, and partly it was the result of the growing realization of the educational possibilities of fiction.

It was towards the end of the century, when new concepts of fiction were growing, that the circulating library was more keenly felt as a great immovable block to all new work. Its existence undoubtedly did much to delay the appearance of new concepts of fiction; naturalism, for example, was repugnant to the established taste that deplored the depiction of evil or even of "unpleasant" scenes, charging that not only were they disagreeable, but that they were not true. Thus, while the critical concept of the function of a novel as a representation of actual life was widely accepted, the work of the French naturalists was rejected in part because it was felt to show false pictures. Further, of course, such works would have brought a blush to the cheek of Mr. Podsnap's Young Person when they were read aloud in the drawing-room after dinner.

· *"The* Mudie *Mountain"* ·

THE DISADVANTAGES OF THE SYSTEM CHARLES EDWARD Mudie built up are much more apparent than the advantages. In mid-century, Mudie did establish the respectability of the circulating library, and incurred the respect, and even perhaps the gratitude, of those readers who could afford a subscription. Looking back at the height of his power, his admirers saw his library as the highly preferable successor to patronage. In a sense, Mudie's does stand as a kind of logical transition between the aristocratic patrons of an earlier era and twentieth-century mass sales and best sellers. He himself corresponded to the patron, but he was developing an audience to which publishers would be able to appeal directly.

To contemporary observers the increase in the number of novel-readers seemed one of the literary phenomena of the day, and Mudie's did much to encourage this growth. If in his own day he was promoting high prices and a subsequently restricted audience for books, he was paving the way for direct appeal to a larger public by developing the taste for reading, and by instilling in "the British middle-class mind those few ideas it possesses," as Wyndham Lewis astringently put it.[30] In this period, especially between 1845 and 1870, when the potential earning power of the novel developed enormously, when literary critics saw the novel as the nineteenth-century replacement for the epic and even for the drama, when interest in fiction was sharpened by careful and copious criticism, when the novelist was demanding the right to be judged as a serious critic of life, Mudie's contributed essential elements by providing a central distributing agency and by the development of a cohesive body of readers.

Mudie had hit the requirement of the times, and his patrons generally responded with wholehearted approval of his policies. Critics sniping at his censorship usually represented a small group struggling against the tastes and mores of the time more than against the library. As an institution not only was it representative of its age, but through its power of reflecting ideas and attitudes, it was also instrumental in molding the literary history and character of the times. As clerks entered titles in Mudie's catalogue with precise, copper-plate calligraphy, reputations grew or declined. Over against the restrictions felt by authors from their limited market, however, must be set the energy, enterprise, and skill which Mudie used to provide an audience for Victorian novelists such as George Eliot.

As the development of the three-decker, and of Mudie's, corresponds roughly with the growth and strength of the Victorian novel, so the death of that form coincides with the birth of the artistic aspirations of the nineties. Once merely a mechanical printer's device, the form came to affect the construction of the novel, and a perception of the ways in which it influenced fiction increases our understanding of the conventions of fiction. Beside the form stand the institutions which strengthened it, Mudie's Select Library, and its later imitator and rival, Smith's. Only these libraries were powerful enough to destroy the form they had maintained, and when they did that, they also destroyed the library Mudie's had been. Carlyle's prediction was proved true: "One day the *Mudie* mountain, which seemed to stand strong like other rock mountains, gave suddenly, as the icebergs do, a long-sounding crack, suddenly with huge clangour, shivered itself into ice dust, and sank, carrying much along with it."[31] Not fifteen years after their decision, Ford Madox Hueffer's passing reference to the "half-ruined libraries"[32] shows how dependent that type of library had been on the three-decker. Times had changed; and the library which paralleled Victorian conditions so exactly, succumbed. For the student of the Victorian era, Mudie's has more than just value as an institution which met the requirements of an age—though this study is of worth in itself; through its repercussions on authors, the reading public, and publishers, it contributes to our knowledge of Victorian literary tastes and values.

SELECT BIBLIOGRAPHY

THIS LIST IS HIGHLY SELECTIVE, CONSISTING OF WORKS FOUND
most helpful for information about Mudie's in particular, circulating
libraries in general, and publishing practices. A few references to
relevant autobiographies and criticism are included. Other sources
and often more detailed references are cited in the Notes.

· *Manuscript Sources* ·

THE REPORTS OF GERALDINE JEWSBURY AS A READER FOR THE
publishing firm of Richard Bentley and Son are primarily in the
British Museum (those from 1860 to 1875 are British Museum
Add. MSS 46,656 to 46,675). A few are in the Bentley Collection
at the University of Illinois at Urbana. That collection also includes
the Bentley letter-file of correspondence with various nineteenth
century authors and George Bentley's daybook, *After Business*, for
the years 1849 to 1895.

Sources of letters, publication agreements, and other relevant
documents are indicated in the Notes. The typescript of "That
'Mountain, Mudie,'" by William H. Matthews is in the Guildhall

Library, London; that of Michael Sadleir's "Bibliographical Aspects of the Victorian Novel" (Sandars Lectures delivered at Cambridge University, November, 1937) is in the Cambridge University library.

· *Published Sources* ·

Altick, Richard D. *The English Common Reader: A Social History of the Mass Reading Public, 1800–1900.* Chicago: University of Chicago Press, 1957.

Barnes, James J. *Free Trade in Books.* London: Oxford University Press, 1964.

Bentley, Richard II, and Williams, F. E. (compilers). *A List of the Principal Publications Issued from New Burlington Street, 1829–1898.* London: Richard Bentley and Son, 1893–1920.

Besant, Walter; Linton, Mrs. E. Lynn; and Hardy, Thomas. "Candour in English Fiction," *New Review,* II (January, 1890), 6–21.

Besant, Walter. *The Pen and the Book.* London: Burleigh, 1899.

———. "The Rise and Fall of the 'Three-Decker'," *Dial,* XVII (October 1, 1894), 185–86.

Betham-Edwards, Matilda. *Mid-Victorian Memories.* London: John Murray, 1919.

Blakey, Dorothy. *The Minerva Press, 1790–1820.* London: The Bibliographical Society, 1939.

Blathwayt, Raymond. *Looking Down the Years.* London: George Allen and Unwin, 1935.

Dearest Isa: Robert Browning's Letters to Isabella Blagden. Edited by Edward C. McAleer. Austin: University of Texas Press, 1951.

Buchanan, Robert. *Is Barabbas a Necessity?* London: Robert Buchanan, 1896.

Bunce, Oliver B. "English and American Book Markets," *North American Review,* CL (April, 1890), 470–79.

Letters of Jane Welsh Carlyle to her Family, 1839–1863. Edited by Leonard Huxley. New York: Doubleday Page, 1924.

Carter, John D., with the collaboration of Michael Sadleir. *Victorian Fiction.* London: Cambridge University Press for the National Book League, 1947.

"The Case for the Publishers," *Pall Mall Gazette,* XL (December 17, 1884), 1–2.

Chapman, John. *Cheap Books and How to Get Them*. London: John Chapman, 1852.

"The Circulating Libraries and Publishers," *Pall Mall Gazette*, LIX (July 11, 1894), 3.

Colby, Robert A. " 'The Librarian Rules the Roost': The Career of Charles Edward Mudie (1818–1890)," *Wilson Library Bulletin*, XXVI (April, 1952), 623–27.

Collins, Arthur S. *Authorship in the Days of Johnson, 1726–1780*. London: Robert Holden, 1927.

———. *The Profession of Letters: A Study of the Relation of Author to Patron, Publisher, and Public, 1780–1832*. London: Routledge, 1928.

Cox, Harold. "The House of Longman," *Edinburgh Review*, CCXL (October, 1924), 209–42.

Cruse, Amy. *After the Victorians*. London: George Allen and Unwin, 1938.

———. *The Victorians and Their Books*. London: George Allen and Unwin, 1935.

Curwen, Henry. *A History of Booksellers, the Old and the New*. London: Chatto and Windus, [1873].

The Letters of Charles Dickens. Edited by Walter Dexter. 3 vols. London: Nonesuch Press, 1938.

Downey, Edmund. *Twenty Years Ago*. London: Hurst and Blackett, 1905.

The George Eliot Letters. Edited by Gordon S. Haight. 7 vols. London: Oxford University Press, 1954–1955.

Espinasse, Francis. *Literary Recollections and Sketches*. London: Hodder and Stoughton, 1893.

Ford, George H. *Dickens and His Readers: Aspects of Novel-Criticism since 1836*. Princeton: Princeton University Press, 1955.

Friswell, J. Hain. "Circulating Libraries: Their Contents and Their Readers," *London Society*, XX (December, 1871), 515–24.

The Letters of Mrs. Gaskell. Edited by J. A. V. Chapple and Arthur Pollard. Manchester: Manchester University Press, 1966.

Gettmann, Royal A. *A Victorian Publisher*. Cambridge: Cambridge University Press, 1960.

Letters of George Gissing to Members of His Family. Collected and arranged by Algernon and Ellen Gissing. London: Constable, 1927.

Gohdes, Clarence. "British Interest in American Literature during the Latter Part of the Nineteenth Century as Reflected by Mudie's

Circulating Library," *American Literature*, XIII (January, 1942), 353–62.

Gosse, Edmund. "The Tyranny of the Novel," *National Review*, XIX (April, 1892), 163–75.

Griest, Guinevere L. "A Victorian Leviathan: Mudie's Select Library," *Nineteenth-Century Fiction*, XX (September, 1965), 103–26.

Hamlyn, Hilda M. "Eighteenth-Century Circulating Libraries in England," *Library*, Fifth Series I (December, 1946–March, 1947), 197–222.

Heinemann, William. *The Hardships of Publishing*. London: Ballantyne Press, 1893.

Howe, Susanne. *Geraldine Jewsbury, Her Life and Errors*. London: George Allen and Unwin, 1935.

Hughes, Thomas. *Memoir of Daniel Macmillan*. London: Macmillan, 1882.

James, W. P. "A New Pipe-Plot," *Macmillan's*, LXX (October, 1894), 438–44.

Selections from the Letters of Geraldine E. Jewsbury to Jane Welsh Carlyle. Edited by Mrs. Alexander Ireland. London: Longmans, Green, 1892.

Johnson, Edgar. *Charles Dickens: His Tragedy and Triumph*. 2 vols. London: Gollancz, 1953.

Keith, Sara. "Mudie's Circulating Library," *Nineteenth-Century Fiction*, XI (September, 1956), 156–57.

Knight, Charles. *Shadows of the Old Booksellers*. London: Bell and Daldy, 1865.

Lauterbach, Charles E. and Edward S. "The Nineteenth Century Three-Volume Novel," *Papers of the Bibliographical Society of America*, LI (Fourth Quarter, 1957), 263–302.

Leavis, Q. D. *Fiction and the Reading Public*. London: Chatto and Windus, 1932.

"Literary Property—I. The Three-Volume Novel," *Author*, V (August, 1894), 63–65.

Letters of Alexander Macmillan. Edited by George A. Macmillan. Glasgow: Printed for private circulation, 1908.

Letters to Macmillan. Edited by Simon Nowell-Smith. London: Macmillan, 1967.

McKillop, Alan D. "English Circulating Libraries, 1725–1750," *Library*, Fourth Series XIV (March, 1934), 477–85.

Maxwell, Sir Herbert. *The Life and Times of the Right Honourable*

William Henry Smith, M.P. New ed. Edinburgh: Blackwood, 1894.

Milne, James. *A London Book Window.* New York: G. P. Putnam's Sons, 1925.

———. "Mudie's: The Diamond Jubilee of a Great Library," *Strand,* LVIII (August, 1919), 138–42.

Moore, George. *Avowals.* London: Heinemann, 1936.

———. *A Communication to My Friends.* [London]: Nonesuch Press, 1933.

———. *Confessions of a Young Man.* New York: Brentano's, 1915.

———. *Literature at Nurse: or Circulating Morals.* London: Vizetelly, 1885.

———. "A New Censorship of Literature," *Pall Mall Gazette,* XL (December 10, 1884), 1–2.

Morgan, Charles. *The House of Macmillan, 1843–1943.* London: Macmillan, 1943.

Mumby, Frank A. *The House of Routledge, 1834–1934.* London: Routledge, 1934.

———. *Publishing and Bookselling.* London: Jonathan Cape, 1949.

Oliphant, Margaret. *Annals of a Publishing House: William Blackwood and His Sons, Their Magazine and Friends.* 3 vols. Edinburgh: Blackwood, 1897. See also Porter, Mrs. Gerald.

Paston, George [Emily M. Symonds]. *At John Murray's: Records of a Literary Circle, 1843–1892.* London: John Murray, 1932.

Payn, James. *Some Literary Recollections.* London: Smith, Elder, 1884.

Pocklington, G. R. *The Story of W. H. Smith & Son.* London: Printed for private circulation, 1921.

Porter, Mrs. Gerald. *John Blackwood.* Vol. III of *Annals of a Publishing House.* Edinburgh: Blackwood, 1898.

Preston, William C. "Mudie's Library," *Good Words,* XXXV (October, 1894), 668–76.

"The Price of the Novel, 1750–1894," *Author,* V (September, 1894), 94–99 (with a table compiled by R. English).

Ray, Gordon N. "The Bentley Papers," *Library,* Fifth Series VII (September, 1952), 178–200.

Reade, Charles. *The Eighth Commandment.* London: Trübner, 1860.

———. *Readiana.* London: Chatto and Windus, 1883.

Sadleir, Michael. "The Camel's Back or the Last Tribulation of a Victorian Publisher," *Essays Mainly on the Nineteenth Century*

Presented to Sir Humphrey Milford. London: Oxford University Press, 1948.

————. *The Evolution of Publishers' Binding Styles, 1770–1900.* London: Constable, 1930.

————. *Nineteenth Century Fiction: A Bibliographical Record.* 2 vols. London: Constable, 1951.

————. *Things Past.* London: Constable, 1944.

————. "Anthony Trollope and His Publishers," *Library*, New Series V (December, 1924), 215–42.

Shaylor, Joseph. "The Issue of Fiction," *Publishers' Circular*, XCIII (October 15, 1910), 565–66. Reprinted in *The Fascination of Books.* London: Simpkin, Marshall, Hamilton, Kent and Co., 1912.

Sprigge, S. Squire. *The Methods of Publishing.* London: Society of Authors, 1890.

Stang, Richard. *The Theory of the Novel in England, 1850–1870.* New York: Columbia University Press, 1959.

Stevens, Alfred A. *The Recollections of a Bookman.* London: Witherby, 1933.

Taylor, John T. *Early Opposition to the English Novel.* New York: King's Crown Press, 1943.

Taylor, Robert H. "The Trollopes Write to Bentley," *Trollopian*, III (December, 1948), 201–14.

The Letters and Private Papers of William Makepeace Thackeray. Edited by Gordon N. Ray. 4 vols. London: Oxford University Press, 1946.

Tillotson, Kathleen. *Novels of the Eighteen-Forties.* Oxford: Clarendon Press, 1954.

Tinsley, William. *Random Recollections of an Old Publisher.* 2 vols. London: Simpkin, Marshall, Hamilton, Kent and Co., 1900.

Tredrey, F. D. *The House of Blackwood, 1804–1954.* Edinburgh: Blackwood, 1954.

Trollope, Anthony. *Autobiography.* London: Williams and Norgate, 1946.

————. "On English Prose Fiction as a Rational Amusement," *Four Lectures.* Edited by Morris L. Parrish. London: Constable, 1938.

The Letters of Anthony Trollope. Edited by Bradford A. Booth. London: Oxford University Press, 1951.

"A Visit to Mudie's," *Pall Mall Gazette*, XXXIX (March 11, 1884), 11.

Ward, Mrs. Humphry. *A Writer's Recollections.* 2 vols. New York: Harper, 1918.

Waugh, Arthur. "The Coming Book Season—II. Fiction," *New Review,* XI (October, 1894), 426–32.

———. *A Hundred Years of Publishing.* London: Chapman and Hall, 1930.

Winter, John Strange [Henrietta E. V. Stannard]. *Confessions of a Publisher, being the Autobiography of Abel Drinkwater.* London: F. V. White, 1888.

NOTES

The following abbreviations are used:

ALS   Autograph Letter Signed.
Bentley   Bentley Collection, University of Illinois.
Berg   Berg Collection, New York Public Library.
Dearest Isa   *Dearest Isa: Robert Browning's Letters to Isabella Blagden*, ed. Edward C. McAleer (Austin: University of Texas Press, 1951).
Eliot Letters   *The George Eliot Letters*, ed. Gordon S. Haight, 7 vols. (London: Oxford University Press, 1954–1955).
Gissing Letters   *Letters of George Gissing to Members of His Family*, collected and arranged by Algernon and Ellen Gissing (London: Constable, 1927).
Huntington   Henry E. Huntington Library and Art Gallery, San Marino, California.
Oliphant   Margaret Oliphant, *Annals of a Publishing House: William Blackwood and His Sons*, 3 vols. (Edinburgh: Blackwood, 1897).

| Trollope Letters | The Letters of Anthony Trollope, ed. Bradford A. Booth (London: Oxford University Press, 1951). |
| UCLA | Library of the University of California, Los Angeles. |

1. THE AGE OF MUDIE: BACKGROUND

1. "Novels as Sedatives," *Spectator*, LXXIII (July 28, 1894), 108.

2. Contemporary scholarship has paid little attention to the circulating library in the Victorian era. A history of Mudie's is given in my "A Victorian Leviathan: Mudie's Select Library," *Nineteenth-Century Fiction*, XX (September 1965), 103–26. R. A. Colby briefly sketched the record of the two major firms in the *Wilson Library Bulletin*: "The Librarian Rules the Roost," XXVI (April 1952), 623–27; and "That He Who Rides May Read," XXVII (December 1952), 300–306. The influence of the libraries has been discussed by R. D. Altick, *The English Common Reader* (Chicago: University of Chicago Press, 1957), especially in Chap. XIII, and by R. A. Gettmann, *A Victorian Publisher* (Cambridge: Cambridge University Press, 1960), especially in Chap. VIII.

3. Anthony Trollope, "On English Prose Fiction as a Rational Amusement," *Four Lectures*, ed. Morris L. Parrish (London: Constable, 1938), p. 108. The lecture was first delivered in Edinburgh, January 28, 1870.

4. Edmund Gosse, "The Tyranny of the Novel," *National Review*, XIX (April 1892), 164.

5. Henry James, "The Future of the Novel," *The House of Fiction*, ed. Leon Edel (London: Rupert Hart-Davis, 1957), p. 48. Originally published as the preface to Vol. XXVIII of *The Universal Anthology* (1899).

6. George Saintsbury, *The Later Nineteenth Century*, Periods of European Literature, ed. G. Saintsbury (Edinburgh: William Blackwood, 1907), p. 65.

7. Walter Besant, *The Pen and the Book* (London: Burleigh, 1899), p. vi.

8. Stanley Unwin, "The Effect of Circulating Libraries on the Booktrade," *Publishers' Weekly*, CXX (August 15, 1931), 594.

9. George Moore, "A New Censorship of Literature," *Pall Mall Gazette*, XL (December 10, 1884), 1.

10. Mudie catalogues are available in the British Museum. Sara Keith has put on microfilm fiction lists from the Mudie catalogues of 1848, 1858, and 1869. See her "Mudie's Circulating Library," *Nineteenth-Century Fiction*, XI (September 1956), 156–57.

11. Joseph Shaylor, *The Fascination of Books* (London: Simpkin, Marshall, Hamilton, Kent, 1912), pp. 310–11. His figures are given fully in Chap. 8, below, p. 208.

12. "The Manufacture of Novels," *Spectator*, LXXXVI (August 31, 1901), 278.

13. Michael Sadleir, *The Evolution of Publishers' Binding Styles, 1770–1900* (London: Constable, 1930), p. 73.

14. [Rudyard Kipling], "The Old Three-Decker," *Saturday Review*, LXXVIII (July 14, 1894), 44. Zuleika is the name traditionally ascribed to Potiphar's wife (Gen. 39:7–20) whose advances were resisted by the virtuous Joseph. A translation of the Persian *Yúsuf and Zulaikha* had appeared in Trübner's Oriental Series in 1882, and another version had come out in 1883 (reprinted from an 1873 edition), so Kipling could assume some familiarity with the story on the part of his readers.

15. Christopher Bateman abandoned this custom at his bookshop in Little Britain to keep his stock in good condition. "If you buy it," he said, "I will engage it to be perfect before you leave me." John Nichols, *Literary Anecdotes of the Eighteenth Century* (London: Nichols and Bentley, 1812), I, 424, quoted by Frank A. Mumby, *Publishing and Bookselling* (London: Jonathan Cape, 1949), p. 142.

16. Quoted in Hilda M. Hamlyn, "Eighteenth-century Circulating Libraries in England," *Library*, Fifth Series I (December 1946–March 1947), 197. For other instances of early booklending, see Richmond P. Bond, "Early Lending Libraries," *Library*, Fifth Series XIII (September 1959), 204–205, and Alan D. McKillop, "English Circulating Libraries, 1725–1750," *Library*, Fourth Series XIV (March 1934), 477–85.

17. Quoted in William A. E. Axon, "A London Circulating Library of 1743," *Library*, Second Series I (September 1900), 377. Joseph Gilburt of Cawthorn and Hutt's "British Library" (circulating) wrote that Wright founded his library in 1740. See his "The Oldest Circulating Library in Europe," *Library*, I (1889), 151.

18. One hundred years later, in 1852, another library (Lewis's

Circulating Library of medical, scientific, and philosophical works) limited to certain fields was founded; it continues to prosper.

19. See Burns Martin, *Allan Ramsay* (Cambridge: Harvard University Press, 1931), pp. 33–34.

20. Benjamin Franklin, *Autobiography*, ed. Max Farrand (Berkeley: University of California Press, 1949), pp. 53–54.

21. Martin, p. 33.

22. Richard B. Sheridan, *The Rivals*, I, ii. Of the nineteen books mentioned by Lydia Languish and Lucy, fifteen were recent novels, most of them identifiable. See R. Crompton Rhodes, Introduction to *The Rivals* (Oxford: Basil Blackwell, 1928). According to Hilda M. Hamlyn, *Library*, Fifth Series I (1946–1947), Lydia obtained her supply from Bull's in Bath. F. R. Richardson, in "The Circulating Library," *The Book World*, ed. John Hampden (London: Thomas Nelson, 1935), pp. 195–96, quotes a contemporary response to Sheridan in a letter to the *Morning Post* for February 3, 1775: "Mr. Editor, I desire you will inform the author of the *Rivals* that his attack upon *Circulating Libraries* in his first act is unjust and very impertinent. . . ."

23. For a study of Lane and the influence of his press, see Dorothy Blakey, *The Minerva Press, 1790–1820* (London: The Bibliographical Society, 1939).

24. [Mrs. Catherine G. F. Gore], "The Monster-Misery of Literature," *Blackwood's*, LV (May 1844), 557.

25. Michael Sadleir, "Bibliographical Aspects of the Victorian Novel" (Sandars Lectures delivered at Cambridge University, November 1937), typescript in Cambridge University Library.

26. Leitch Ritchie, Preface to *The Ghost Hunter and his Family*, by the O'Hara Family [Michael Banim], Vol. I in "The Library of Romance" (London: Smith, Elder, 1833).

27. Prospectus in *The Stolen Child: a Tale of the Town*, by John Galt, Vol. IV in "The Library of Romance" (London: Smith, Elder, 1833).

28. Advertisement in *The Slave King from the Bug-Jargal*, by Victor Hugo, Vol. VI in "The Library of Romance" (London: Smith, Elder, 1833). Ritchie's metaphor recalls the early days of the circulating library when booksellers kept stools in their shops to allow customers to read there.

29. Gosse, p. 171.

30. Besant, p. 107.

31. George Saintsbury, *The English Novel*, The Channels of

English Literature, ed. O. Smeaton (London: J. M. Dent, 1913), p. 212.

32. George Paston [Emily M. Symonds], *At John Murray's: Records of a Literary Circle, 1843–1892* (London: John Murray, 1932), p. 24.

2. MUDIE'S: THE LEVIATHAN

1. *Spectator*, LXV (November 1, 1890), 583.
2. Charles Edward Mudie, "Mr. Mudie's Library," letter to the *Athenaeum*, October 6, 1860, p. 451.
3. "A Visit to Mudie's," *Pall Mall Gazette*, XXXIX (March 11, 1884), 11.
4. Francis Espinasse, *Literary Recollections and Sketches* (London: Hodder and Stoughton, 1893), p. 357.
5. Quoted in James J. Barnes, *Free Trade in Books* (London: Oxford University Press, 1964), p. 96.
6. A. M. W. Stirling, *William De Morgan and his Wife* (New York: Henry Holt, 1922), p. 49.
7. Thomas Hughes, *Memoir of Daniel Macmillan* (London: Macmillan, 1882), p. 261.
8. *The George Eliot Letters*, ed. Gordon S. Haight, 7 vols. (London: Oxford University Press, 1954–1955), II, 467; III, 7 (hereafter cited as *El' 't Letters*).
9. "The Circulation of Modern Literature," *Spectator*, XXXVI (Supplement, January 3, 1863), 16–18.
10. "Mudie's Library: the Last of a Famous Institution," *The Times*, July 12, 1937, p. 12.
11. "The Opening of Mr. Mudie's New Hall," *Illustrated London News*, XXXVII (December 29, 1860), 618.
12. *The Letters of Anthony Trollope*, ed. Bradford A. Booth (London: Oxford University Press, 1951), p. 83 (hereafter cited as *Trollope Letters*).
13. William C. Preston, "Mudie's Library," *Good Words*, XXXV (1894), 670.
14. ALS, May 8, 1886, Berg Collection, New York Public Library (hereafter cited as Berg).
15. *The Times*, January 24, 1862, p. 5.
16. Quoted in William Tinsley, *Random Recollections of an Old Publisher*, 2 vols. (London: Simpkin, Marshall, Hamilton, Kent and Company, 1900), I, 69.

17. Apparently the firm was poorly managed and was plagued with other distresses. William Tinsley, who knew the library business thoroughly, tells of book thieves who used the low subscription rate to acquire books to be sold on the secondhand market.

18. *The Times*, August 5, 1864, p. 8.

19. Notice, dated February 7, 1881, in the Bentley Collection, University of Illinois (hereafter cited as Bentley). The publishers evidently received a steady and reliable if not spectacular return on their investment in Mudie's. Fourteen years earlier the *Publishers' Circular* noted that Mudie's had "again" declared a 7½ percent dividend. "Literary Intelligence," XXX (February 15, 1867), 89. Another publisher, Joseph J. Miles of Simpkin, Marshall, was the first chairman of Mudie's board of directors, with which his descendents were associated for decades.

20. Ashton and Mitchell's theater ticket agency in London today is the descendent of Mitchell's and still uses the designation "Royal Library."

21. Hookham's account is contained in Tinsley, I, 69–71. He was of the third generation in the firm, which had been founded in 1764.

22. Margaret Oliphant, *Annals of a Publishing House: William Blackwood and his Sons*, 3 vols. (Edinburgh: Blackwood, 1897), II, 458 (hereafter cited as Oliphant).

23. ALS, January 6, 1880, UCLA. Mary Mudie wrote a brief account of her brother's life, *Charles Henry Mudie: A Memorial Sketch* (London: R. Clay, Sons, and Taylor, 1879).

24. William H. Matthews, "That 'Mountain Mudie'," typescript in the Guildhall Library, London. The account contains a chatty, discursive, and sometimes inaccurate history of the library from the viewpoint of one who knew many of its managers and understood its operation. He quotes Smith's announcement banning the three-decker, for example, and attributes it to Mudie's.

25. D. B. Wyndham Lewis, "Standing By . . . a Weekly Commentary on One Thing and Another," *Bystander*, CXXXV (July 28, 1937), 133.

26. William Foyle, "Mudie's Library," letter to *The Times*, July 19, 1937, p. 10.

27. James Milne, "The Diamond Jubilee of a Great Library," *Strand*, LVIII (August 1919), 141.

28. "The Circulation of Modern Literature," p. 17.

29. Hughes, pp. 287–88.

30. This reading room was located at No. 192, only a few doors from the present main offices in Strand House, at No. 186.

31. "Railway Circulating Libraries," *Punch*, XVI (February 10, 1849), 61.

32. "Literature of the Rail," *The Times*, August 9, 1851, p. 7.

33. "Our Weekly Gossip," *Athenaeum*, June 16, 1860, p. 825.

34. The hymn by which he was best known, "I lift my heart to Thee," was "marked by great beauty and tenderness of expression," according to the Rev. W. Garrett Horder, *A Dictionary of Hymnology*, ed. John Julian (New York: Scribner's, 1892), p. 774. It and several other hymns are included in Mudie's volume of verse, *Stray Leaves*, published in 1872.

35. In private life, he was a director of the London Missionary Society and a Fellow of the Royal Geographical Society.

3. Mudie's and the Three-Decker

1. Quoted in "A Visit to Mudie's," *Pall Mall Gazette*, XXXIX (1884), 11.

2. Charles Edward Mudie, "Mr. Mudie's Library," letter to the *Athenaeum*, October 6, 1860, p. 451.

3. *Athenaeum*, September 22, 1855, p. 1077.

4. *Athenaeum*, October 6, 1860, p. 451.

5. "The Circulation of Modern Literature," *Spectator*, XXXVI (1863), 17. The figures are given on p. 22, note 1.

6. John C. Francis, *John Francis, Publisher of the Athenaeum*, 2 vols. (London: Richard Bentley, 1888), II, 122–23, note.

7. *Spectator*, LV (January 28, 1882), 135.

8. "A Visit to Mudie's," p. 11.

9. [Henry Longueville Mansel], "Sensation Novels," *Quarterly Review*, CXIII (April 1863), 484.

10. See Catalogues of Mudie's Select Library, 1858, and later.

11. See Michael Sadleir, "Bibliographical Aspects of the Victorian Novel" (Sandars Lectures, Cambridge University, November 1937), p. 6.

12. See, for example, "Occasional Notes," *Pall Mall Gazette*, XLIII (January 4, 1886), 3–4. Royal A. Gettmann, citing an analysis of novels in the Sadleir Collection by Charles E. and Edward S. Lauterbach (*Papers of the Bibliographical Society of America*, LI [1957], 302), notes that "the common assumption that

it [the three-decker] completely dominated the writing and publishing of fiction is not altogether true" (*A Victorian Publisher* [Cambridge: Cambridge University Press, 1960], p. 231). Certainly the three-decker did not "completely" dominate nineteenth-century fiction (Dickens and Thackeray rarely used the form, and reprints, except of unusually successful novels, were most commonly in one volume, as were collections of stories), but the Sadleir Collection figures should be used cautiously. Although it is large, and although one distinct interest of Sadleir was three-decker first editions, the collection was made by an individual with certain preferences and tastes, and hence is not completely representative. Of Margaret Oliphant's fifteen three-deckers published in the 1870s, just six are listed in Sadleir's catalogue of his collection, *Nineteenth Century Fiction*; of Harrison Ainsworth's eleven three-volume novels published in the same decade, only six are cited. Although George Eliot's eight novels are included, only three of George Gissing's first six three-deckers are found, and James Payn, a popular and prolific writer who published twenty-eight three-deckers in twenty-six years, is not represented at all.

13. R. D. Altick, *The English Common Reader* (Chicago: University of Chicago Press, 1957), p. 52.

14. For analyses of the increase in novel prices during these years, see [R. English], "The Price of the Novel, 1750–1894," *Author*, V (September 1894), 94–99, and Sadleir, "Bibliographical Aspects of the Victorian Novel."

15. Edward P. Morton, "News for Bibliophiles," *Nation*, XCVI (April 3, 1913), 331.

16. Charles Knight, *Shadows of the Old Booksellers* (London: Bell and Daldy, 1865), p. 313.

17. See Joseph Shaylor, *The Fascination of Books* (London: Simpkin, Marshall, Hamilton, Kent, 1912), pp. 27–29. In "The Issue of Fiction," *Publishers' Circular*, XCIII (October 15, 1910), 565, Shaylor recalls that for an important novel, the publisher would supply sheets soon after midnight on the day of publication. The binder, with covers ready, would fold the sheets, paste on the labels, and deliver the volumes to the libraries by 8 a.m.

18. Michael Sadleir, *The Evolution of Publishers' Binding Styles, 1770–1900* (London: Constable, 1930), p. 95.

19. *Eliot Letters*, II, 393.

20. In a letter to his publisher Chapman, Trollope wrote, "After all the old-fashioned mode of publishing does very well now and

then as a change." *Trollope Letters*, p. 140. The industrious Trollope actually was publishing in all three ways during this period. When *Rachel Ray* was issued in October 1863, *The Small House at Allington* was running as a serial in the *Cornhill*. *Can You Forgive Her?* came out in monthly parts starting in January 1864. The next year *Miss Mackenzie* came out in original volume form. All of these were in two volumes; his next novel, *The Belton Estate*, a three-decker, was originally serialized in the new *Fortnightly Review*.

21. Arthur T. Quiller-Couch, "On the Length of Novels," *Speaker*, XVIII (October 1, 1898), 399, reprinted in *Living Age*, CCXIX (December 10, 1898), 734.

22. Charles E. and Edward S. Lauterbach, "The Nineteenth Century Three-Volume Novel," *Papers of the Bibliographical Society of America*, LI (Fourth Quarter, 1957), 285–93, also the source of the figures in the next paragraphs. Lauterbach and Lauterbach developed an electrical word counter with a probable error of plus or minus 1,500 words. Their study contains a detailed discussion of the methods by which publishers "padded" a skimpy text into the regulation number of volumes.

23. Anthony Trollope, *Autobiography* (London: Williams and Norgate, 1946), p. 293.

24. Quoted in Edgar Johnson, *Charles Dickens*, 2 vols. (London: Gollancz, 1953), I, 345–46.

25. *The Letters of Charles Dickens*, ed. Walter Dexter, 3 vols. (Bloomsbury: Nonesuch Press, 1938), III, 507.

26. [George Henry Lewes], "Recent Novels: French and English," *Fraser's*, XXXVI (1847), 687.

27. [James Fitzjames Stephen], "Three-Volume Novels," *Saturday Review*, I (April 26, 1856), 526.

28. Leader, *The Times*, December 18, 1860, p. 8.

29. January, 1882. Bentley.

30. "Three-Volume Novels," *Daily News* (London), July 3, 1871, p. 5.

31. Reports to Richard Bentley, May 17, 1862, and [March] 1861, British Museum Add. MSS 46,656.

32. *Daily News* (London), July 3, 1871, p. 5.

33. Cambridge University Add. MSS 7,349.

34. Letter of June 12, 1865, quoted in *Letters to Macmillan*, ed. Simon Nowell-Smith (London: Macmillan, 1967), p. 43.

35. "One-Volume Novels," *Saturday Review*, VII (January 1, 1859), 11.

36. Julian Hawthorne, *Shapes That Pass* (London: Murray, 1928), pp. 169–70, quoted in Kenneth Robinson, *Wilkie Collins* (London: Bodley Head, 1951), pp. 243–44.

37. Quoted in Alfred A. Stevens, *The Recollections of a Bookman* (London: Witherby, 1933), p. 166.

38. George Henry Lewes, "Dickens in Relation to Criticism," *Fortnightly Review*, XVII (February 1872), 152.

39. Ms. in Pierpont Morgan Library. At the informal level, Mary Elizabeth Braddon corroborates this custom in a letter to her publisher, William Tinsley: "The novel can be published on February 1st and will then be six weeks in advance of it's [*sic*] completion in the London Journal." ALS, Huntington.

40. ALS, Berg.

41. ALS, June 1 and May 3, 1882, UCLA.

42. ALS, Berg.

43. Letter of August 8, 1881, quoted in M. L. Parrish, *Wilkie Collins and Charles Reade: First Editions in the Library at Dormy House* (London: Constable, 1940), p. 111.

44. F. A. Mumby, *The House of Routledge, 1834–1934* (London: George Routledge, 1934), pp. 95–96.

45. George Moore, *A Communication to My Friends* ([London]: Nonesuch Press, 1933), p. 23.

46. Charles Morgan, *The House of Macmillan, 1843–1943* (London: Macmillan, 1943), p. 128.

47. Michael Sadleir, *Things Past* (London: Constable, 1944), p. 108.

48. Frank L. Mott points out that when the New York *Tribune* began issuing a series of novels in 1873 it charged ten cents for a single number (of novelette length), or twenty cents for the double number necessary for an English three-decker. See his *Golden Multitudes: The Story of Best-Sellers in the United States* (New York: Macmillan, 1947), p. 150. These novels were, of course, reprints.

49. Leader, *Daily News* (London), July 3, 1871, p. 5.

50. Matthew Arnold "Copyright," *Irish Essays and Others* (London: Smith, Elder, 1882), p. 263.

51. *Dearest Isa: Robert Browning's Letters to Isabella Blagden*, ed. Edward C. McAleer (Austin: University of Texas Press, 1951), p. 146 (hereafter cited as *Dearest Isa*).

52. *Letters of George Gissing to Members of His Family*, collected and arranged by Algernon and Ellen Gissing (London: Constable, 1927), p. 160 (hereafter cited as *Gissing Letters*).

4. PUBLISHERS, PROFITS, AND THE PUBLIC

1. Letter of September 11, 1943, quoted in Charles Morgan, *The House of Macmillan, 1843–1943* (London: Macmillan, 1943), p. 132.

2. *Eliot Letters*, III, 64.

3. *Trollope Letters*, p. 350.

4. S. Squire Sprigge, *The Methods of Publishing* (London: Society of Authors, 1890), p. 46.

5. "Notes and News," *Author*, V (August 1894), 74–76. Probably written by Walter Besant, the editor.

6. William Heinemann, *The Hardships of Publishing* (London: Ballantyne Press, 1893), pp. 100–101.

7. Letter to his brother Algernon, February 9, 1895, Berg.

8. Bentley. Bentley is explaining that with payment to her of £500, he will have only £32 profit from such a sale. Bentley stipulated that "the large libraries" paid only 14s.6d.; from lesser libraries which ordered fewer copies, Bentley of course received a higher price per copy. In 1887 Bentley wrote to Marie Corelli that he had sold 656 copies of her *Vendetta* at "an average . . . 15/9d. per copy." See Michael Sadleir, "The Camel's Back or the Last Tribulation of a Victorian Publisher," *Essays Mainly on the Nineteenth Century Presented to Sir Humphrey Milford* (London: Oxford University Press, 1948), p. 138.

9. John Carter, with the collaboration of Michael Sadleir, *Victorian Fiction* (Published by the Cambridge University Press for the National Book League, 1947), p. 7.

10. The account of this transaction is given by Florence E. Hardy, *The Early Life of Thomas Hardy* (London: Macmillan, 1928), pp. 109–16.

11. Ibid., p. 116.

12. John Strange Winter [Henrietta E. V. Stannard], *Confessions of a Publisher* (London: F. V. White, 1888), pp. 1–23. Mrs. Stannard was a popular and prolific novelist of this period, with 112 entries in the British Museum catalogue.

13. *Spectator*, XXXVI (January 3, 1863), 1484.

14. Bentley. "The book" was Fanny Kemble's *Records of a Girlhood*, 1878, published in three volumes at 31s.6d.

15. John Chapman, "The Commerce of Literature," in *Cheap*

Books and How to Get Them (London: John Chapman, 1852), p. 8; reprinted from the *Westminster Review* of April 1852.

16. "A Great Bookseller and What He Sells," *Pall Mall Gazette*, XLIII (May 17, 1886), 1–2.

17. See R. D. Altick, *The English Common Reader* (Chicago: University of Chicago Press, 1957), pp. 304–305.

18. R. A. Gettmann, *A Victorian Publisher* (Cambridge: Cambridge University Press, 1960), pp. 132–33.

19. January 13, 1881, Bentley.

20. Oliphant, II, 459–460.

21. *Eliot Letters*, II, 417.

22. Ibid., III, 262, 298. Blackwood's letter is dated May 25, 1860.

23. Ibid., III, 371.

24. Letter from John Blackwood to the Earl of Lytton, December 4, 1872, ibid., V, 353, note.

25. *Athenaeum*, April 1, 1845, pp. 13–14.

26. Michael Sadleir, *Nineteenth Century Fiction: A Bibliographical Record*, 2 vols. (London: Constable, 1951), II, 132.

27. This was not the first time Bentley had attempted lower prices. In January 1839, three years before Mudie's opened, he had advertised that in "view of meeting a very general wish that Works of Fiction should be sold at a more moderate rate," his novels would be reduced from 10*s*.6*d*. to 8*s*. a volume. (*Athenaeum*, January 5, 1839, p. 1.) Dickens's *Oliver Twist* (at 25*s*. the set because of illustrations) was included among the works published at that price, as was Ainsworth's *Rookwood*. Prices were not consistent, however; Mrs. Gore's *The Cabinet Minister* appeared not two months after his advertisement in three volumes at 31*s*.6*d*. Soon this was once more the standard price for his firm, and the one that Mudie was to solidify not many years later.

28. Berg.

29. Berg.

30. Gettmann, p. 24.

31. *Athenaeum*, October 15, 1853, p. 1212.

32. Samuel Tinsley, "Three-Volume Novels," letter to *The Times*, December 4, 1871, p. 4.

33. *Spectator*, XLV (January 27, 1872), 123. In this and later advertisements, Tinsley quoted denouncements of the three-volume system from *The Times* and the *Saturday Review*.

34. *"The Mistress of Langdale Hall," Spectator*, XLV (June 15, 1872), 757. The novel was written by Rosa Mackenzie Kettle.

35. *Athenaeum*, November 28, 1891, p. 707.

36. "A List of Mr. William Heinemann's Publications and Forthcoming Works" (October 1892), p. 10, following Thomas De Quincey, *Posthumous Works*, ed. Alexander H. Japp (London: Heinemann, 1893), vol. II.

37. "A Circulating Censorship," *Saturday Review*, LVIII (December 13, 1884), 747.

38. *Memoir and Correspondence of Susan Ferrier*, ed. John A. Doyle (London: Murray, 1898), p. 313.

39. Bentley.

40. UCLA.

41. August 30, 1849, Berg.

42. See Charles E. and Edward S. Lauterbach, "The Nineteenth Century Three-Volume Novel," *Papers of the Bibliographical Society of America*, LI (Fourth Quarter, 1957), 285–93, for specific details of these ingenious practices.

43. "Small-Beer Chronicles," *All the Year Round*, IX (May 23, 1863), 309–10.

44. Michael Sadleir, *Things Past* (London: Constable, 1944), pp. 85–86.

45. *Trollope Letters*, p. 196. The editor, Bradford Booth, notes the metaphor from *The School for Scandal* (I.ii): "a beautiful quarto page where a neat rivulet of text shall meander through a meadow of margin."

46. Anthony Trollope, *Autobiography* (London: Williams and Norgate, 1946), p. 292.

47. *Trollope Letters*, p. 277.

48. Trollope, *Autobiography*, p. 293.

49. Michael Sadleir, "Anthony Trollope and His Publishers," *Library*, New Series V (December 1924), 235.

50. Berg.

51. Oliphant, II, 420.

52. *Eliot Letters*, IV, 309, 307; V, 146.

53. Ibid., V, 203–204; 353, note. Haight observes that Blackwood understated the sales of *Middlemarch*.

54. "Novels of the Week," *Athenaeum*, February 11, 1882, p. 186.

55. "Mrs. Oliphant's Last Novel," *Spectator*, LV (January 28, 1882), 124.

56. *"In Trust,"* *Saturday Review*, LIII (February 25, 1882), 243.

57. *Eliot Letters*, III, 283.

58. Thomas Hughes, *Memoir of Daniel Macmillan* (London: Macmillan, 1882), p. 288.

59. George Moore, *A Communication to My Friends* ([London]: Nonesuch Press, 1933), p. 22.

60. March 18, 1873, Berg.

61. ALS, March 1, 1876, Bentley.

62. September 23, 1875, Bentley.

63. ALS, May 18, 1881, Bentley.

64. Quoted in *Letters to Macmillan*, ed. Simon Nowell-Smith (London: Macmillan, 1967), p. 43.

65. ALS, December 22, 1879, Bentley.

66. John Carter, "Bentley Three-Deckers," *Spectator*, CLVIII (May 7, 1937), 857.

67. Altick, p. 311.

68. Hardy, p. 133.

69. Mrs. Humphry Ward, *A Writer's Recollections*, 2 vols. (New York: Harper, 1918), II, 87.

70. Gettmann, p. 117.

71. Henry James, "The Future of the Novel," in *The House of Fiction*, ed. Leon Edel (London: Rupert Hart-Davis, 1957), p. 48.

72. "The Numbers of the Comfortable," *Spectator*, XLV (November 30, 1872), 1518. Note that these figures are for families, not individuals. According to census figures, the population of Great Britain in 1871 was 31,845,379; of London, 3,254,260. See E. L. Woodward, *The Age of Reform, 1815– 1870* (Oxford: Clarendon Press, 1949), pp. 579–80.

73. *The Times*, July 12, 1937, p. 12.

74. "Three-Volume Novels," *Daily News* (London), July 3, 1871, p. 5.

75. Woodward, p. 475, note.

76. J. Hain Friswell, "Circulating Libraries: their Contents and their Readers," *London Society*, XX (December 1871), 523.

77. *Hansard's Parliamentary Debates*, CXXI (April 30–June 3, 1852), 596–98.

78. *Eliot Letters*, V, 265, 355.

79. *Letters of Alexander Macmillan*, ed. George A. Macmillan (Glasgow, 1908), p. 125. The letter is dated December 13, 1862.

80. George Moore, "A New Censorship of Literature," *Pall Mall*

Gazette, XL (December 10, 1884), 2. According to Moore's account in *A Communication to My Friends*, pp. 33–59, Tinsley issued *A Modern Lover* on condition that Moore would pay £40 if the book did not prove successful, that is, if Mudie and Smith took too few copies to defray expenses. Some months after its publication, Tinsley sent Moore his account—£40. After inquiries and negotiations, Moore's brother Augustus learned that Tinsley's stock had been stored in a fully insured warehouse which was destroyed by fire, and since Tinsley was paid through the insurance, Moore owed him nothing. Needless to say, this was the last of Moore's dealings with Tinsley. Cf. Hardy's experiences when Tinsley issued *Desperate Remedies*, pp. 60–61, above.

81. "Correspondence," *Pall Mall Gazette*, XL (December 15, 1884), 2.

82. Letter to his brother Algernon, July 27, 1885, Berg.

83. Leader, *The Times*, July 12, 1937, p. 13.

84. Frances Ann Kemble, *Further Records, 1848–1883*, 2 vols. (London: Richard Bentley, 1890), II, 73.

85. T. H. Escott, *Social Transformations of the Victorian Age* (London: Seeley and Company, 1897), p. 370.

86. James Milne, *A London Book Window* (New York: G. P. Putnam's Sons, 1925), p. 39.

87. [George Henry Lewes], "A Box of Books," *Blackwood's*, XCI (April 1862), 434–35. According to Lewes's Journal, the review was originally called "A Box from Mudie's," but a delay in publication, which meant the books were no longer new, necessitated the change in title. See *Eliot Letters*, IV, 22, note.

88. Recalled by E. E. Kellett, "Mudie's," *Spectator*, CLIX (July 16, 1937), 100.

5.   NOVELISTS, NOVELS, AND THE ESTABLISHMENT

1. *Eliot Letters*, III, IV, V, and VII, passim.
2. *Gissing Letters*, p. 196.
3. *Dearest Isa*, p. 216.
4. *Gissing Letters*, p. 94.
5. ALS, UCLA.
6. February 9, 1891, Huntington.
7. ALS, Berg.
8. ALS, Pierpont Morgan Library.

9. Henry James, "Greville Fane," *The Portable Henry James*, ed. Morton D. Zabel (New York: Viking, 1951), p. 141.

10. Charles Reade, "The Four Fogs," *Readiana* (London: Chatto and Windus, 1883), p. 211.

11. Charlotte Brontë, "Biographical Notice of Ellis and Acton Bell," following *Wuthering Heights* by Emily Brontë (Oxford: Blackwell, 1931), p. 4.

12. James Payn, *Some Literary Recollections* (London: Smith, Elder, 1884), p. 240.

13. *Trollope Letters*, pp. 29, 244. The "tale" was *The Golden Lion of Granpère*.

14. George E. Buckle, *The Life of Benjamin Disraeli* (London: John Murray, 1920), VI, 552. For Longman's financial return on this venture, see below, pp. 200–201.

15. "Three-Volume Novels," *Daily News* (London), January 11, 1884, p. 6.

16. Letter to his American publishers, Ticknor and Fields, Huntington.

17. So Milvain terms it in Gissing's *New Grub Street*, 3 vols. (London: Smith, Elder, 1891), II, Chap. XV.

18. *Gissing Letters*, p. 173.

19. James Payn, "Story-Telling," *Nineteenth Century*, VIII (July 1880), 92.

20. Mrs. Alec Tweedie, "A Chat with Mrs. Lynn Linton," *Temple Bar*, CII (July 1894), 364.

21. Anthony Trollope, *Autobiography* (London: Williams and Norgate, 1946), pp. 212–13, 214.

22. *Gissing Letters*, passim.

23. Buckle, VI, 553.

24. *Trollope Letters*, pp. 371, 458.

25. [R. Ogden], "The Rule of Three Volumes," *Nation*, LIX (August 16, 1894), 115.

26. Malcolm Elwin, *Charles Reade* (London: Jonathan Cape, 1931), p. 81.

27. Bentley.

28. "Reade's *Christie Johnstone*," *Spectator*, XXVI (September 3, 1853), 851.

29. ALS, Berg; also the source of the quotations in the rest of the paragraph.

30. Berg.

31. Huntington.

32. Berg.

33. Huntington.

34. Quoted in Robert H. Taylor, "The Trollopes Write to Bentley," *Trollopian*, III (December 1948), 213.

35. *Gissing Letters*, pp. 164–66.

36. Berg.

37. Michael Sadleir, *Things Past* (London: Constable, 1944), p. 104.

38. *The Letters of Mrs. Gaskell*, ed. J. A. V. Chapple and Arthur Pollard (Manchester: Manchester University Press, 1966), pp. 68, 70, 74.

39. John D. Gordan, *George Gissing, 1857–1903: An Exhibition from the Berg Collection* (New York: New York Public Library, 1954), p. 22.

40. Berg.

41. Janet P. Trevelyan, *The Life of Mrs. Humphry Ward* (London: Constable, 1923), p. 111.

42. [Margaret Oliphant], "Modern Novelists—Great and Small," *Blackwood's*, LXXVII (May 1855), 565.

43. ALS, Huntington.

44. Kathleen Tillotson is one of the more recent critics who have observed this effect. See the excellent Introduction to her *Novels of the Eighteen-Forties* (Oxford: Clarendon Press, 1954), especially p. 23.

45. Proof of "How I Write my Books: Related in a Letter to a Friend," UCLA.

46. ALS, May 27, 1880, UCLA.

47. Huntington.

48. Huntington.

49. June 26, 1879, UCLA.

50. "That Sad Second Volume," *Spectator*, LXIV (May 10, 1890), 656–57.

51. George Saintsbury, *The English Novel* (London: J. M. Dent, 1913), p. 268.

52. May 27, 1880, UCLA.

53. Elizabeth C. Gaskell, *The Life of Charlotte Brontë*, intro. by Clement K. Shorter, Haworth Ed. (London: John Murray, 1920), p. 580.

54. *The Letters of Mrs. Gaskell*, p. 675.

55. *Eliot Letters*, III, 249, 267.

56. Ibid., III, 267.

57. *"It Is Never Too Late to Mend,"* *Saturday Review*, II (August 16, 1856), 360–61.

58. *Eliot Letters*, III, 317.

59. Mrs. Russell Barrington, *Life of Walter Bagehot* (London: Longmans Green, 1914), p. 251.

60. Letter to Isidore G. Ascher, quoted in "Correspondence," *Author*, V (November 1894), 161.

61. ALS, Berg.

62. Charles Reade, *The Eighth Commandment* (London: Trübner, 1860), pp. 165–66.

63. "Small-Beer Chronicles," *All the Year Round*, IX (1863), 310.

64. See, for example, Monroe Engel, *The Maturity of Dickens* (Cambridge: Harvard University Press, 1959). Dickens's statement appeared as a "Note" in *All the Year Round*, X (December 26, 1863), 419.

65. [Henry James], *"Far from the Madding Crowd,"* *Nation*, XIX (December 24, 1874), 423.

66. See George Gissing, *Workers in the Dawn*, ed. Robert Shafer, 2 vols. (New York: Doubleday Doran, 1935), I, Chaps. V, III.

6. READERS, REACTIONS, AND RESTRICTIONS

1. British Museum Add. MSS 46,656.

2. Susanne Howe, *Geraldine Jewsbury* (London: Allen and Unwin, 1935), p. 95.

3. *Letters and Memorials of Jane Welsh Carlyle*, ed. James A. Froude, 2 vols. (New York: Charles Scribner's Sons, 1883), II, 29; *Jane Welsh Carlyle: Letters to Her Family, 1839–1863*, ed. Leonard Huxley (London: Murray, 1924), pp. 61, 66; *Letters and Memorials*, II, 74.

4. *Jane Welsh Carlyle: Letters*, pp. 66, 189.

5. Michael Sadleir, *Nineteenth Century Fiction: A Bibliographical Record*, 2 vols. (London: Constable, 1951), I, 193.

6. Richard Stang, *The Theory of the Novel in England, 1850–1870* (New York: Columbia University Press, 1959), p. 84.

7. [George Henry Lewes], "The Lady Novelists," *Westminster Review*, LVIII (July 1852), 129–41.

8. David Masson, *British Novelists and Their Styles* (Cambridge: Macmillan, 1859), p. 212.

9. Howe, p. 95.

10. Bentley.

11. B.M. Add. MSS 46,656.

12. *Selections from the Letters of Geraldine Jewsbury to Jane Welsh Carlyle*, ed. Mrs. Alexander Ireland (London: Longmans Green, 1892), p. 146.

13. "Literature," *John Bull*, XXV (February 22, 1845), 119.

14. Bentley.

15. B.M. Add. MSS 46,656.

16. Anthony Trollope, *Autobiography* (London: Williams and Norgate, 1946), p. 201.

17. Ibid., p. 135.

18. B.M. Add. MSS 46,656.

19. William C. Roscoe, "W. M. Thackeray, Artist and Moralist," *National Review*, II (January 1856), 203–204.

20. B.M. Add. MSS 46,656.

21. See, for example, [Henry Longueville Mansel], "Sensation Novels," *Quarterly Review*, CXIII (April 1863), 481–514.

22. Trollope, *Autobiography*, p. 199.

23. B.M. Add MSS 46,656.

24. Bentley.

25. That this is still a moot question is proved by the Easter 1955 controversy about the B.B.C.'s presentation of *Family Portrait*. Catholic listeners objected to the production of a play which represented Mary as having had other children after the birth of Jesus.

26. "*Tales by a Barrister*," *Quarterly Review*, LXXIX (December 1846), 62.

27. Huntington.

28. B.M. Add. MSS 46,657.

29. "The Literary Profession," *Pall Mall Gazette*, IX (April 17, 1869), 10.

30. Stephen was active on the *Pall Mall Gazette* at that time, contributing 142 articles in 1869, "not much less than half" of the leading articles for that year. See Leslie Stephen, *The Life of Sir James Fitzjames Stephen*, 2nd ed. (London: Smith, Elder, 1895), pp. 213–14.

31. Cambridge University Add. MSS 7,349.

32. Anthony Trollope, "Novel-Reading," *Nineteenth Century*, V (January 1879), 39, 26.

33. Anthony Trollope, "On English Prose Fiction as a Rational

Amusement," *Four Lectures*, ed. Morris L. Parrish (London: Constable, 1938), p. 109.

34. Trollope, *Autobiography*, p. 200.

35. This also provides an example of her prudence: she cautions Bentley to have her suggestions copied, since the author knows her writing!

36. B.M. Add. MSS 46,657.

37. *Trollope Letters*, p. 78.

38. George Moore, Preface to *Piping Hot!* by Émile Zola (London: Vizetelly, 1885), pp. xvi–xvii.

39. B.M. Add. MSS 46,657.

40. Ibid.

41. Quoted in William R. Rutland, *Thomas Hardy* (Oxford: Blackwell, 1938), p. 353.

42. Bentley.

43. *Gissing Letters*, p. 119.

44. Evelyn Abbott, a fellow of Balliol, thus judged it during the course of revising it for Bentley. In spite of his changes, the novel was never issued. For a full account, see Royal A. Gettmann, "Bentley and Gissing," *Nineteenth-Century Fiction*, XI (March 1957), 306–14.

45. *Gissing Letters*, p. 312.

46. *Gissing Letters*, pp. 74, 288.

47. Quoted in Kenneth Robinson, *Wilkie Collins* (London: Bodley Head, 1951), p. 232.

48. Charles Reade, "Facts Must Be Faced," *Readiana* (London: Chatto and Windus, 1883), p. 323.

49. Quoted in Jack Lindsay, *George Meredith* (London: Bodley Head, 1956), p. 123.

50. Bertrand and Patricia Russell, *The Amberley Papers*, 2 vols. (London: Hogarth Press, 1937), I, 77–80.

51. Henry James, "The Art of Fiction," *The Portable Henry James*, ed. Morton D. Zabel (New York: Viking, 1951), p. 416, and "*Nana*," *House of Fiction*, ed. Leon Edel (London: Rupert Hart-Davis, 1957), pp. 278–79 (originally published in the *Parisian*, February 26, 1880).

52. Moore, Preface to *Piping Hot!*, pp. xiv–xvi.

53. Walter Besant, Mrs. E. Lynn Linton, and Thomas Hardy, "Candour in English Fiction," *New Review*, II (January 1890), 6–21.

54. *The Letters and Private Papers of William Makepeace Thackeray*, collected and edited by Gordon N. Ray (London: Oxford University Press, 1946), IV, 161. Some thirty years after Thackeray's statement, Grant Allen used Hardy's *Tess of the D'Urbervilles* to illustrate the greater reticence required by the serial. When *Tess* was running through the *Graphic*, it was drastically cut. Readers got the "real" *Tess* only "by the author piecing together the *disjecta membra* of his mangled tale and printing them at full in the library edition." "Fiction and Mrs. Grundy," *The Novel Review*, I (July 1892), 294–315.

55. B.M. Add. mss 46,658. In 1871 Geraldine Jewsbury advised Bentley to take *A Woman's Vengeance*. In spite of lagging action and tedious passages she felt it was clever, "and it is the work of a *gentleman*." Bentley issued the novel (by James Payn) anonymously the following year.

56. Quoted in Lionel Stevenson, *The Ordeal of George Meredith* (New York: Scribner's, 1953), p. 72.

57. *Critic*, XVII (April 15, 1858), 172.

58. *Critic*, XVII (May 1, 1858), 196.

59. The *Critic* pointed out the general hostility of the trade to *Cream* because Reade, who was involved in a lawsuit against Bentley, had published the work himself on a commission basis.

60. Letters to Samuel Lucas, October 1859, quoted in Lindsay, p. 94.

61. Malcolm Elwin, *Charles Reade* (London: Jonathan Cape, 1931), pp. 321–22.

62. "Mr. Mudie's Monopoly," *Literary Gazette*, New Series V (September 29, 1860), 252.

63. Arthur Waugh, *A Hundred Years of Publishing* (London: Chapman and Hall, 1930), p. 101.

64. George Moore, *Literature at Nurse, or Circulating Morals* (London: Vizetelly, 1885), p. 16.

65. *Literary Gazette*, New Series V (October 6, 1860), 285.

66. Charles Edward Mudie, quoted in "Mr. Mudie's Library," *Athenaeum*, October 6, 1860, p. 451.

67. Ibid.

68. "Mr. Mudie's Reply," *Literary Gazette*, New Series V (October 13, 1860), 302.

69. "Mr. Mudie's Advertisement," *Literary Gazette*, New Series V (November 10, 1860), p. 398.

70. Mrs. Annie Edwards, Letter to the *Athenaeum*, November 3, 1860, p. 594.

71. "Mr. Mudie's Monopoly," *Literary Gazette*, New Series V (October 6, 1860), 285.

72. Oliphant, II, 457.

73. Mary Elizabeth Braddon, "Explanation," prefixed to No. 1 of the "Mudie Classics," *Belgravia*, V (March 1868), 41.

74. John Coleman, *Charles Reade as I Knew Him* (London: Treherne, 1904), p. 324.

75. Bentley.

76. Auriant, "Un Disciple anglais d'Émile Zola. George Moore," *Mercure de France*, CCXCVII (May 1940), 316, note. Moore always wrote to Zola in French, but his use of the language does not seem to be conventional. It is clear, however, that he attributes the maintenance of the inflexible prejudices which caused the fall of the novel in England to the circulating libraries.

77. George Moore, "A New Censorship of Literature," *Pall Mall Gazette*, XL (December 10, 1884), 1.

78. January 12, 1884, quoted in Georges-Paul Collet, *George Moore et la France* (Geneva: Librairie E. Droz, 1957), p. 133.

79. "New Censorship," p. 1.

80. "A Circulating Censorship," *Saturday Review*, LVIII (December 13, 1884), 747–48.

81. Preface to *Piping Hot!*, p. xvi.

82. *Literature at Nurse*, pp. 9, 15.

83. *Punch*, LIII (December 21, 1867), 252.

84. *Literature at Nurse*, pp. 17–18.

85. Ibid., p. 20.

86. George Bernard Shaw, "Mr. Besant's Literary Paradise. From a Socialist's Point of View," *Pall Mall Gazette*, XLVI (November 12, 1887), 3.

87. George Moore, *Confessions of a Young Man* (New York: Brentano's, 1915), pp. 184–85. Moore also mentioned an Irishman behind the counter, O'Flanagan, who for three pounds a week edited the magazine, read the manuscripts, looked after the printer and binder, kept accounts, and entertained visitors. This was Edmund Downey, who in his reminiscences, *Twenty Years Ago* (London: Hurst and Blackett, 1905), denied keeping the accounts.

88. George Moore, *A Communication to My Friends* ([London]: Nonesuch Press, 1933), p. 28.

89. Ibid., p. 27.

90. *Confessions*, p. 134.

91. "Mr. George Moore's New Novel," *Publishers' Circular*, LX (May 5, 1894), 465.

92. *Communication*, pp. 74–75. This is in the second part of the work, unrevised by Moore before his death.

93. B.M. Add. MSS 46,657.

94. Bentley.

95. *Communication*, p. 77.

96. George Moore, *Avowals* (London: Heinemann, 1936), pp. 174–75.

97. D. B. Wyndham Lewis, "Standing By . . . A Weekly Commentary on One Thing and Another," *Bystander*, CXXXV (July 28, 1937), 133.

7. THE COLLAPSE

1. "*Pendennis*," *Fraser's*, XLIII (January 1851), 75.

2. "Cheap Literature," *British Quarterly Review*, XXIX (April 1859), 325. Sheridan's metaphor recurs frequently in comments on the three-decker. Cf. Trollope's use, above, p. 71.

3. "*Life and Memoirs of Marie de Medici*," *Edinburgh Review*, CXCVI (October 1852), 451.

4. "*Advice to Authors, &c.*," *Athenaeum*, October 13, 1860, p. 474.

5. "Three-Volume Novels," *Daily News* (London), July 3, 1871, p. 5.

6. "A Novel—One Guinea and a Half," *Saturday Review*, XXXII (November 11, 1871), 615–16.

7. "*Fair to See*," *The Times*, November 23, 1871, p. 4.

8. "Publishers and the Public," letter to *The Times*, December 17, 1880, p. 6, and leader, *The Times*, December 17, 1880, p. 7. Gladstone had replaced Disraeli in April of 1880. The great depression of 1879 undoubtedly provided additional incentive for agitation about lower novel prices.

9. Edmund Gosse, "The Shaving of Shagpat," *Independent*, XL (February 2, 1888), 130.

10. "Novels of the Season," leader, *The Times*, August 16, 1883, p. 9.

11. ALS, UCLA.

12. "In Three Volumes," leader, *The Times*, January 4, 1886, p. 9.

13. Edmund Downey, *Twenty Years Ago* (London: Hurst and Blackett, 1905), p. 247.

14. J. Hain Friswell, "Circulating Libraries: Their Contents and Their Readers," *London Society*, XX (December 1871), 515.

15. "On the Forms of Publishing Fiction," *Tinsleys' Magazine*, X (May 1872), 413.

16. [W. P. James], "A New Pipe-Plot," *Macmillan's*, LXX (October 1894), 440.

17. "Is the Novel Moribund?" *Tinsleys' Magazine*, XXX (April 1882), 391.

18. "Three-Volume Novels," letter to the *Daily News* (London), July 3, 1871, p. 5.

19. "Literary Intelligence," *Publishers' Circular*, XXXVI (February 1, 1872), 70.

20. Ibid., p. 70.

21. "Is the Novel Moribund?" p. 391.

22. "On the Forms of Publishing Fiction," p. 414.

23. [Henry James], *"Far from the Madding Crowd,"* *Nation*, XIX (December 24, 1874), 423.

24. Oliver B. Bunce, "English and American Book Markets," *North American Review*, CL (April 1890), 479.

25. The two volumes sold at the standard 10s.6d. a volume in England. Bunce notes that it was actually published in the United States at twenty-five cents, "and doubtless had a good sale."

26. "That Sad Second Volume," *Spectator*, LXIV (May 10, 1890), 656–57.

27. Edmund Gosse, "The Tyranny of the Novel," *National Review*, XIX (April 1892), 165.

28. James Milne, *A London Book Window* (New York: G. P. Putnam's Sons, 1925), p. 40.

29. "A Visit to Mudie's," *Pall Mall Gazette*, XXXIX (March 11, 1884), 11.

30. Bentley.

31. Bentley.

32. The Library Association, *A Century of Public Library Service* (1950), p. 5.

33. In "The Librarian Rules the Roost," *Wilson Library Bulletin*, XXVI (1952), 623–27, Robert A. Colby incorrectly identifies the founder's successor as Oliver Edward Mudie.

34. From *After Business* (a daybook kept by George Bentley), pp. 107–108, in the Bentley Collection. Bentley's comment on this story, which Mudie had told him at lunch, is to the publisher's credit, since the Bentley firm had a large stake in three-decker novels: "This is obviously unjust, and a man who considers himself thereby robbed cannot be blamed for saying so. It shows how possible robbery is within the law, until society sees the new sin, & takes its precautions."

35. Frederic M. Bird, "Brevity in Fiction," *Lippincott's*, XLVII (April 1891), 531.

36. *Publishers' Circular*, LXI (July 21, 1894), 57.

37. [R. English], "The Price of the Novel, 1750–1894," *Author*, V (September, 1894), 98.

38. The circulars from both firms were printed in the *Publishers' Circular*, LXI (July 7, 1894), 7. The "odd copy" refers to the trade practice of giving thirteen copies for an order of twelve.

39. "Libraries and Three-Volume Novels," *Publishers' Circular*, LXI (July 14, 1894), 34. The *Circular* noted it did not "endorse the opinions of the writer."

40. Bentley.

41. She cited it in an account of her father-in-law's life. See Matilda Betham-Edwards, *Mid-Victorian Memories* (London: John Murray, 1919), p. 152.

42. July 24, 1894, Bentley.

43. ALS, December 21, 1894, Bentley.

44. [R. Ogden], "The Rule of Three Volumes," *Nation*, LIX (August 16, 1894), 115.

45. Quoted in the *Publishers' Circular*, LXI (July 28, 1894), 78.

8. THE VANISHING THREE-DECKER

1. "The Three-Volume Novel Question," *Bookseller*, August 4, 1894, p. 639.

2. "Table Talk," *Literary World*, New Series L (July 6, 1894), 9.

3. "Occasional Notes," *Pall Mall Gazette*, LIX (July 3, 1894), 2.

4. "Literary Property—I. The Three-Volume Novel," *Author*, V (August 1894), 63. The resolution was also reprinted in other literary journals, such as the *Academy*, XLVI (July 28, 1894), 66, and the *Saturday Review*, LXXVIII (July 28, 1894), 92–93.

5. The *Author* does not give the source of its figure, which is the

same as the *Spectator's* 1872 estimate of the number of families which could afford a yearly guinea subscription (see above, p. 79). At the time of Mudie's death in 1890 his subscribers were said to total about 25,000; Smith's was smaller, but the two firms accounted for the bulk of the business (see "Mr. Charles Edward Mudie," *Publishers' Circular*, LIII [November 1, 1890], 1418).

6. F. D. Tredrey, *The House of Blackwood, 1804–1954* (Edinburgh: Blackwood and Sons, 1954), p. 175.

7. William Blackwood, letter to *The Times*, November 27, 1871, p. 7.

8. Bentley.

9. William Heinemann, "The Hardships of Publishing," *Athenaeum*, December 3, 1892, p. 780, also reprinted in *The Hardships of Publishing* (London: Ballantyne Press, 1893).

10. Quoted in Heinemann, *The Hardships of Publishing*, pp. 114–15.

11. "Notes and News," *Academy*, XLVI (July 21, 1894), 48.

12. "Novels as Sedatives," *Spectator*, LXXIII (July 28, 1894), 108–109.

13. "The Three-Decker," *Saturday Review*, LXXVIII (July 28, 1894), 92.

14. "Book Talk," *Author*, V (August 1894), 84.

15. [W. P. James], "A New Pipe-Plot," *Macmillan's*, LXX (October 1894), 441, 444.

16. *Publishers' Circular*, LXI (July 7, 1894), 8.

17. R. B. Marston, "The Circulating Libraries and Publishers," letter to the *Pall Mall Gazette*, LIX (July 3, 1894), 3.

18. "Occasional Notes," *Pall Mall Gazette*, LIX (1894), 8.

19. "Three-Volume Novels," *Daily News* (London), July 3, 1871, p. 5.

20. "Occasional Notes," *Pall Mall Gazette*, XLII (October 10, 1885), 3.

21. *Publishers' Circular*, LXI (1894), 5.

22. Ibid.

23. "The Circulating Libraries and the Publishers," *Pall Mall Gazette*, LIX (July 11, 1894), 3.

24. *Publishers' Circular*, LXI (July 21, 1894), 57.

25. "The Three-Volume Novel," leader, *The Times*, July 25, 1894, p. 10.

26. H. Rider Haggard, "The Three-Volume Novel," letter to *The Times*, July 27, 1894, p. 11.

27. "Table Talk," *Literary World*, New Series L (July 27, 1894), 57.

28. *After Business* (1894), Bentley.

29. "The Three-Decker," *Saturday Review*, LXXVIII (1894), 92–93.

30. *Publishers' Circular*, LXI (July 28, 1894), 81.

31. "Literary Property—I.," *Author*, V (1894), 63–64. Although the *Author* and some advocates of the form seriously associated the three-decker with invalids, *Punch* was suggesting the three-volume novel as a cure for stubborn cases of insomnia: "And who now shall say that the three-volume novel of the amateur is not a means of spreading civilisation?" "In Three Volumes," *Punch*, CVII (September 1, 1894), 101.

32. Bentley. The reference is to Frances Peard's two-volume novel published in June 1894.

33. *Eliot Letters*, III, 33.

34. *Publishers' Circular*, LXI (August 4, 1894), 120.

35. Ibid., p. 101.

36. "Trade and Literary Gossip," *Bookseller*, August 4, 1894, p. 637.

37. *Bookseller*, September 5, 1894, p. 757.

38. *Publishers' Circular*, LXI (September 1, 1894), 211.

39. Leader, *Publishers' Circular*, LXI (September 29, 1894), 339.

40. Arthur Waugh, "The Coming Book Season—Fiction," *New Review*, XI (October 1894), 427.

41. Walter Besant, "The Rise and Fall of the 'Three Decker'," *Dial*, XVII (October 1, 1894), 185–86.

42. "Notes and Announcements," *Publishers' Circular*, LXI (October 13, 1894), 434.

43. "Three-Volume Novels," *Daily News* (London), July 3, 1871, p. 5. In an editorial the *News* observed pointedly, "As for the suggestion that publishers should abandon a method of publishing which does not, as a rule, bring them much profit, and issue works of fiction at a few shillings a volume, that is scouted by nearly every one of our Correspondents."

44. "Literature for the People," *The Times*, February 9, 1854, p. 10.

45. "Three-Volume Novels," *Daily News* (London), July 3, 1871, p. 5.

46. James Griffin, also a publisher, estimated that if *Endymion* had been issued at 2*s*.6*d*., 500,000 copies might have been disposed of in England alone. On such an edition, he calculated a profit of 1*s*. a copy, or a total of £25,000. See his "Publishers and the Public," *The Times*, December 17, 1880, p. 6. *Endymion* was a celebrated case in the literary world during the three-decker controversy. It cropped up regularly to illustrate the viewpoints of the author, of the libraries, of the public, and of publishers. Cf. pp. 91, 158 above. Robert Buchanan used it to attack publishers saying it showed how their "zeal for plunder" could cause trouble. Copies were foisted on the libraries, he argued, where they remained unread, since no one cared for a bad novel. As a result, every work of fiction suffered from the glut created at the fountainhead, and every author was more or less a loser from what Buchanan called the "Publisher's cupidity" and the "Librarian's imbecility." See Robert Buchanan, *Is Barabbas a Necessity?* (London: Robert Buchanan, 1896), pp. 4–6. Buchanan's use of *Endymion* shows that the main facts of its sale were well known in the trade, but his pamphlet is filled with vituperation and exaggeration. The tone is indicated by the illustration on the cover, which pictures, in front of a window labeled "Barabbas and Company," a large spider in the center of a web hung with the lifeless bodies of authors, both men and women.

47. See George E. Buckle, *The Life of Benjamin Disraeli* (London: John Murray, 1920), VI, 568–70, and Harold Cox, "The House of Longman, 1724–1924," *Edinburgh Review*, CCXL (October 1924), 209–42.

48. "Table Talk," *Literary World*, New Series L (November 30, 1894), 429.

49. Bentley.

50. *Bookseller*, January 9, 1895, p. 7.

51. "Publishers of Today, Mr. William Heinemann," *Publishers' Circular*, LXII (January 12, 1895), 50.

52. Ouida [Marie L. de la Ramée], "Literature and the English Book Trade," *North American Review*, CLX (February 1895), 157–65.

53. "Notes and Announcements," *Publishers' Circular*, LXII (February 9, 1895), 154.

54. Bentley.

55. "The Three-Volume Novel," *Publishers' Circular*, LXII (March 16, 1895), 305.

56. "Booksellers of Today: Messrs. Simpkin, Marshall, Hamilton, Kent & Co. Ltd.," *Publishers' Circular*, LXII (May 11, 1895), 514–15.

57. Quoted in Buchanan, p. 29.

58. "Notes and Announcements," *Publishers' Circular*, LXIII (November 9, 1895), 532.

59. Buchanan, pp. 6–11.

60. Joseph Shaylor, "The Issue of Fiction," *Publishers' Circular*, XCIII (October 15, 1910), 566; reprinted in his *Fascination of Books* (London: Simpkin, Marshall, Hamilton, Kent, 1912), pp. 310–11. Shaylor did not give the source of his figures, but as a director of Simpkin, Marshall, Hamilton, Kent, the publishers of *Sons of Fire*, he was in a position, and had good reason, to note such figures carefully. At least no exception to them was taken in the *Circular*, which was read by publishers and others in a position to judge their accuracy.

61. "The Manufacture of Novels," *Spectator*, LXXXVI (August 31, 1901), 278.

62. George Moore, *A Communication to My Friends* ([London]: Nonesuch Press, 1933), p. 77.

63. Ernest A. Vizetelly, *Émile Zola, Novelist and Reformer* (London: John Lane, 1904), p. 250.

64. H. Rider Haggard, *The Days of My Life* (London: Longmans, Green, 1926), I, 251.

65. Janet P. Trevelyan, *The Life of Mrs. Humphry Ward* (London: Constable, 1923), p. 111.

66. *Bookseller*, January 9, 1895, p. 7.

67. Simon Nowell-Smith, *The House of Cassell, 1848–1958* (London: Cassell, 1958), pp. 188–89.

68. A. M. W. Stirling, *William De Morgan and His Wife* (New York: Henry Holt, 1922), p. 321.

69. Shaylor, *Publishers' Circular*, XCIII (1910), 566.

70. Society of Bookmen, *Report of the Commercial Circulating Libraries Sub-Committee* (London, 1928), pp. 10–11.

9. THE END OF AN ERA

1. Arthur Waugh, *A Hundred Years of Publishing* (London: Chapman and Hall, 1930), p. 101.

2. "Mudie's," *Leisure Hour*, X (March 7, 1861), 150.

3. *Dearest Isa*, p. 167.

4. ALS, Bentley.

5. Oliphant, II, 461–62.

6. *Spectator*, LXV (November 1, 1890), 583.

7. D. B. Wyndham Lewis, "Standing By," *Bystander*, CXXXV (July 28, 1937), 133.

8. *Hansard's Parliamentary Debates*, CXXI (1852), 597.

9. "Literature for the People," *The Times*, February 9, 1854, p. 10.

10. Arthur Hugh Clough, "Recent English Poetry," *North American Review*, LXXVII (July 1853), 3–4.

11. Letter to his publisher, Bentley.

12. ALS, Cambridge University Add. MSS 7,349.

13. Edmund Gosse, "The Shaving of Shagpat," *Independent*, XL (February 2, 1888), 130.

14. Arthur T. Quiller-Couch, "On the Length of Novels," *Speaker*, XVIII (October 1, 1898), 398.

15. Quoted in Janet P. Trevelyan, *The Life of Mrs. Humphry Ward* (London: Constable, 1923), p. 44. After this novel Mrs. Ward's tendency ran to the opposite extreme of length. Cf. above, p. 101.

16. Mary Russell Mitford, *Recollections of a Literary Life* (London: Richard Bentley, 1859), p. 316.

17. James Milne, *A London Book Window* (New York: G. P. Putnam's Sons, 1925), p. 160.

18. See, for example, "Historical Romance," *Quarterly Review*, XXXV (March 1827), 518–66.

19. "Contemporary Novelists," a review of a lecture by the Rev. H. C. Shuttleworth, *Pall Mall Gazette*, XLVII (February 21, 1888), 13–14. This is a popular opinion, interesting because it reveals the prestige of the form.

20. *Pall Mall Gazette*, XLVII (May 4, 1888), 3.

21. A typical instance is found in David Masson, *British Novelists and their Styles* (Cambridge: Macmillan, 1859).

22. James Fitzjames Stephen, "The Relation of Novels to Life," *Cambridge Essays* (London: John W. Parker and Son, 1855), p. 148.

23. J. Hain Friswell, "Circulating Libraries: Their Contents and Their Readers," *London Society*, XX (December, 1871), 523.

24. Ibid., p. 518.

25. See, for example, "Advice to an Intending Serialist," *Blackwood's*, LX (November 1846), 595; and cf. above, p. 131 ff.

26. Sometimes the author's treatment resulted in transforming these preferences into "absolute Juggernauts." Fitzjames Stephen cited *Hawkstone* as such an instance. In that novel, the atheist falls into melted lead, "sinking slowly on his face"; and the Jesuit, trapped in a secret passage of his own contrivance, is eaten by rats, the vital parts apparently attacked last. Even an evangelical clergyman, who had compounded his offence by belonging to a debating club at Cambridge, is "thrown at last into a quasi convent, by way of restitution." "Relation of Novels to Life," *Cambridge Essays*, pp. 178–79.

27. ALS, UCLA.

28. [Margaret Oliphant], "Modern Novelists—Great and Small," *Blackwood's*, LXXVII (May 1855), 554–68.

29. [George Meredith], "Belles Lettres," *Westminster Review*, LXVII (April 1857), 615.

30. Lewis, p. 133.

31. Thomas Carlyle, *Essays*, quoted on the title page of George Moore, *Literature at Nurse, or Circulating Morals* (London: Vizetelly, 1885).

32. Ford Maddox Hueffer, *Memories and Impressions* (New York: Harper, 1911), p. 259.

INDEX

poetry, as subservient to prose, 217-18; Victorian prices for, 43
Pawling, Sidney, 69, 202-3
Payn, James, 26, 88, 90-92
periodical division of Mudie's, 39
periodicals, reaction to libraries' edict reflected in, 177-212; serialization of novels in, 52-53; three-deckers defended in, 161-66
Pinafore, 33
plots in three-deckers, 111-13
Poor Man and the Lady, The, 136
Poor Miss Finch, 53
press, attacks on three-decker, 157-61; reaction to libraries' edict, 177-212
prices, libraries' edict to publishers on, 171-75; maintained by Mudie's at artificially high levels, 215-16; paid by Mudie to publishers, 187-88; paid by publishers for novels, 91; reaction to libraries' edict on, 176-212; of three-deckers, 4, 11-12, 41-43, 52, 65-74, 91; of three-deckers defended, 162; of three-deckers protested, 156-61
Principal Publications Issued from New Burlington Street, 202
prose vs. poetry in Victorian days, 217-18
public libraries, lack of, 79-81
Publishers' Association, 180-82
Publishers' Circular, 161-64, 176, 181-86, 192-99, 202-4
publishing industry, advertising practices influenced by Mudie, 62-64; American, 55-56, 165-66; attacked for triple-decker's high price, 156-61; bookbinding by, 42-43; creation of Publishers' Association, 180-82; edict from circulating libraries demands new terms from, 171-75; expansion of, 42; and free trade in bookselling, 64; Mudie's influence on, 58-86; and one-volume original editions, 67-70; prices paid by Mudie's to, 187-88;

prices paid for three-deckers, 65-66; price-breaking series of original novels, 66-70; production costs for three-decker novels, 58-62; profits from three-deckers, 58-62, 163; reaction to libraries' price-reduction edict, 176-82; relations between authors and publishers, 70; of reprints, 53-54, 74-75; stretching devices used by, 70-73; successive modes of issuing one novel, 52-54; symposium on three-decker, 199; three-deckers defended by, 161-66; title selection by, 75-76

Quiller-Couch, Sir Arthur, 45

railway bookstall libraries, 22, 32, 54
Ramsay, Allan, 9
rates charges by Mudie's, 17-18, 23, 38-39, 186
Reade, Charles, and American vs. British versions of novel, 105-6, 109; collection of clippings, 217; comments on three-deckers, 92, 116-17; difficulties with triple-deckers, 94-97; fulminates against Mudie's, 90; mentioned, 52, 149; Mudie's censorship of, 141, 148; multiplicity of plots in, 112-13; and price reductions, 68; quoted on love interest in novels, 125; quoted on Mudie, 143; quoted on number of volumes, 72; quoted on successive modes of publishing a novel, 54; quoted on "young girl" standard, 138; shortened work, 101
reading public, Mudie's influence on 78-86
reprints, Mudie's difficulties with, 170; Mudie's influence on timing of, 74-75; one-volume cheap editions, 48, 205; "yellowbacks," 53-54
Reynolds' Publishing House, 121
Richard Feverel, 142
Ritchie, Leitch, 12

fluence on popularity of, 41-42; "society" novels, 190; structure as affected by tripartite form, 101-19; unknown authors benefited by, 56, 184-85; varying lengths of, 45-46; *see also* novels
Times, The, 158-61, 189-90, 200, 216
Tinsley, Samuel, 68
Tinsley, William, comment on own periodical, 161; dealings with Hardy, 60-61; mentioned, 121; Moore's attack on, 152
Tinsley's Magazine, 161, 162, 164
titles, Mudie's influence on selection of, 75-76
Trevelyan, Janet, 209
triple-decker novels. *See* three-decker novels
Trollope, Anthony, American publication of, 55; character portrayal by, 113-15; *Framley Parsonage*'s structure, 102-3; Mudie commented on by character, 144; Mudie's purchase of *Autobiography*, 166; multiplicity of plots in one novel, 111-13; novel as didactic to, 131-32; *Orley Farm* quoted on Mudie's, 57; price for novels, 91; publishers not allowed to stretch out his novels, 71-72; satire on lady novelists, 89; serialization of, 44; and Thackeray's rejection of story, 133-34; three-decker format's effect on, 102-3; quoted on love in novels, 125; quoted on Mudie's, 21; quoted on novelists and three-deckers, 93-94; quoted on novel reading, 3; quoted on novel's length, 46; quoted on own endings, 113; quoted on vice, 128; quoted on three-decker's profits, 58-59
Trollope, Frances Eleanor, 97
Tuer, Andrew W., 170
Twain, Mark, 56
two-volume novels, appearing after

libraries' edict, 207; as transitional, 194
United States' publishing practices compared with England's, 55-56, 165-66
Unwin, Stanley, 5
used-book sales, 29-30, 168-70

Van Homrigh, B.A., 25, 76
Vanity Fair, 92
Vizetelly, Henry, 209

Ward, Mrs. Humphry, anecdote on Mudie's as proof of success, 78; cuts novel to fit three volumes, 101; and end of three-decker, 209-10; mentioned, 218; quick reprint hurts Mudie's, 170
Watts, Robert, 9
Waugh, Arthur, 144, 198-99, 213
Way We Live Now, The, 89-90
Webber, Byron, 75
Westward Ho!, 20, 29-30, 75
W. H. Smith's, bans *Esther Waters*, 153-54; demands new terms of publishers, 171-72; influence on Hardy's career, 61; Mudie refuses to start libraries at railway bookstalls of, 22; as Mudie's competitor, 31-34
Wilde, Oscar, 51
William Heinemann's, 59, 69
Williams, F.E., 202
Williams, William Smith, 90, 105
Wills, William Henry, 52
Wodrow, Robert, 9
Woman in White, The, 104
Wood, Mrs. Henry, 5, 46, 65
Workers in the Dawn, 118
writers. *See* authors
Wuthering Heights, 55

"yellowback" reprints, 32, 54
"young girl" standard, 137-40

Zangwill, Israel, 94
Zoe, 121-24, 130
Zola, Émile, 148-50